Body Merchants

Body Merchants

A Novel

Elaine Bossik

PORTABLE SHOPPER, LLC

PORTABLE SHOPPER, LLC

Copyright © 2023 by Elaine Bossik.

All rights reserved. No part of this book may be used or reproduced in any manner whatsoever without written permission, except in the case of brief quotations embodied in critical articles and reviews, without permission in writing from the publisher, Portable Shopper, LLC.

Portable Shopper, LLC
Boynton Beach, Florida

This is a work of fiction. Names, characters, organizations, places, events, and incidents are products of the author's imagination or are used fictitiously. Any similarity to real persons, living or dead, or actual events is coincidental and not intended by the author.

Cover design by Ray Bossik
Book design by Glenn Bossik
Author photograph by Eric Bossik

ISBN: 978-0-9842419-5-8
eBook ISBN: 978-0-9842419-6-5
Library of Congress Control Number: 2023902231

For the countless unwitting victims of organ trafficking all over the world.

Earth provides enough to satisfy every man's needs, but not every man's greed.
— Mahatma Gandhi

Also by Elaine Bossik
The Last Victim

Chapter 1

Alexandria, Virginia, Monday, July 13, 2009

Ellie Andrews walked into the Virginia Star newsroom at 8:15 a.m., earlier than most of the staff. Even at this hour, phones rang insistently and fax machines spewed out streams of messages for this popular local newspaper.

Ellie turned on her computer, brushed an unruly dark curl from her brow, and scanned the screen for breaking news. Her eyes widened as she read a local headline: *Football Star Bob Reynolds Critical After Kidney Transplant at Virginia General Hospital.*

She reached for her phone and punched in a number. "Dr. Andrews," she said.

"He's not available," the receptionist answered.

"Tell him it's his niece."

After some moments waiting on hold, Dan answered. "I know why you're calling," he said.

"What happened?" she asked.

"It's not unusual for a transplant patient to have a setback after surgery. It's only news because he's a big-name athlete."

"He could die, right?"

"Bob's case isn't unique...and he's getting state-of-the-art treatment."

"Why do you think this happened?"

"He'll recover and, by tomorrow, this won't be news."

"Are you sure about that?"

"No articles about this right now, you hear me?"

"It's not my decision," she said, surprised by the threat in his answer.

"Tell your father my wishes." He hung up before she could say another word.

Staffers started drifting into cubicles on the newsroom floor. Ellie's stomach grumbled, reminding her that she hadn't eaten breakfast. She headed for the kitchen. "Hey, Ellie," a fellow reporter called, his eyes on the tight jeans she wore, revealing shapely hips and long legs. Ellie waved to him as she walked to the kitchen. A tray with bagels sat on the counter and she plucked one, setting it on a paper plate. After filling a cup with coffee from the urn, she headed back to her office.

She stopped at her brother's cubicle, next door to hers, and leaned against the door frame. He had just arrived, late as usual. At age twenty-five, three years younger than Ellie, Matt was a senior reporter like her. They had both caught the bug for reporting as teenagers.

Ben Andrews had started taking Ellie and Matt to the newsroom on school holidays and summer days when they were teenagers. They ran errands for the staff and pretended to work there. She and Matt were sworn to secrecy before a story headlined. Some days they stayed late with their father and watched the printing press spitting out stories on newsprint paper. The clattering and thrumming of the presses, and the smell of freshly inked paper churning out the news became part of their DNA.

Ellie's eyes settled on Matt's desk, littered with stacks of papers and files. "How was your weekend?" she asked.

Matt looked up, his sandy-colored hair disheveled and in need of a haircut. "Uneventful." He sat down, stretched his long legs and yawned.

"I went to the Kennedy Center after I dined at the White House with the Obamas," she joked.

"You need to get out more," he said.

Ellie grinned and went back to her office. Matt was right, she *did* need to socialize more. Friday evening, she had joined staffers at a local pub, where they regularly went to unwind after a week of late nights and tight deadlines. After an hour of downing drinks and sharing laughs, the crowd was heading to La Madeleine for dinner. "I'm going to take a rain check for dinner," Ellie announced.

"What a surprise," John, a fellow reporter, said sarcastically.

"Research beckons," Ellie said.

Her friend, Claire, also a senior reporter, whispered in her ear, "You're coming with us tonight. That's an order."

"I will next week," she promised and hurried out. She spent the rest of the evening at her computer, munching on a take-out sandwich as she read screens filled with reports. She kept a spiral notebook on her bedside table so she could jot down ideas that came to her if she woke in the night.

Ellie bit into the bagel now and sipped the strong coffee. It was 9:45 when she looked at her watch, almost time for the editorial meeting. Her eyes settled on a photograph on her desk. It captured her father when he was a ruggedly attractive young man. He stood next to Ellie's beautiful blonde mother, who smiled and looked happy. Ellie's blue-green eyes were the only resemblance to her mother. She remembered the cold December day, fifteen years ago, when she had last seen her mother, and she turned the photograph face down on the desk.

A flying paper ball bounced off Ellie's head, pulling her back from her thoughts. She looked up at Matt, who peered over the top of her cubicle and smirked. "Editorial meeting," he announced. Ellie shook off the memory of her mother and followed Matt.

At 10:00 a.m., the managing editor, reporters, copy editors, photographer, graphic designer and other staffers gathered in the conference room around a mahogany rectangular table that occupied most of the room. Ben Andrews was already seated at the head of the table when Ellie and Matt arrived. Ben ran his fingers through his thick dark hair, now peppered with gray. At fifty-three years old, he had a well-toned body and pleasant face that women found attractive.

Ben looked at his watch. "Let's get started, people. Updates and issues?" He turned to Greg Burrows, the managing editor, who gave a summary of assignments that needed to be completed by the end of the day. Other staffers followed with updates of their articles and, by 10:20, it was Ellie's turn to report.

"You probably all saw the local TV report on Bob Reynolds, who's in critical condition at the Virginia General Hospital after transplant surgery. I called the medical director, who you know is Ben's brother. He said that Bob's condition wasn't unusual after a transplant."

Ben scratched his head. "Follow up on this," he said.

"I'm on it," Ellie said.

"What have you got, Matt?" Ben asked.

"I finally got permission to interview an inmate at Red Ridge Prison," Matt said.

"Good. That'll be all folks. Let's get back to work," Ben dismissed the staff. "Matt, Ellie stay for a few minutes."

When the door closed behind the last of the staffers, Ben turned to Ellie. "Did Dan tell you what happened?"

"He didn't explain. And he insisted that we don't report on this."

"He knows we can't do that."

"Maybe you two should talk to each other," she said.

Ben sighed. "See what else you can find out, Ellie." He turned to Matt. "Be careful at Red Ridge. They'll be listening to every word you say to the prisoner…What's his name?"

"Rusty Degan. He shouldn't have been sent to a maximum-security prison. He was moved there as punishment for a minor infraction at a local prison."

"Keep me posted," Ben said on his way out of the conference room.

Ben's phone was ringing when he stepped into his office. He picked it up, and his brother's voice floated to his ear. "Ben, I talked to Ellie this morning. Did she tell you that I can't have any stories in the Star about Bob Reynolds right now?"

"She did," Ben said. "But you know we're obligated to report local news. How would it look if all the local media reported on this except us?"

"Past publicity in the Star cost the hospital dearly. We depend on the generosity of donors for funding," Dan said.

"Is there something you're not telling me?" Ben asked.

"No," he insisted. "I'm asking you to delay the report for a few days."

"The facts will come out whether we report them or some other newspaper does," Ben said.

"I'm in an awkward position as medical director and co-owner of the Star. Our donors know this. Put yourself in my place. Then maybe you can be more understanding."

"Newspaper reporting isn't personal," Ben said.

"Fuck you." Dan slammed the phone down, the sound reverberating in Ben's ear.

Ellie spent the next hour hunkered down in her office, researching organ transplants. She learned that one-year survival after a kidney transplant was 90%. Maybe Dan was telling her the truth when he said that Reynolds would probably recover. On the other hand, he could become one of the 15% to 20% who die from infection. Bob appeared to be in excellent health before the transplant. So, what happened? Why did he need a kidney transplant?

Chapter 2

Tuesday, July 14, 2009

The first thing Ellie noticed when she stepped into her office was her phone blinking with messages. She wanted to go directly to the newsroom kitchen for coffee, but she set her handbag on the desk and played the first message.

"Ellie, it's Dan. Come to my office today at 11:00 o'clock. It's best that you get the facts from me about Bob Reynolds." *Maybe Dan and her father spoke and worked things out,* she thought.

By 10:00 a.m., Ellie was in her car, heading to Arlington on the Beltway. Half an hour later, she drove through the tree-lined streets to the medical center, a complex of tall modern buildings. She pulled into a parking space and walked to the hospital entrance.

Wide double doors opened automatically into an expansive lobby surrounded by windows from above that bathed the space in sunlight and reflected off the polished marble floor. She went to the circular information desk in the center of the lobby. "I have an appointment to see Dr. Dan Andrews."

"Your name?" the receptionist asked.

"Ellie Andrews." The receptionist made a phone call, hung up and wrote a visitor's pass for her. "Take the elevator to fourteen," she said.

Ellie crossed the lobby and stepped into a waiting elevator. She rode to the fourteenth floor, which housed the administrative offices. When she opened the door to Dan's outer office, his secretary looked up and smiled. "How are you, Ellie?" she asked.

"I'm good, Maureen. Thanks for asking."

"Go right in. Doctor's expecting you."

Ellie opened the door to an office tastefully decorated with fine oak furniture. Dan sat at a large antique desk, surrounded by windows overlooking manicured lawns. Floor-to-ceiling bookcases along the facing wall held an impressive collection of medical texts, and a magazine rack displayed current medical journals.

Dan smiled warmly and pointed to an upholstered chair facing his desk. "Sit, Ellie."

"Thanks for seeing me. I know you're busy." Ellie looked into his dark eyes and marveled at how attractive he was. At age 55, he was only two years older than her father, but he looked years younger, in spite of the peppered-gray hair at his temples. He was shorter than Ben and looked nothing like him, except for his dark brown hair. His skin was tanned and smooth, and tortoise shell glasses lent a studious appeal to his face. Dressed in an expensive summer suit, pale blue shirt and navy tie, he looked every bit the medical director.

"You have questions about Bob Reynolds?" Dan asked.

"How's he doing?" Ellie asked, pulling a spiral notebook and pen from her bag.

"About the same."

"Why did someone as healthy as Bob need a kidney?"

"He had a serious back injury a few months ago. He was in a lot of pain, which wasn't controlled by over-the-counter pain medication. His doctor prescribed stronger medication—an opioid—and physical therapy. His condition was improving."

"What changed?"

"He started taking more and more pain medication, against his doctor's advice. Off the record, I suspect he may have even used cocaine. Then he was out with friends one evening, drinking heavily. He collapsed and was brought here by ambulance. When he arrived in the ER, he was barely alive."

"So, his life was saved in the ER?"

"We have an outstanding trauma center. But when Bob was brought in, we discovered that he had serious kidney damage from opioids and alcohol. Without a transplant, he would have died."

Ellie scribbled notes as Dan talked. "From what I've read, survival is expected in patients who are in good health before a transplant. So, why is he in critical condition now?"

"He was in kidney failure when he was admitted. That hardly qualifies as good health."

"What I mean is that he didn't have any other life-threatening condition," she said.

"Still, he was critically ill when he received the new kidney."

Ellie was about to ask about Bob's prognosis when Dan's cell phone buzzed. He looked at the caller's name. "Would you excuse me for a few minutes. I need to take this call." Ellie nodded, and Dan rose, his ear to the phone as he walked out of the office.

Her eyes wandered to a wall where framed photographs hung alongside Dan's medical degree from Baylor College of Medicine. She went to the wall for a closer look at a picture of herself and Matt, standing beside Dan near the swimming pool at his estate in Texas. She was sixteen years old then. Ellie smiled, recalling the many summer vacations spent in Dallas after Dan convinced Ben to send her and Matt to visit.

Dan took them sailing, fishing and on hiking excursions. Joan never came along, insisting she had a country club luncheon or event she was organizing. But Joan did take Ellie shopping, buying her outfits she would never wear. "You're a young lady now, and you have to dress well. It's time to shed the worn jeans and T-shirts," Joan had told her. What Ellie remembered most about Joan during those visits was the look of relief on her face when she and Matt kissed her goodbye. Dan would drive them to the airport, his face sad as he waved goodbye.

A row of photographs showed off Dan and Joan dressed formally at elegant affairs. Ellie recognized the governor of Texas, presenting Dan with a plaque in one photograph.

The office door opened and Dan walked in. "Sorry about the interruption," he said.

"I was admiring your photos. They brought back happy memories of summer vacations with you in Dallas."

"They're happy memories for me, too," he said.

"Isn't that the governor?" Ellie pointed to the photograph.

"He gave me an award for establishing a new hospital for underprivileged children. To this day, it's fully funded."

"That's a great accomplishment."

"Joan deserves most of the credit. She and her family and friends found wealthy donors. Joan has always been involved in charity work."

Ellie didn't comment about her aunt, who she knew was no Mother Teresa. Joan didn't help anyone unless it benefited her and Dan. Ellie's eyes settled on Dan's medical degree. "It must have been hard leaving your family in Virginia and going to Texas to study medicine," she said.

"Medical school was tough. After that, doing an internship and residency were grueling—long hours on very little sleep."

"But you did become a doctor."

"I was a hospital-based doctor. I never went into private practice, which is much more lucrative."

"But you could have."

"I was headed in that direction when I met Joan."

"You never told me how you two met."

"We met at a fundraising event for breast cancer. The medical center sent me to represent them and plead for funds. There was a fabulous dinner and dance at the Fairmont Hotel. Everyone from Dallas' high society was there." Dan smiled, recalling the evening. Wearing his only suit for the occasion, Dan had felt underdressed next to the men in tuxedos and women in designer gowns. He stood at the sidelines in the ballroom, but Joan spotted him and swept across the room to introduce herself.

"Hi, I'm Joan Foster." She smiled and held out her hand, dazzling him with her beauty and southern charm.

He took her hand and said, "Dan Andrews, from Baylor U Medical Center."

"You're a doctor?"

"I am."

"Well, Dr. Andrews, it's so refreshing to meet someone who isn't a politician or a millionaire." Joan took Dan under her wing from that moment, introducing him to the wealthiest and most influential people in Texas society and to the politicians they supported.

Dan pointed to a photograph of himself and Joan at a villa on the Amalfi Coast in Italy. "That's where Joan and I spent our honeymoon."

"So, you didn't have a very long courtship." Ellie said.

"We were married six months after we met. And my life took another turn, thanks to Joan's parents, the Fosters, who introduced me to the CEO at a Texas hospital conglomerate. The hospital was looking to recruit a doctor with my background for a new administrative position. I was surprised when I was offered the job. I accepted, and the rest of my story is history."

"Do you regret giving up medicine?" Ellie's question hung in a long silence.

"I have no regrets. When I turned to hospital administration, I was able to help more patients than I ever could as a practicing physician." Dan didn't share the fact that he had never enjoyed the hands-on practice of medicine, the personal involvement with patients whose lives could depend on his medical decisions. As a hospital administrator, he developed a reputation as a valuable middleman. He brokered deals for the hospital to acquire smaller hospitals, grow their investments and expand their reach into private clinics, laboratories and pharmaceuticals. Private investors behind the acquisitions made huge profits and rewarded Dan handsomely with stock options, executive board positions in other companies and valuable perks.

Dan looked at his watch. "I have an important meeting in a few minutes, so we need to wrap this up."

Ellie looked into his eyes. "I have one more question," she said. "Who was Bob's kidney donor?"

Dan sucked in his breath, surprised by her question. "That's confidential. HIPAA privacy rules forbid disclosure."

Startled by his tone, Ellie said, "Off-the-record, of course. How do you ensure that donor organs are healthy?" she persisted.

Dan's face tightened. "There are rigorous screening standards for donated organs. It's too complicated to go into details now...and I'm late for my meeting."

Ellie stood. "Maybe you can explain when you have more time."

"Please send me your article before publishing...so I can check it for accuracy."

Ellie nodded, surprised by his request, which sounded more like a demand.

"If you want a good story, why not write one about the lives we save every day in our ER. It's ranked the number one trauma center in Virginia," Dan boasted.

"I'd like to do that," she said.

"Good. I'll give you a tour of the hospital and our specialty units. Call next week and we'll set a date."

On her way out, Ellie said, "Regards to Joan," though she knew that her aunt was not interested in her or Matt or her father.

Chapter 3

Wednesday, July 15, 2009

Matt started out at 6:00 a.m. for the drive from Alexandria to Pound, Virginia, in the remote Appalachian Mountains, where Red Ridge Prison was hidden from most of America. For the 1,073 people who lived in this coal mining town, Red Ridge was a boon to the economy, employing hundreds of laid off coalfield workers. Matt drove steadily for hours, his Dodge Charger climbing higher through curving mountain roads. Lush forests spread out on either side of the highway, interrupted by fields of breathtakingly beautiful wildflowers.

After three hours, Matt pulled his car onto an overlook off the road. He stepped out of the car and stretched his legs. A pristine lake was visible in the distance and butterflies circled everywhere. He took a bottle of water out of a cooler he kept in the car and sipped as he studied the rugged landscape. The mountain air felt cool and fresh against his skin, and he drew a deep breath before getting back in the car.

As Matt drove on, he thought about Rusty Degan, the inmate he was about to meet. *Could he convince Rusty to trust him and talk about prison life?* Matt first became interested in Red Ridge when he had seen Nick Labelle, a human rights investigator, during a TV interview. "Red Ridge has the highest prisoner death rate in the United States," Nick had said. That statement had gotten Matt's attention, particularly since the prison was in his home state.

"Red Ridge is a maximum-security prison. It cost over $70 million to build. It was designed to house the most violent and dangerous criminals. But, in order to fill the now privately-run prison, many minor offenders are transferred there from local correctional facilities," Nick reported.

Matt was eager to write a feature story for the Virginia Star and connect the mounting incarceration rate throughout the U.S. to the privatized for-profit prison system. He spent weeks combing through public records in Fairfax County to find a prisoner who didn't belong there, one who could be the focus of his story.

After reading about Rusty Degan's case, Matt was convinced that the young offender was sent to the wrong facility for the wrong reason. Rusty was a twenty-four-year-old convicted of driving a vehicle during an armed robbery, and sentenced to seven years in prison. Because Rusty had no prior record and didn't carry any weapons or participate in the assault, he was first remanded to a medium-security correctional facility. Soon after, he was transferred to Red Ridge. It had taken Matt two months and numerous petitions to get permission to see him today.

Matt navigated his car along the curvy mountain road that snaked to a final elevation of 1,565 feet. At last, he turned onto Jack Rose Highway. The wild beauty of the mountains gave way to a bleak landscape of windowless stone buildings surrounded by a double-security fence with sensors and coils of razor wire. He pulled up to the guardhouse, rolled down the window and showed his press ID. As the guard examined his ID and made a phone call, Matt's eyes settled on the prison's stone facade and looming watchtowers manned by guards wielding AR-15 rifles. He shuddered imperceptibly as the guard returned his ID card and the steel gates opened.

After parking his car, Matt entered the prison through the visitors' entrance. He followed a uniformed guard along a narrow corridor with bare concrete walls that seemed to press in on him. They stopped in front of a locked door. The guard inserted an electronic key, and the door to the visitors' room swung open.

Matt was ushered to a seat behind a thick glass partition. On the other side of the partition, a side door opened and a uniformed guard led Rusty Degan inside. Dressed in a bright orange jumpsuit that hung loosely from his bony frame, Rusty looked more like a teenage boy lost in his father's clothing than a dangerous criminal. He dragged his feet, taking small steps in the leg shackles. The guard pushed him into a chair opposite Matt and stepped back against the wall.

Rusty eyed Matt suspiciously through the partition. Matt smiled and picked up the phone next to him. He pointed to Rusty's phone, but Rusty hesitated, judging Matt warily through blue eyes rimmed with dark circles. Rusty reached for the phone near him with his handcuffed hands, holding it awkwardly against his ear.

"How are you doing, Rusty?" Matt asked. "I'm Matt Andrews, a reporter from the Virginia Star. I'm writing a story about Red Ridge and the inmates here. Can I ask you some questions?"

Rusty's face twitched. He turned his head to peer over his shoulder at the guard before answering. "I don't want no story about me."

Matt noted the ceiling-mounted cameras and state-of-the-art listening devices positioned around the room. "I won't use your name."

"Why should I believe you?"

"I read about your case, and I want to help you."

"You just want a story to make you look good."

"I could write other stories, but yours is important because you don't belong here."

"A lot of men don't belong here. So what?"

"If we expose the truth, things could improve here, or change."

"You don't know anything. It'll get worse." He blinked nervously.

"I know more than you think." Matt's eyes rested on the white numbers stamped on the right side of Rusty's uniform and the dragon tattoo on his neck, half hidden by the collar. "How did you end up in prison?"

"I lost my construction job. I did odd jobs after that...whatever I could get. My landlord kicked me out when I couldn't pay the rent for three months. You look like you don't have to worry about money," he said, his tone accusing.

"I've been lucky," Matt said. "What about your family? Couldn't they help?"

"After high school, I got as far away as I could. Left my family in West Virginia. I wasn't cut out for coal mining. That's what my Dad had in mind for me." He studied Matt's neatly-laundered shirt and good jeans. "Where do you live...in a high-buck apartment or a big fancy house?"

"I live in an apartment," Matt said, his eyes on Rusty's trembling hands. Rusty's matted red hair, pale cheeks and puffy eyes made Matt wonder when he had last slept through the night. "Where did you stay when you lost your apartment?" Matt asked.

"Moved in with a friend. Slept on the sofa."

"How did you get mixed up in an armed robbery?"

"A friend of a friend asked me to drive for a job they were doing. I needed the money."

"You served three years of your sentence at Meadow Brook Prison. What happened there that got you transferred here?"

"I was mindin' my own business. I didn't want to get mixed up with no gangs. But you got to pick sides or else."

"Or else what?"

"You get beaten by *all* the gangs till you join one."

"What happened when you were transferred here three months ago?"

"I was in solitary...for twenty-three days."

"Twenty-three days?"

"Yeah." Rusty's face twitched and his eyes had a distant look, as though he were reliving those torturous days.

"I read that the rules here allow you out of a solitary cell for only one hour a day."

"To shower. But no soap, no toothpaste, no nothin'."

Matt made some notations in a notepad. "Why were you sent to solitary?"

"Punishment."

"But the gang attacked you."

"I punched back. And when a guard tried to break it up, I pushed the guard."

Matt nodded, refraining from commenting on the draconian punishment. "I see you have a tattoo. Does that mean you joined a gang here?"

"Yeah."

"I want to help you get transferred back to a lower-security prison."

Rusty was silent, studying Matt. Then he said, "I hope you're not lyin' like my lawyer."

"I can't promise that I'll succeed."

"Men walk in the door here and go out in boxes," Rusty said.

Matt straightened in his chair. "What do you mean?" There was a long pause, and Rusty didn't explain. "Can you tell me about everyday life here... how you and other prisoners are treated?" Matt pressed.

A loud buzzer sounded before Rusty could respond. The guard, who wore ear buds and whose eyes never left them, moved swiftly, pulling the phone out of Rusty's hands. "Visiting hours are over," he told Matt, slamming the phone into the cradle. Then he dragged Rusty out of the chair and pushed him out of the room.

On the drive back to Alexandria, Matt puzzled over Rusty's unexplained revelation, 'Men walk in the door here and go out in boxes.' *Rusty could have been a friend*, Matt thought, *someone he would go jogging with or have a beer with while watching a football game. But he had all the advantages that come with money, and Rusty had all the disadvantages of poverty. Though only a year younger than him, Rusty's hopelessness made him look decades older.*

Matt was determined to get Rusty transferred out of that hellhole. He would have to be careful if he wanted to uncover abuses at the prison. It wasn't going to be easy to get permission from Warden Parker for another visit, but he was not one to give up when pursuing a story.

Chapter 4

Wednesday, July 22, 2009

Ellie was awake by 6:30 a.m. She showered, dressed and turned the TV on while drying her hair. A reporter from a local news channel stood outside the Virginia General Hospital as doctors, hospital personnel and visitors walked in and out of the entrance.

"Football athlete Bob Reynolds died yesterday evening, a week after kidney transplant surgery," the TV reporter said.

Ellie turned off the hair dryer and stared at the screen, which showed a photo of a smiling Bob Reynolds in his football uniform. "A hospital administrator said that Bob was in critical condition when he arrived in the ER. He was diagnosed with kidney failure and received a kidney transplant to try to save his life. The Reynolds family refused an autopsy by the hospital and demanded that the chief medical examiner perform Bob's autopsy," the reporter said.

Ellie dressed quickly, grabbed her handbag and hurried out of her apartment. Her mind raced with questions as she drove to the newsroom. *Why did the Reynolds family refuse an autopsy by the hospital?*

In the newsroom, Ellie waited until 9:00 before calling Dan's office. There was a recorded message from his secretary: "You have reached the office of Dr. Dan Andrews, Medical Director. The doctor is out of the office. Please leave a message at the beep."

She hung up and phoned the chief medical examiner's office. "This is Ellie Andrews from the Virginia Star. The newspaper requests a comment from the medical examiner about the Bob Reynolds case."

"No comment until the autopsy is complete," a receptionist told her.

"When can we expect that?" Ellie asked.

"Tomorrow," she said, and hung up.

Ellie sighed, setting the phone in the cradle. She stood and headed to the kitchen for coffee. Matt walked toward her on his way to his office. "Did you see the news about Reynolds?" she asked.

"Yep. Is Dan still singing the praises of the hospital?"

"You can't blame *him*."

"You're the reporter. Find out who to blame," he said, stepping into his cubicle. He turned on his computer. He had made three petitions to revisit Rusty Degan last week, and they were denied. "Why?" Matt had asked.

"The warden doesn't have to give you a reason," a prison spokesperson had told him.

He logged into his e-mail now. There was an official message from the prison: *Your interview subject matter was not approved. Your interview is denied.* Matt slammed his fist on the desk. Then he turned back to his computer to search for investigations of Red Ridge. Human Rights International had filed numerous reports of abuse at the prison by investigator Nick Labelle. Matt reached for his phone and dialed.

"Nick Labelle," a strong voice answered.

"Nick, I'm Matt Andrews, a reporter at the Virginia Star. I've read your reports about Red Ridge, and I'm looking for some advice."

"How can I help?" Nick asked.

"I'm working on a story about a young prisoner who was moved to Red Ridge from a low-security prison. He doesn't belong there. I interviewed him only once, and I'm being denied visits again."

"I'm not surprised," Nick said.

"Can we meet today?"

"Where?"

"There's a diner one block south of the Virginia Star. The sign over the door is Diner. Food's pretty good. How's 1:00 o'clock?"

"See you then," Nick said.

Matt hung up just as Ellie walked in. She studied his face. "What's pissing you off now?" she asked.

"The warden at Red Ridge."

"If I know you, you'll work it out," she said.

***

Matt was waiting in a booth at the diner when Nick walked in. He recognized Nick from a TV interview he had watched, and he waved to him. They shook hands and Nick slipped into the seat across from Matt. "Thanks for meeting me," Matt said.

He couldn't explain what characterized an honest face, but that was his first impression of Nick. They studied the menu for a few minutes. "Too many choices. What do you recommend?" Nick asked.

"They make a good burger...unless you don't eat red meat."

"Burger sounds good," Nick said.

"Red Ridge is jerking me around," Matt said. "Maybe you can give me some advice on how to get back in to talk to an inmate—Rusty Degan. He's just a kid."

"I'm not surprised that the prison is running you in circles," Nick said. "We've been investigating Red Ridge since it was built in the late 90s. That's when the prison system was privatized. We're constantly petitioning the courts, and sometimes the governor, to get in there and document conditions."

"I didn't see much of the prison because I was escorted to a visitor room," Matt said. "They didn't like the questions I asked Rusty, or his answers, because my interview ended abruptly."

"They monitor conversations."

"Rusty looked terrified. They had him in leg shackles and handcuffs. There were guards around the room watching and listening."

A waiter stepped up to their table. "Are you ready to order?"

"Two burger specials," Matt said.

"Drinks?" the waiter asked.

"Coors Light," Matt said.

"Make that two," Nick said.

The waiter left and Nick continued. "Conditions at Red Ridge are harsher and more restrictive than at any other super-max prison in the country. Inmates are locked two to a cell for twenty hours a day. They're denied most reading material, activity, education, rehabilitation." His words spilled out like a plea. Nick reached for his cell phone on the table and accessed a photograph. "Here's what the inside of a cell looks like."

Matt stared at the picture—a claustrophobic cell with slab beds that looked like shelves, a thin mattress and an exposed toilet.

"Inmates get one roll of toilet paper a week," Nick said. "If they use it up, they're out of luck. If they break any rules, and there are hundreds, they go to solitary. Over two hundred inmates are in solitary at any given time... and they stay there for weeks, months or years, where they generally become psychotic."

"Your organization has gotten some conditions improved there," Matt said.

"After we reported several inmate deaths, the prison was no longer allowed to use live ammunition. They're also not allowed to use electroshock weapons for punishment. But they continue to use them, claiming they need to protect themselves and threatened prisoners."

"What chance do I have of helping the inmate if they can ignore legal prohibitions whenever they want to?"

The waiter arrived and set two plates with burgers and fries on the table, and the beers they had ordered. They paused their conversation to enjoy the burgers.

"You're right, the burgers are good here," Nick said, taking a sip of beer. "It's easy to get discouraged when dealing with Warden Parker. He resents anyone trying to reign in his fiefdom. We're alarmed about a current rash of prisoner deaths."

Matt's eyes widened. "What happened?"

"We're investigating the death of a prisoner that the warden claims was caused by an inmate-on-inmate attack. According to Parker, the death resulted from a fight between prisoners in the recreation yard."

"I read the incident reports on your website, but there weren't many details."

"There's been one death every month for the past three months."

"Is that unusual in a violent setting like that?"

"For a prison that's so closely monitored, it is. The courts granted our petition to conduct an autopsy on the prisoner who died there last week. Why don't you use this incident as leverage to get in there again to see Rusty?"

"How?"

"Call Parker and tell him you're going to publish an article about recent deaths at the prison unless you're allowed to interview Degan again. A story about Rusty will be less threatening to him than a story about an investigation of prisoner deaths."

"It'll piss off the warden. I may never get back in there."

"Parker's an expert on blackmail. That's why you should use it to your advantage."

"My conversations with him have all ended badly. But I appreciate your advice." Matt reached for the check. "Lunch is on me." They shook hands.

"Let me know how it turns out," Nick said. Matt watched him walk to the door, taking long, confident strides. He liked Nick from the first moment they shook hands.

When Matt got back to his office, he phoned the prison. "Warden

Parker," he said.

"Who's calling?"

"Matt Andrews from the Virginia Star."

Matt waited and waited and was about to hang up when he heard Parker's voice. "You were told to file an official request if you want to visit an inmate. So why are you calling me again, Andrews?"

"While I'm filing my fourth request and waiting for your decision, I'll have plenty of time to work on a new article about three inmate deaths that are under investigation. On the other hand, if I'm busy interviewing Rusty Degan, I won't have time to write the article."

There was a long pause. Matt heard Parker's heavy breathing. "August 5th, twelve noon," Parker barked. "Send your interview questions for approval. We can cancel for any reason." He hung up before Matt could respond.

Chapter 5

Thursday, July 23, 2009

It was noon when the Medical Examiner released results of the autopsy on Bob Reynolds. The headline went viral: A*thlete Bob Reynolds died of hepatitis C from an infected kidney following transplant surgery. The Reynolds family is suing the Virginia General Hospital.*

Ellie's phone buzzed and she reached for it. "Come into my office," Ben said. She hung up, grabbed a notepad and raced across the newsroom floor.

Ben was on the phone when Ellie stepped into the office, closing the door behind her. He motioned to the chair beside his desk and turned on the speakerphone. Dan's voice floated out.

"I know why you're calling. I'll explain what happened to Bob Reynolds, but I'm on another call. I'll get back to you in a few minutes." He hung up abruptly.

Turning to Ellie, Ben said, "Let's see what bullshit he comes up with to whitewash this."

"It's a headline story now. Dan must be upset," Ellie said. She wanted to stay neutral in the ongoing friction between her father and uncle. She loved her father and usually agreed with him, but she was fond of her uncle, who had always been kind to her, especially after her mother left.

Ben rifled through papers on his desk, his jaw clenched as he waited for Dan's call. Ellie's eyes wandered to a framed photograph on the wall—a front page story from the Virginia Star with the headline, *Star Publisher Ben Andrews Receives Award for Exposing Slave Trade*. A younger Ben Andrews smiled in the photo as he accepted a plaque from the mayor.

Ellie remembered the ceremony. She was twelve years old in the photo, sitting in a front row seat. Her mother sat beside her, hands clenched and lips pressed together. When her father accepted the plaque, Ellie jumped up, clapping furiously along with the audience. She sensed that her mother was still angry about the brick hurled through their living room window weeks earlier, when the story headlined.

The phone rang, pulling Ellie back to the present. Ben answered, "Dan, I'm turning on the speakerphone so Ellie can join us. She's writing the Reynolds story, and we want the hospital's explanation."

"Go ahead with your questions," Dan said.

"Isn't there a screening process for donated organs…testing for disease?" Ellie asked.

"The donated kidney passed our initial tests. It was compatible with Bob's antigens, which made it less likely to be rejected."

"How did the hospital miss detecting the hepatitis C infection?" she asked.

"The initial tests were negative. Extensive testing takes more time. But Bob needed an emergency transplant. We had a donor who was a good match. We had to move quickly because organs are only viable for a short time."

"Who was the donor?" Ellie asked.

"My answer hasn't changed since you last asked that question. We follow HIPAA patient privacy regulations."

"Is the donor deceased?" she asked.

"He died in an accident."

"Was there an autopsy?" she asked.

"There was no medical reason for one."

"Can an autopsy be performed now?" she asked.

Dan cleared his throat. "The donor was cremated."

Ellie exchanged a puzzled look with her father. "What did the hospital do for Bob when it was discovered that he had hepatitis C?" Ben asked.

"He was treated for the virus immediately and aggressively. Patients do recover from Hep C. But Bob was in poor condition from opioid and alcohol abuse. That's why he died. That's the truth…plain and simple," Dan insisted.

"Can I quote you?" Ellie asked.

"I want you to write an impartial account of what happened. The hospital did everything medically possible to save Bob's life."

"We report the facts…the truth." Ben didn't hide the irritation in his voice.

"You know what I mean," Dan said.

"What are you asking?"

Dan cleared his throat. "Can I speak to you privately for a few minutes?"

Ben turned to Ellie. "We'll touch base later," he told her.

Ellie gathered her notes and walked out of the office. Ben turned the speakerphone off and held the phone to his ear. "Ellie left," he said.

"Must you challenge everything I say? I don't want to argue. It seems like we're always doing that." There was a long silence before Dan continued. "You know I can't answer questions about cases under investigation."

"Can't or won't?"

"Can you imagine how it will look for *me* if you write a negative story about the hospital?"

"If the hospital did something negligent or unethical, we're obligated to report it."

"If you imply that the hospital is responsible for Bob's death, I'll personally be blamed. It's always the person at the wheel who's held to account."

"You weren't the doctor treating Reynolds."

"I'll do whatever it takes to protect the hospital's reputation and my own." Ben heard his brother take in a deep breath. "There are some toes you don't want to step on."

Ben's jaw tightened. "What does that mean?"

"We have wealthy donors with long arms."

"Are you threatening me?" Ben's voice rose.

"There are some people even *you* don't want to tangle with."

"The Virginia Star is *your* newspaper too. Or did you forget that detail?"

"But *you're* calling the shots. Max made sure of that." The truth of Dan's words silenced Ben. "I'm sure we can reach an agreement." Dan's voice softened. "On another subject, Joan and I want you to join us for dinner at our house on Saturday. We'd also like Ellie and Matt to come."

Dan had a habit of changing the subject when he couldn't win an argument. Ben took his time answering. "I'll come. But I can't answer for Ellie and Matt."

"I'll phone them," Dan said. "It's been too long since we spent a social evening together. See you Saturday, about 7:00."

Ben hung up, sensing that there was another motive for Dan's invitation. His eyes moved to a photograph on the wall of himself and Dan as teenagers. They were in the newsroom with Max, who often took them there during school vacations, instructing them in every aspect of the business. Max was generous in his praise for Ben, telling him, "You have a talent for the newspaper business." Ben still remembered his father's harsh criticism of Dan, which bordered on cruelty. "You're not cut out to be a newspaper man.

Better find another profession," Max had told him.

Eventually, Dan stopped going to the newsroom and trying to prove his worth to his father. Instead, he studied hard, got excellent grades at school and earned a four-year scholarship to the University of Virginia. Ben admired his brother's accomplishments—becoming a doctor and then a medical director of a major hospital. In a short time, Dan had amassed a fortune while living and working in Texas. Ben could only guess how much of it was Joan's family fortune and how much Dan had earned on his own.

When Dan lived in Texas, the distance between them made it easier to avoid arguments. But when he moved to Virginia, his ties to Republican interests regularly clashed with the liberal Virginia Star. *Perhaps a social evening would ease the tension between them*, Ben thought.

Chapter 6

Saturday, July 25, 2009

Ben turned his Volvo onto Sugarland Road and followed it to a private access road. He pulled up to the gate and pressed the call-in button. "It's Ben," he announced. The gate opened slowly, and Ben drove down the long driveway to the main entrance. The house, modeled after a French chateau, was set on three acres of landscaped grounds.

Inside, there were eight bedrooms, nine bathrooms, two chef's kitchens, a two-story library, a dining room that seated twenty-four guests, and two entertainment rooms. The lower level housed a billiards room, an exercise room and a wine cellar. Flagstone patios and gardens surrounded the rear of the house, leading to a fresh-water swimming pool with multilevel decks.

Dan opened the front door, and Ben stepped into an expansive marble hallway. The house never failed to take Ben's breath away. A Chihuly blown-glass chandelier hung from the ceiling in the entry, lighting a spiral staircase that led to the second level. "Are Ellie and Matt here?" Ben asked.

"Ellie's not here yet, and Matt had other plans," Dan said. He led Ben into a room furnished with contemporary leather sofas and chairs, glass and brass tables and a bar. Floor-to-ceiling windows overlooked a flower garden. "What can I get you to drink?"

"Red wine would be nice," Ben said.

"I have a Spottswood Cabernet from the Napa Valley that I think you'll like." Dan uncorked the bottle and filled two glasses.

Ben sipped the wine, savoring its full-bodied taste. "Excellent," he said.

Dan sank into a leather sofa facing his brother. "You look tired, Ben. You're working too hard."

"News publishing is a tough job. But there's nothing else I'd rather do."

"Take your wine and come into the garden. I want to show you some new additions to the grounds." Dan opened the French doors, and they stepped onto a flagstone patio. The garden, surrounding the swimming pool, was planted with exotic wildflowers—purple asters, yellow coreopsis, orange cornflowers, red columbine and Queen Anne's lace. Ben inhaled the intoxicating scents as he followed Dan along a path behind the flower garden. The smell of basil, rosemary, thyme, sage and lavender hung in the warm air. "Our new herb garden," Dan boasted. "Our chef picks fresh herbs every day. We brought in an herbalist from California to design it."

"Nice," Ben said, wondering about the price tag.

Dan led the way to a pond set in a Japanese rock garden. "Another addition you haven't seen—our meditation garden," he announced, as though he were introducing a celebrity.

"Impressive," Ben said. "Now you can meditate in style."

Dan smiled, ignoring Ben's sarcasm. They sat on a stone bench beside the pond, watching koi swim beneath the water lilies. Neither brother spoke for some moments, enjoying the serenity. Finally, Dan turned to his brother with a plea. "As a personal favor to me, I'm asking you not to report anything about the Reynolds case that will reflect negatively on the hospital. It will cause irreparable damage to my relationship with important benefactors."

"We report the facts...not our opinion. You can't expect us to write a biased report in favor of the hospital."

"If you care anything about *me*, now is the time to show it. A story that implies that the hospital was negligent will ruin me."

"You're being paranoid. *You're* not writing the news. I don't see how this can damage your reputation. You're doing a fine job as the medical director, better than the last director."

"I'll let you in on a secret. We're about to close on a tremendous deal to acquire another medical center. Any implication that the hospital can be blamed for Bob's death will kill the deal."

"I don't see how," Ben said.

"All the players in this acquisition know I'm co-owner of the Virginia Star."

"We can't change that fact," Ben said.

"It was always *you* who Dad wanted to run the paper from the time we were kids. You were the one he groomed to perpetuate his dream."

"You're judging Max too harshly. Maybe he thought you wouldn't be happy working at the newspaper," Ben said.

"When did Max ever care about my happiness?"

"I never approved of the way he treated you."

"I don't dwell on the past. And you don't need to pull the rug out from under me now...So, can I count on you?"

Ben looked into his brother's dark eyes. *Carrying around his father's disappointment in him must be a heavy burden,* he thought. "I'll do my best to keep your name out of the newspaper. If a patient is harmed by treatment at the hospital, we're obligated to report it."

"You sound like you're reading from Max's book of platitudes."

"Max is gone. I take full responsibility for publishing decisions."

"I need your *promise* not to imply that the hospital shares any blame in this case."

"I can't promise how news is interpreted by readers."

"Can't or *won't*?" Dan snapped.

The brothers walked back to the house, the sound of their footsteps echoing in the strained silence between them. When they returned to the sitting room, Ben refilled his wine glass and settled on the sofa. Dan retreated behind the bar, arranging liquor bottles on the shelves and slicing lime wedges.

Joan appeared in the doorway, assessing the anger on her husband's face and sensing that she had interrupted yet another of the brothers' arguments. She glided into the room with a dancer's grace. At age forty-eight, Joan Andrews was a beautiful woman, with a shapely figure that her personal trainer helped her maintain. Her straight blonde hair, perfectly styled, fell to her shoulders. She was dressed casually in white linen slacks and a sleeveless mauve shirt. Diamond Cartier drop earrings hung from her ear lobes, and a four-carat emerald ring glittered on her finger. "Ben, it's good to see you." Joan planted a kiss in the air next to Ben's cheek, her expensive perfume lingering when she pulled away. "I'm so glad Ellie's coming. It's been too long since we've been together," she said. "Too bad Matt couldn't join us."

"Maybe next time," Ben said. He often made excuses for Matt avoiding his uncle and aunt. Matt disliked their politics and their friends. Ben had told Matt many times, "Dan's not a bad person. He just comes from a different social environment."

The gate buzzer sounded, and Dan went to the front door. Ellie stepped inside and he hugged her. "You look beautiful and cool on this warm night," he said, leading her into the sitting room.

"Hi everyone." Ellie smiled brightly and kissed Joan lightly on her cheek.

Joan's eyes swept over Ellie. "You look pale," she said. "You're spending too much time in the newsroom." She looked disapprovingly at the wild curls that framed Ellie's face. "You must come and spend a day with me at the country club. A spa treatment and a makeover with my stylist are just what you need."

"I'll take you up on your offer one day," Ellie said. As Joan scrutinized Ellie's pastel blue summer dress and simple white sandals, she didn't hide her disapproval. Ellie turned away from her aunt's judgmental eyes.

"What can I get you ladies to drink?" Dan asked.

"A vodka martini for me," Joan said.

"I'll have the same," Ellie said.

Behind the bar, Dan measured vodka and vermouth, added ice and stirred the shaker. With honed expertise, he strained the mixture into chilled martini glasses and garnished each with three olives on a pick. He had learned the art of drink mixing during his undergraduate college days when he worked part time as a bartender in a local tavern. He presented the martinis with a flourish. Ellie sipped from the glass. "You make a mean martini," she said.

"Thanks." Dan smiled warmly at Ellie.

Joan took a long drink, then set her glass on the coffee table. "I'll go check on dinner," she said.

When Joan returned from the kitchen, she herded them outside to a shaded gazebo in the garden where a table had been set for dinner. "It's such a beautiful night. I thought we'd dine alfresco," she said, as they seated themselves around a glass table, set with china, crystal, and a colorful arrangement of fresh flowers. Ben sat at the far end of the table, away from Dan.

Dusk was darkening into night as the waiter appeared and lit several candles that spread a soft glow around the table. The smell of lavender from the garden scented the night air. Uncorking a bottle of wine, the waiter poured a tasting for Dan, who sipped it and nodded approval. "You'll enjoy this wine," Dan said as the waiter filled their glasses. "It's an Egon Muller Riesling from the great Muller vineyard, dating back to 1300."

Ellie and Ben tasted the wine and nodded in agreement. "Superb," Ben said, savoring the nutty citrus flavor. The waiter went back to the kitchen and soon returned with a tray of plated appetizers of scallops with cucumber and mango salsa. A fresh salad of arugula and watercress with goat cheese and cherry balsamic vinaigrette was served next.

When the chef appeared with the main course, Joan said, "Tell us what you prepared for us, Mara."

"Alaskan sea bass with lemon-shallot butter, accompanied by mushroom risotto in white wine and truffle oil and grilled asparagus," Mara said. "Enjoy."

"Thank you, Mara. It looks and smells delicious," Dan said.

They ate in silence, with Dan and Ben avoiding eye contact. "I'm sorry Matt couldn't be here tonight," Dan said.

"He has no idea what a fabulous dinner he's missing," Ellie said. Everyone mumbled in agreement, but the earlier neutral mood had shifted to an uncomfortable silence. Ellie sensed that Dan and her father had argued before she arrived.

Dan reached across the table and squeezed Ellie's hand. "I'm glad *you're* here," he said. Ellie smiled at her uncle.

"Dan, I'd like to take you up on your offer of a tour of the hospital and the specialty units. We could do a feature story…send our photographer for a photo shoot," Ellie said.

"Maybe in the next few months," Dan said.

"I was hoping we could do this next week."

"We're starting work on a new wing, and it'll be too chaotic."

"I hadn't heard," Ben said. "A new wing?"

Dan pressed his lips together. "It'll be dedicated to organ and tissue transplants." He turned to Ellie. "I can show you our OB/GYN and neonatal units. You could write a feature about how we save premature babies that weigh less than two pounds."

"I'd like that," Ellie said.

"The hospital must be doing many transplants if they're building an entire unit," Ben said.

"Yes," Dan said. "There's no more to say about it just yet."

"Where does the hospital get organs for transplant patients?" Ben persisted.

"The usual sources…accident victims," Dan said, his words clipped.

"Can we talk about something pleasant?" Joan asked.

"Do families volunteer? I mean after an accident, if a loved one dies?" Ellie asked.

"People sign up as donors on their drivers' licenses," Dan said.

"What if the driver's license doesn't give donor approval?" Ellie continued.

"We keep the patient on life support and then persuade the family to donate."

"That must be difficult," Ben said.

"We have a team of social workers and psychologists who are very persuasive," Dan said. "Enough on this depressing subject. Here's our dessert." The waiter arrived with a tray of tiramisu and espresso.

Ellie tasted a forkful of the tiramisu. "This is heavenly," she said, savoring the rich creamy confection.

"We have a pastry chef—Rita from California," Joan boasted.

"I'm glad you're enjoying dessert." Dan's face relaxed as the conversation returned to food.

They finished dessert, and Dan pushed his chair away and stood. "Let's go back to the house. I want to show you a new room," he said.

Ellie walked beside Dan, her sandals crunching on the gravel path. "Maybe a news story about how the hospital helps people who need organ transplants will encourage more donors," she suggested, but Dan pretended not to hear her.

Inside the house, Dan led them down a flight of stairs to the lower level. He opened the door to a large wood-paneled room with a wall-to-wall screen, a surround-sound system and stadium seating with leather chairs. "Our new media studio," he announced. "I receive advance copies of new films. I hope you'll both join me for a viewing."

When they returned to the sitting room, Joan rose from the sofa. "I'm going to have to beg off early. I feel a headache coming on," she said, dismissing her guests in her usual manner.

"Of course," Ben said. "I was just leaving."

"Me, too," Ellie said. "Thanks for a fabulous dinner and a lovely evening." She kissed Dan on his cheek. "Let me know when we can schedule the hospital tour."

Ellie and Ben walked to their cars parked in the driveway. "What was going on with you and Dan tonight?" Ellie asked.

"Nothing you need to be concerned about." Ben kissed his daughter on her forehead and opened his car door.

On the drive back to her apartment, Ellie puzzled over the barely-concealed hostility between her uncle and her father. She would have to persuade Dan to let her tour the hospital, a promise he seemed reluctant to keep now.

Chapter 7

Wednesday, August 5, 2009

It was raining steadily as Matt drove through the Appalachian Mountains to Red Ridge Prison. He was exhausted and tense by the time he pulled up to the prison entrance and showed his ID. After parking, he entered the prison and was ushered into the visitors' room. He sat behind a glass partition and waited for Rusty. Guards armed with tasers stood ready for action, as if they were in a war zone.

Matt's eyes swept around the room, where other prisoners sat talking to visitors over phones held awkwardly in their handcuffed hands. At the station to his right, an inmate with a spider web tattoo on his neck, signifying a long prison term, glared at Matt. The letters EWMN—evil, wicked, mean, nasty—were tattooed on his shaved head.

A side door opened and Rusty shuffled in, his legs in shackles, handcuffs on his wrists and an electroshock stun belt circling his waist. A guard accompanied him to the chair facing Matt. Though the thick glass between them was scratched and clouded, Matt could see a dark purple bruise beneath Rusty's right eye. Rusty picked up the phone and looked at Matt dully.

"How are you?" Matt asked. "I brought you some toiletries and chocolate."

"Thanks," Rusty mumbled.

"What happened to your eye? Your hand?"

There was a long silence while Rusty's face twitched. He turned to look at the cameras mounted on the ceiling. "I fell," he said.

"You can tell me the truth."

Rusty shifted in the chair, his eyes on the prisoner at the next station with the spider web tattoo. He blinked nervously and lowered his voice to a whisper. "There was a fight in the rec yard, and my friend was killed."

"The death that was reported about a week ago?"

"Yeah. My friend, Tony, was attacked by a gang. I jumped in to help him and got whacked in my eye. Then the dogs were let loose."

"Dogs?"

Rusty held up his bandaged hand. "Yeah."

"The guards sent in dogs?"

Rusty nodded. "Then I heard shots...and Tony stopped moving."

"Shots from where?"

"The watchtowers."

"Did Tony die in the rec yard?"

Rusty blinked rapidly. "Don't know for sure…Guards carried him away." Rusty doubled over and cried out in pain now. A guard rushed over, pulling him out of the chair and pushing him roughly to the door.

Matt set the phone back in the cradle. There was no point in protesting the abrupt end to the interview. On his way out, an inmate with a pronounced limp and bruised face was led inside. Outside in the hallway, a guard approached. "The warden wants to see you," he said.

"What's this about?" Matt asked.

"Follow me," he ordered. Matt thought better of protesting and followed him to an office at the end of the hallway. The guard knocked.

"Door's open," Warden Parker's voice boomed.

The guard opened the door and motioned for Matt to enter. The office was painted in cold gray, like the rest of the prison. Clayton Parker sat behind a large oak desk, a bull of a man in his mid-forties. His thick neck bulged against his shirt collar. "Sit." He glowered at Matt through deep-set eyes.

Matt sat in a chair facing Parker. "You wanted to see me?"

"You're likely going to print a lot of lies about us."

"I write the truth."

"What truth is that?" His lips curled in a sneer.

"Rusty Degan was abused."

"He was disciplined."

"Dogs, bullets and stun belts seem unusual to me."

"Red Ridge isn't a vacation resort. These men are dangerous criminals. We treat them accordingly."

"Rusty isn't dangerous. He doesn't belong here."

"This is where he was sent, and this is where he's going to stay. So, keep your nose out of Degan's case."

"Are you threatening me?"

"It's a suggestion."

"I'll report your suggestion in the Virginia Star." Matt stood and turned to the door.

"You take care." Parker's words followed Matt on his way out. The guard, waiting outside the door, escorted him to the exit.

Parker reached for the phone on his desk and punched in a number. "I don't want to see him here again!" he barked.

On the long drive back to Alexandria, Matt's thoughts turned to Rusty. Would he succeed in getting Rusty transferred out of there before it was too late? After what he had learned today, Matt was eager to call Nick Labelle and find out the autopsy results for Rusty's friend, Tony. Meeting Parker was an experience he wouldn't forget. The man derived pleasure from his power to inflict pain.

Chapter 8

Thursday, August 6, 2009

Dan was waiting in his office for Ellie when she arrived at the Medical Center at 9:00 a.m. It had taken many phone calls and a great deal of negotiating to persuade Dan to give her a tour. "I'll show you the maternity ward today and our neonatal intensive care unit," Dan said.

Ellie followed him to the elevator in the hallway. They rode to the ninth floor—the obstetrics and gynecology unit, and the maternity ward. They walked along a hallway with white walls and polished gray tile floors. Numbered exam rooms, most with closed doors, led off the long hallway, and the smell of antiseptics hung in the air.

"Women come here for routine gynecological exams and for prenatal and postnatal care," Dan explained. Ellie peered into the open doorway of an exam room with a familiar examination table, complete with metal foot stirrups. They passed a door labeled, *Radiology*. "Ultrasound exams are done here. Some are routine for the mother, and some are for fetal monitoring." Ellie scribbled notes while Dan talked.

At the end of the corridor, swinging doors opened into the maternity unit. The sounds of women moaning and crying drifted into the hallway. Nurses and doctors, dressed in blue scrubs, hurried in and out of the rooms. "Looks like a busy day," Dan said. "Maybe we'll get to see a delivery." Ellie's heart quickened in anticipation.

A door opened, and two male nurses wheeled out a gurney carrying a woman whose huge belly bulged beneath a white blanket. She thrashed from side to side, shrieking curses directed at no one in particular. Ellie winced at the sound of the woman's pain. A nurse murmured words of encouragement to her, "Breathe through the pain. Pant. You can do this, sweetheart." The gurney was rolled into a delivery room.

Ellie followed Dan to an observation theater adjacent to the delivery room. They sat on a bench, and Dan turned to her. "You're allowed to observe this delivery because the mother signed a written consent form. HIPAA privacy rules require this. Since this is a teaching hospital, patients generally agree."

Through the window, they watched as the pregnant woman was lifted onto a delivery table. A blue surgical drape covered her bulging abdomen. An obstetric nurse parted her legs, lifting and positioning them in metal stirrups. An anesthesiologist, stationed at the head of the table, placed a mask over the woman's mouth and nose.

"The mask will deliver oxygen to the patient during delivery. She'll also receive nitrous oxide in the mixture to take the edge off the most painful contractions that will come very rapidly," Dan explained. Ellie nodded, jotting quick notes she would read later.

A gowned and masked obstetrician entered the delivery room and stepped up to the table. She said something to the patient and examined her progress beneath the surgical drape. She nodded to the anesthesiologist, who adjusted the anesthesia. The laboring woman immediately relaxed and appeared to doze off.

A surgical assistant handed the doctor a scalpel. Ellie winced as the doctor made an incision and an assistant swabbed oozing blood. "Routine episiotomies are done to avoid painful vaginal ruptures that would take much longer to heal," Dan explained.

Moments later, the baby's head emerged from the birth canal, and her slippery body followed. Ellie gasped with excitement. The doctor lifted the newborn, placed her on her mother's abdomen and cut the umbilical cord. The infant's dark hair and small body were slick with bloody amniotic fluid.

The crying infant was carried to a nearby table, where a nurse cleaned her, wrapped her in a soft blanket and placed her in her mother's waiting arms. The new mother examined her baby and smiled with such adoration that her face seemed to glow. Her instant love for the new life she produced replaced her obvious exhaustion. Ellie was surprised by sudden tears that sprung in her eyes. *This young mother would never leave her child*, Ellie thought.

Dan led Ellie into the hallway. "Are you all right?" he asked.

"That was amazing," Ellie said.

"I'm glad you got to see a healthy birth. The newborn will be examined by one of our staff pediatricians and taken to the nursery."

Dan led Ellie through another set of doors to the nursery. They stopped in front of the nursery's large windows and looked in at rows of bassinets holding newborns swaddled in blankets, with knit caps covering their heads. Some infants cried, while others slept peacefully. Pediatric nurses moved around the nursery, monitoring the infants, changing diapers, and feeding some newborns with bottled formula.

Ellie smiled at the sight…new life holding so much hope. A young mother dressed in a robe entered the nursery and was led to a padded chair. A nurse carried her swaddled infant and placed him in her arms. The mother stroked her baby's cheek with her fingertips, her face glowing with love and awe. The scene brought on a sudden feeling of grief for Ellie, as if she had lost something. She stumbled back from the window as though someone had slapped her.

"What's wrong?" Dan asked.

"Nothing," she insisted, regaining her composure and forcing a weak smile. Dan sensed that the scene had evoked Ellie's memories of her mother. *It couldn't have been easy for a teenage girl, having her mother walk out of her life,* he thought. As for himself, he had conflicted feelings about his own mother, who could be loving but judgmental. "You should know better. You're the older brother," his mother often scolded.

Dan turned to Ellie. "I want to show you our newly expanded neonatal intensive care unit—the NICU." They entered the NICU through a set of double doors and stopped in front of large windows, where they could observe premature newborns in incubators. A nurse changed an infant's diaper and adjusted the oxygen hood covering his face.

"He's so tiny," Ellie said. "Will he survive?"

"Babies weighing less than three pounds are kept alive here."

Ellie's eyes were riveted to incubators where infants hooked up to breathing machines fought for life. Dan explained, "We expanded this unit to care for more preemies and also congenitally ill infants. We recently acquired a small private hospital. In fact, three new hospitals are now part of Virginia General. Patients get state-of-the-art care here."

"So, the hospital has grown since you took over as director," Ellie said.

"We're now the largest hospital in Virginia," he boasted. "And we're ranked number one."

"What about the new transplant unit?" she asked.

"It's in the planning stage," he said dismissively.

"I was just wondering…"

"I have business I must attend to now, but I hope you learned enough to write a favorable article."

"I appreciate what you've shown me. Can I send our photographer over to take some pictures for the article?"

"Have your photographer call me."

When they reached the lobby, Dan looked at his watch. "I'm late for my meeting."

"Thanks again, Dan." Ellie's words followed him as he hurried away.

***

Ellie slept fitfully that night, her mother's face drifting in and out of her mind. A dream carried her back in time to a cold December day in 1994 when she was thirteen years old. It was Saturday morning, a day she loved because her father was home. The smell of freshly-brewed coffee drifted up to her bedroom from the kitchen.

She threw the covers off, stepped out of bed onto the carpeted floor and went to Matt's room next door. The sound of her mother singing in the shower filled her with happiness. She flung open Matt's bedroom door. "Mom's home. We're having breakfast together," she said. Matt opened his eyes, blinked and huddled deeper beneath the blanket. Ellie poked him with her fingers. "Get up and get dressed," she said.

Matt stretched and yawned. "Get out of my room," he said.

"Downstairs in ten minutes," she ordered, on her way out of his bedroom. She didn't hear the shower any longer, so she knocked softly on her mother's bedroom door.

"Come in," Laura said.

Ellie stepped inside and sat on the bed, watching her mother style her long blonde hair. She drifted over to Laura's dressing table and fingered the perfume bottles and makeup containers. "Don't touch the Chanel," Laura ordered. Ellie pulled her hand away quickly. "You can try this one." Laura reached for a bottle of cologne and sprayed some on Ellie's neck. Ellie smiled, happy she would smell like her mother for as long as the scent lasted.

"Hot pancakes, everyone!" her father's voice boomed from the kitchen.

"Go ahead. I'll be down in a few minutes," Laura told her.

Ellie raced down the steps in her pajamas. Matt was already dressed in jeans and a T-shirt, seated at the table. A platter heaped with steaming pancakes sat in the center of the table next to a pitcher of maple syrup.

"Good morning." Ben smiled at his children and poured milk in a glass for Matt and a treat of half a cup of coffee for Ellie, who filled the rest of her cup with milk, added sugar and took a long gulp. She piled her plate with pancakes and poured syrup over them.

By the time Laura came into the kitchen, the pancakes had grown cold. She wore a suit and high-heeled shoes instead of her Saturday morning sweat suit outfit. "Just coffee for me," she said.

Ben set a mug of coffee on the table for Laura and sat down across from her. "Going somewhere?" he asked.

Laura sipped coffee, then set the mug down. "I need to talk to you. Upstairs." She pushed the chair out and headed to the staircase, with Ben following.

Ellie listened to their loud voices from above as she sat at the table, tearing off bits of paper napkin and rolling them into tiny balls. Matt raked his fork through a sticky puddle of maple syrup on his plate. Then Ellie pushed her chair away from the table. Matt followed her upstairs. They waited outside their parents' bedroom door.

Laura's words leaked through the door. "I won't live like this, terrified every time I go out because of the stories you print."

"You never tried to understand," Ben shouted.

"It's always about you and your damned newspaper."

"You didn't mind all the things it bought you."

"Spare me," Laura said.

"I never stood in the way of your singing gigs with the band…gone sometimes for weeks."

Ellie squeezed Matt's hand and swallowed hard to keep down the pancakes she had just eaten. Matt dropped her hand and snatched Laura's car keys from a small table in the hallway. The bedroom door flew open, and Ellie jumped back. Laura rushed out, carrying a suitcase. She brushed past Ellie, moving swiftly down the steps and across the hallway to the front door, her high-heeled shoes clacking against the polished wooden floor.

Ben took Ellie's hand, and they followed Laura outside, where she tossed her suitcase onto the back seat of her Mercedes and rummaged through her handbag. Matt ran out of the house, breathing hard, and stood beside Ellie.

"Where the hell are my keys? Ellie! Matt! Did you take my keys?" Laura stamped her feet. Ellie nudged Matt with her elbow and, when she looked into his eyes, she knew where to find her mother's keys.

Ellie hurried into the house, taking the stairs two at a time. In Matt's bedroom, she dragged a chair to the center of the room and climbed on it to reach a ceiling tile. She pried the loose tile with her fingers, poked her hand into the empty space, and pulled out the keys.

When she returned to the front walk, she held out the keys for her mother and grasped her hand. "Don't go, Mom."

"Take care of your brother, Ellie. I'm counting on you." Laura's fingers glided lightly across her daughter's cheek as though Ellie were a pet she was abandoning. Then she patted the top of Matt's head. "Matt, listen to Ellie. Behave yourself."

Then Laura stepped into the car, turning away from her husband and children. Matt wiped tears from his eyes with the back of his hand. Ellie's fingers pressed against her cheek, clinging to her mother's last touch. She squeezed Matt's hand as her mother sped away, leaving a trail of dust and gravel.

Ellie opened her eyes and sat up in bed, breathing hard. She shook her head, trying to dispel the haunting dream. The room was dark, except for a sliver of moonlight seeping beneath the blinds. Cold perspiration clung to her skin. Throwing off the blanket, she stepped out of bed and went to the kitchen for a bottle of water. After taking long gulps of the cold water, she went into the bathroom, shed her damp pajamas and turned on the shower. The hot water cascaded over her face and body, but it failed to wash away the feeling of loss.

Chapter 9

Monday, August 10, 2009

The conference room buzzed with conversations as the newsroom staff gathered for the daily editorial meeting. It was not like Ben to be late, but he didn't walk through the door until 10:15. He took a seat at the head of the table and ran his fingers through his hair, a habit that signaled the start of the meeting. "Good morning, everyone. Sorry I'm late, but I was on the phone with Dr. Andrews. He was very pleased with the feature article on the Virginia General Hospital. Nice job, Ellie."

"Thanks," Ellie said. "The hospital got some generous donations for their neonatal unit after the article ran."

"Matt, let's have your update on the prison investigation," Ben said.

"I visited Red Ridge a few days ago and saw things firsthand. The warden threatened me, which didn't surprise me. What did surprise me is that prisoners are seriously injured in fights and afterwards, they *disappear* from the prison."

"Disappear?" Ben asked.

"I spoke to Nick Labelle from Human Rights International. He confirmed that an inmate who was injured in a fight in July, and taken by ambulance to the Virginia General Hospital, later died of his injuries. Nick demanded an autopsy by the chief medical examiner, but the hospital reported that the prisoner had been cremated."

"Isn't that destroying evidence?" Ellie asked.

"The hospital claimed that the prisoner's family requested cremation. I'm working on contacting the family to corroborate this."

"Why was the prisoner taken 400 miles away to the Virginia General

Hospital?" Ellie asked.

"The prison claims there's no local hospital equipped to treat life-threatening injuries," Matt said. "In these cases, they can legally transport prisoners wherever treatment is available."

Ben scratched his head. "This story is getting more complicated, Matt." He turned to Ellie. "What do you have on Reynolds' death?"

"The hospital refused to identify the kidney donor. They're citing patient confidentiality rules. The Reynolds family is suing for wrongful death, and they demanded an autopsy of the donor by the chief medical examiner. The hospital told me that the autopsy request arrived *after* the donor was cremated," Ellie said.

"Ellie, see what you can learn from the hospital's pathology department," Ben said, "even if it's off the record." He turned to the managing editor. "Greg, let's have your update."

After Greg's report, the staff filed out of the conference room.

Matt returned to his cubicle and spent the rest of the morning doing online research. He logged in to the Bureau of Justice Statistics and found details through their Death in Custody Reporting Program. He learned that Virginia had the highest number of incarceration deaths. And, in the last year, there was a significant increase in deaths. Prisons could report the causes of death as homicide, accident or unknown. It was only in the last year that the category of inmate-involved homicide was added to the reporting data. Before that time, prisons could categorize these deaths as *unknown*.

Matt reached for his phone and punched in Nick Labelle's number. "Nick, this is Matt Andrews. You may have some information I could use for an article I'm working on."

"What do you need?" Nick asked.

"The names of the Red Ridge prisoners who died between 2008 and 2009 and were taken to Virginia General for treatment."

The question of how Bob Reynolds could have received an infected kidney, in spite of the hospital's screening process, continued to trouble Ellie. Dan's explanation only raised more questions. She turned to her computer and searched the U.S. Centers for Disease Control (CDC) website and the Food and Drug Administration (FDA) site. Both agencies had stringent regulations for human tissue and organ transplantation. Tissue banks and transplant hospitals were strictly regulated and accredited. In spite of all the safeguards, patients still had a 1% to 2% chance of acquiring a disease from a transplant.

Viruses like HIV, hepatitis C, fungus, bacteria, and parasitic infections continued to occur. And Bob Reynolds was another statistic.

Ellie set up a spreadsheet on her computer and extracted data she needed from the government websites. She listed Virginia hospitals where transplants had been done, transplant dates, diseases following transplants, number of cases for each disease and outcomes.

By early afternoon, Ellie had even more questions. Why did Virginia General have the highest number of diseases and deaths following transplants? It was not the predictable 1% to 2%, but closer to 25%. She printed the spreadsheet, walked across the newsroom floor and knocked on her father's office door.

"Come in," Ben said.

Ellie laid the spreadsheet on Ben's desk. "Take a look at the data. The Virginia General Hospital has an unusually high percentage of deaths following transplant surgery."

Ben studied the chart. "Hmm," he said, reaching for his phone. He punched in a number and clicked on the speakerphone. "Dan, I know you're busy, but don't hang up. Ellie found some information that we find puzzling. Can we run it by you?"

"What is it now?" Dan asked.

"Ellie learned that the medical center has a 25% death rate following transplants when the number should be more like 1% to 2%. Can you explain the discrepancy?"

Dan cleared his throat. "We do more transplants than any hospital in the state, and we accept the most critical cases. The patients who come here for transplants are likely to die because of comorbid conditions and other medical issues. Other hospitals would refuse to do transplants on many of the patients we accept, those who have nowhere else to turn. That's why the 1% to 2% death rate doesn't apply to us. And it's unreasonable for you to compare us to other hospitals."

"So, that's your explanation?" Ben asked.

"It's not *my* explanation. It's the *truth*," Dan said.

"Has the CDC questioned your data?" Ellie asked.

"Of course not. Why would they when they're aware of the critical cases we treat? Put your concerns to rest now and move on." Dan hung up.

Ben folded the spreadsheet and handed it to Ellie. "Don't file this away just yet."

"What does that mean?"

"I have more questions for Dan when he's in a better mood."

"Such as?"

"I'll let you know when I get the answers."

Ellie nodded, not pressing her father for more. She had learned long ago that Ben would say nothing until he had all the facts. She tucked the spreadsheet under her arm and walked to the door.

"Ellie, nice investigative work."

She turned to her father and smiled before closing the door behind her.

After Ellie left his office, Ben's eyes settled on a framed photograph sitting on his desk. Ellie at thirteen and ten-year-old Matt stood beside a decorated Christmas tree, smiling at him from the picture. It was Christmas day, 1994, a week after Laura had walked out of their lives. *Was he imagining sadness in their eyes or projecting his own feelings at that moment in time?*

His thoughts took him back to the day he met Laura. It was a warm evening, the air filled with the smell of spring, when Ben walked through the door of a local nightspot in Alexandria. He found an empty seat at the crowded bar and ordered vodka and tonic. As he sipped his drink, a young woman with long blonde hair and blue-green eyes, dressed in a black sequined dress that clung to her like a second skin, stepped onto the stage and started singing.

Men and women, gathered around the bar and seated at small tables, stopped their conversations to follow the singer's mesmerizing movements. Her voice was ordinary and, if not for the band that accompanied her, would have seemed less than ordinary. Ben was drawn to her swaying hips. She seduced him and the audience with an unspoken promise of forbidden sex... and something more.

When the music and applause ended, Ben walked up to her. "Wonderful performance," he told Laura. "Will you join me for a drink?"

Laura studied him, a seductive smile playing on her lips. "You are?"

"Ben Andrews, managing editor of the Virginia Star."

"That's an important job...managing editor of a newspaper. And you're good looking too," she teased.

After their first drink together, Ben returned to the club every night for the rest of the week to see Laura perform. When the act moved on to a new gig in Virginia, Ben traveled miles to see her again. She invaded his thoughts all day, every day, and he was grateful for whatever time she would spend with him. For the first time, he understood the meaning of obsession.

One evening, after they had been meeting for three weeks, Laura told him, "I'm so tired of traveling…sleeping in motels. I've been singing with a band ever since I can remember."

"Stay at my place," Ben offered.

The first night Laura came to his apartment in Alexandria, Ben told her, "I'll sleep on the sofa. You can have my bed."

"No need to do that." She smiled, shedding her clothing and slipping beneath the blanket.

Ben could not get enough of Laura. But, after three months, she was ready to move on. She showed up late at his apartment one night. "I'm going to Las Vegas next week," she told him. "I'm pregnant."

Ben folded her in his arms, planting kisses on her face and neck. "Marry me. You know I'm in love with you."

Laura's face hardened, and she slipped out of his arms. "I want an abortion," she demanded.

"I…I thought you felt the same about me."

"This isn't about feelings…or love. I'm not cut out to be a mother."

Ben didn't understand then that those were the most honest words Laura had ever spoken.

"I won't stand in the way of your career if you marry me." He knew he was begging, but he would have made any bargain then. The thought of losing her took his breath away.

After Ellie was born, Ben believed that Laura's feelings would change. *Every mother loves her child*, he had thought then. But he soon came to understand that she didn't have feelings like other mothers. Their married life began with Laura going off on gigs with her band regularly. Ben hired Irma Carson as a nanny and housekeeper. She was warm, patient and understanding, and she adored Ellie.

When Ellie was just a toddler, Laura returned from a singing gig in California and announced, "Ben, I'm pregnant." He expected her to be furious, to demand an abortion. But she smiled and kissed him.

Ellie was three years old when Matt was born and, for the first time in their marriage, Laura was content to stay home with her children. She loved their expensive new house in the Virginia suburbs, the red convertible Ben bought her, and the jewelry he gave her.

But, when Matt was a year old, Laura grew restless and soon began traveling again with her band. For the next eight years, Laura would take off for weeks at a time, returning happy and animated. She brought small forgiveness gifts for the children, who showered her with hugs and kisses, interpreting her gifts as love. Then, a week before Christmas, in 1994, she left for the last time.

"Is Mom coming home today?" Matt had asked that Christmas day.

"We'll see...maybe," Ben told him, though he knew that Laura had changed her cell phone number and sold the Mercedes to a car dealer.

The family spent that sad holiday with the Nolans, long-time friends. They exchanged gifts with the Nolans' children and enjoyed a sumptuous turkey dinner. But Ben and the children returned to a house without Laura. Ellie went to her room to read a new book she received as a gift, and Matt sulked on the sofa in the den, watching TV. When Ben opened the door to Ellie's room to kiss her goodnight, he overheard her childish bargain with God, words that still tore at his heart, "Please bring her back. I promise never to ask for anything again."

As the weeks, months and years passed, Ellie and Matt stopped asking when their mother was coming home. Ben had believed that they were better off not knowing the truth. *Had he been wrong to encourage their hope?* It was a question that still troubled him.

Ben shook off the painful memories and turned to his computer screen now. A report on *Yahoo News* caught his attention: *The Centers of Disease Control reported ten new cases of hepatitis C infection in patients who recently received tissue transplants from a deceased donor.*

Chapter 10

Tuesday, August 11, 2009

Ellie was so focused on a phone conversation with a doctor at the CDC that she didn't see Ben standing in the doorway of her cubicle. "Which Virginia hospitals did the transplants?" Ellie asked the CDC doctor. She scribbled on a notepad. "How many cases of Hep-C has the Virginia General Hospital reported from the infected donor?" She wrote a number on the notepad. "And the donor's name?" she asked. There was a long silence. "Dr. Finn, are you there?" His answer was the sound of a click. She sighed and set the phone down.

Ben cleared his throat, and Ellie turned to him. "How long have you been standing there?"

"I heard," he said. "So, what did you learn?"

"Seven of the ten Hep-C cases occurred *after* transplants at the Virginia General Hospital. The transplant tissue...different kinds—bone, ligaments, veins—came from one infected donor. The CDC won't release the name of the donor. Probably legal issues."

"We need answers," Ben said. "I wasn't eavesdropping on your phone call. I stopped by to ask if we can meet for dinner tonight."

"I told some of the staff I'd go for drinks with them after work...but I can cancel," Ellie said.

"Don't do that. We can have dinner tomorrow night."

"It's a date," she smiled. She looked forward to spending time alone with her father. They usually met for dinner on Thursdays, and she wondered what was on his mind.

Ben returned to his office and phoned his brother. "Dan, tell me about the seven new Hep-C cases at the hospital?"

"How do you know there were seven cases?" Dan asked.

"From the CDC. It's public records, so you may as well tell me what happened."

"Cases like these are not unusual," Dan said impatiently.

"You mean infected tissue passes screening tests?" Dan didn't answer.

"Where does the hospital get transplant tissue?" Ben persisted.

"From a reliable source."

"That's not an answer."

"I won't have you dragging our source into this," Dan snapped.

"The information will go public whether you tell me now or not. All these new cases and Bob Reynolds' death demand an explanation."

There was a long pause before Dan spoke. "The Virginia Organ Procurement Agency…and I can tell you that every hospital in Virginia, and in other states, gets transplant tissue from them. We're doing an internal investigation. Can't you wait for our report?"

"The Star is doing some initial fact finding."

"I know all about your fact-finding methods." Dan slammed the phone down, the sound reverberating in Ben's ear.

Ben turned to his computer and typed, *Virginia Organ Procurement Agency*. The agency's website opened on the screen. Their phone number was listed, and Ben reached for his phone.

"Ben Andrews here from the Virginia Star to speak to Brian Payne," he told the receptionist who answered.

A few minutes passed before Ben heard, "Brian Payne speaking."

"Brian, I just spoke to my brother, Dr. Dan Andrews."

"I'm aware of the situation, and we're investigating," Payne said.

"I'm sure you are, but I need a face-to-face meeting with you."

"My calendar is full for the next month."

"Half an hour is all I'm asking for."

"Can't even spare half an hour now. Call back in a few weeks."

"I wouldn't want to print something misleading about the tissue bank while I'm waiting to meet with you," Ben said.

After a prolonged silence, Payne said, "I'll fit you in tomorrow morning, 10:00 o'clock. My office." He hung up abruptly.

At 7:00 p.m., Ben gathered the papers he wanted to review before his meeting with Payne tomorrow and stuffed them into his briefcase. He logged off his computer and walked out of his office, closing the door behind him. A few diehards were still at their desks in the newsroom, and Ben waved to them on his way out. Stepping into the elevator, he rode it down to the parking garage.

The garage was nearly empty when Ben got into his Volvo, started the motor and headed for his house in the suburbs. He turned on the radio and tuned in to a classical music station. The sound of a Chopin sonata filled the car, and his thoughts drifted to his phone conversation with Dan. *Why was Dan evasive and hostile whenever he questioned him about the Reynolds death or cases of Hep-C from transplants? Was he protecting the hospital or himself?*

With rush hour nearly over, highway traffic was lighter. The music took the edge off Ben's anger. He knew he should cut Dan some slack. It couldn't be easy for him, dealing with major damage control at the hospital. His thoughts turned to Dan as a youngster. Max was overly critical of Dan, no matter what he achieved. There was nothing Dan could do that would squeeze some praise from their father's lips. Sometimes Max treated Dan like he wasn't even his son. As for their mother, she was silent when she could have defended him. *Was she afraid of Max, too?*

Ben accelerated to seventy miles per hour now, eager to get home. Traffic was building behind him, and he slowed to let oncoming cars pass. He made it a point not to drive in a herd. When the traffic finally thinned, only a black SUV was visible in the distance.

Ben's eyes grew heavy with fatigue, and he changed the radio station to one playing popular music. The sound of Billy Joel singing, *My Life*, filled the car, lifting his spirits. As the music swirled around his ears, Ben slowed to let the SUV, coming up behind him, pass. But the driver didn't pass. Through his rearview mirror, Ben could see that it was a Ford Explorer. It edged closer, tailgating, flashing its brights. *What is his problem?* Ben thought. *Just pass me and get off my tail, asshole.*

Ben moved into the right lane to let him pass. But instead of passing, the Explorer edged along the left side of Ben's car, inching closer…too close. Beads of sweat broke out on Ben's face. *This guy is homicidal or he gets his jollies playing chicken.* A moment after these thoughts went through his head, the Explorer sideswiped him. The startling sound of metal scraping against metal jolted him, jarring all his senses. He clutched the steering wheel to keep the car from swerving, his heart racing. The tires screeched as Ben's car skidded onto the gravel shoulder. Instinctively, Ben pulled the wheel sharply left and maneuvered back into the right lane. Stepping hard on the accelerator, he sped away, his face and underarms dripping with perspiration, the sound of his heart thundering in his ears.

Up ahead, the Explorer slowed, waiting. Ben passed him, speeding ahead. The speedometer read eighty-five miles per hour, not a speed Ben was comfortable with. A road sign announced *Old Rolling Road*. Ben made a sharp right, exiting the highway. Through the rearview mirror, he no longer saw the Explorer, and he exhaled with relief. He drove along the familiar road, his head spinning with thoughts, his heart still beating erratically. Billy Joel sang from the radio, *Only the Good Die Young*. Ben snapped off the radio.

After driving another mile, Ben approached the small town. A traffic light ahead turned red, and he was relieved to stop behind a line of cars. *Surely, I lost the maniac*, he thought, sucking air into his lungs. But, when his eyes moved to the side mirror, the Explorer's bright headlights reflected back at him. His heartbeat quickened along with his breathing. He needed to think clearly, to make the right decision about his next move, but instinct warned him to flee.

Ben maneuvered into street traffic. The Explorer was trapped behind a jam of slow-moving cars. Up ahead, a line of cars was exiting a school parking lot. It looked like an event had just ended there. Ben made a sharp right turn into the schoolyard. He drove to the back of the school, parked and shut off his headlights. He sat there in the dark for fifteen minutes. Then he started his car and drove around to the front of the school, where cars were still lined up, waiting to exit. Ben eased his car into the lineup. He checked his mirrors and, with no sighting of the Explorer, he drew in a deep breath.

Pulling out of the schoolyard onto the main street, Ben passed a small grocery, a diner, a pub. Though there was no sign of the Explorer, he was reluctant to get back on the highway. He slowed and pulled into the pub's parking lot. After easing into a space, he stepped out and examined his car. There was a wide scrape along the left doors where the paint had been gouged off. He thought about calling the local police to report the incident. But he didn't have the Explorer's license plate number and there were thousands of similar vehicles. Paint scraped off the side of his car didn't prove someone was deliberately after him. He would sound like a nut.

The pub was crowded when Ben walked in, but he found an empty seat at the bar and ordered a beer. Conversations and laughter swirled around the room. People appeared to know each other. Ben sipped the beer, beginning to relax in the friendly atmosphere. The smell of grilling meat reminded him that he hadn't eaten for hours. He ordered a burger and another beer.

When the bartender set the burger down in front of him, Ben didn't notice the newcomer who took a seat across the bar and ordered a drink. The large man, with a military haircut, kept his eyes on Ben's reflection in the mirror behind the bar. Ben bit into the burger, savoring the smokey flavor. A long swallow of beer quieted his nerves. He was glad he had stopped here for something to eat. He felt normal again.

The car chase jarred Ben's memory of a long-ago incident when a brick had been hurled through his living room window. Laura had been in the kitchen with the children, and he was upstairs in his home office when the sound of shattering glass rang through the house. There was a note attached to a rock missile, warning Ben to stop writing articles about a local gang's crime spree. He still remembered Laura's angry words, "Your newspaper will get us all killed. I can't live like this...afraid all the time."

Ben dismissed the unsettling memory and downed the rest of the beer. After paying the bartender, he walked out of the pub, certain it was safe to head home. He didn't notice the Explorer parked in the shadows when he started his car and pulled onto the main street.

It was nearly 8:30, and the sky had darkened when Ben eased his car onto the highway. He wasn't more than fifteen minutes from home now. He drove steadily, anxious to get off the highway. His eyes moved reflexively to the rearview mirror, where he sighted a vehicle with bright headlights in the distance. His heart jumped, but he told himself he was being paranoid. *It couldn't be the Explorer. Surely, he had lost him by now.* But as the vehicle drew closer, Ben knew it was him.

He floored the accelerator, his heart pumping wildly. His car lurched ahead. The Explorer sped up, only inches away now, its blinding headlights bouncing off the rearview mirror into his eyes. The deafening sound of metal slamming against metal rang out when the Explorer rammed him. Ben braked and skidded, the tires screeching. His head snapped back. A sharp pain shot down his neck.

The Explorer pulled alongside. Ben turned for a fraction of a second to look through his side window. A beefy-looking man with military-cut hair smirked at him before sideswiping again. A split-second flash of recognition spun through Ben's mind...the man sitting at the bar less than half an hour ago. Streams of perspiration dripped down Ben's face and beneath his clothing, soaking him in fear.

Up ahead was a familiar sign, warning of a sharp curve and a speed limit of twenty miles per hour. Ben was always cautious around this curve, keeping to the speed limit. His home exit was minutes away. He only had to clear the curve. He could feel the blood pumping through his veins, urging him on to safety. He navigated the curve at sixty miles per hour, the tires screeching in protest as the Explorer hugged his left.

As Ben cleared the sharpest point of the curve, a deafening crack rang out. The Volvo's front-left tire exploded, sending it into a dizzying spin. Ben pulled the steering wheel sharply left, away from the guardrail looming ahead. But it was too late to slow the car as it took the curve. It lurched ahead, crashing through the guardrail with an ear-piercing sound of metal colliding with metal at sixty miles per hour.

The impact split the Volvo's front end down the middle. The airbags deployed, smashing against Ben's head and chest, filling his lungs with the acrid smell of propellant. Smoke from the airbags rose from the dashboard. As the car was propelled into the air, Ben felt weightless, much like the feeling he had when he took off in a plane. Time seemed suspended as he careened down the hillside, passing thick shrubbery that he could almost reach out and touch. Ahead was a large oak tree, waiting for him like Father Time. Shock dispelled his fear, surrounding him with an eerie calmness. In his mind, he saw Ellie and Matt. He was overwhelmed with disappointment that there was no time to tell them how much he loved them, how proud he was of them, how he felt responsible for their mother leaving them.

The Volvo hurtled ahead, moving ever closer to the oak tree. When the car slammed into the tree, the startling sound of crushing metal and shattering glass filled Ben's ears. He was shaken back and forth with such force, it felt as though his organs were being torn from his body.

An eerie silence settled on the wreck. *Am I alive?* Ben wondered. The smell of leaking gasoline wrapped around him, bringing him back to reality. The airbag and the seat belt pressed him against the seat. He tried to move his fractured arm to unhook the belt, but it hung limp and useless at his side. He didn't yet feel pain, though blood trickled into his eyes from a deep gash on his head. The smell of gasoline grew stronger, gripping him in panic. He writhed in the seat, desperate to release the belt. The explosion that followed was deafening. Mercifully, Ben was too shocked to feel pain, as flames engulfed the car.

Drivers along the stretch of highway above bore witness to the flames that lit the night sky, heard the roar of exploding gasoline, or perhaps smelled the noxious odor of burning rubber, metal, plastic, chemicals and human flesh. By the time emergency vehicles arrived at the scene, the sound of silence had settled around the smoldering wreck.

Chapter 11

Tuesday, August 11, 2009

Ellie's spirits were high when she stepped into her apartment at 11:00 p.m. Spending the evening with friends from the office reminded her how much she had neglected her social life. After mingling with her co-workers at a local pub, she went to Mario's Pizzeria with her friend, Claire, and Jack, the new graphic designer. It felt good to take a break from her non-stop work schedule. Claire was right when she told her, "Lighten up." The night out had given her a fresh perspective.

She walked into her bedroom humming *Sweet Caroline*, which still buzzed in her head from the pub. She kicked off her shoes and thought about Jack's eyes on her all evening. He was kind of cute, she admitted, but she was adamantly against dating co-workers.

"When was the last time you were out on a date, Ellie?" Claire had whispered in her ear. Ellie couldn't remember.

The unexpected sound of the doorbell, loud and insistent, startled her. She hurried to the door barefooted. When she peered through the peep hole, two uniformed police officers looked back at her—a man and a woman. Her heart raced as she unlocked the door.

"Ma'am, we're here to report an accident," the female officer said.

"What?" Ellie's face drained of color.

"A Volvo, registered to Benjamin Andrews, was found near the Beltway. Is he a relative?" she asked.

Ellie gasped. "Where? Where's my father?"

"There was a body in the car," the male officer said.

"No!" Ellie screamed...a scream seeming to come from outside her.

"We need you to come with us to identify..." the officer's words floated around Ellie as she collapsed onto the floor.

When Ellie regained consciousness, she was lying on the sofa. Matt was beside her, pressing a cold pack against her forehead. Her eyes opened slowly, resting on Matt's grim face. The police officers stood at the side of the living room, waiting.

"No, no, no. It's not true. It can't be," Ellie sobbed.

Matt folded her in his arms. "We need to go with the police now," he said. "Put on your shoes." He held her shoes out, coaxing her like a small child. She slipped her shoes on and followed him.

The rest of the night felt like otherworldly scenes unfolding on a movie set. Ellie and Matt were escorted to the county morgue, where they identified Ben's keys and his watch, which survived the fire. Photographs of part of the Volvo's license plate, which was intact, helped them make a positive identification.

***

Three days later, after Matt had arranged for Ben's dental records to be sent to the medical examiner, an autopsy report was completed. When Ellie and Matt picked up the report, the medical examiner kept using the word, "remains," as if their father were leftover food on a dinner plate.

Ellie moved through the days that followed as though she were a ghost, her senses dulled, her mind far away. Food had no taste or smell. Day turned to night with nothing in between that she could remember. The phone rang constantly, but she didn't answer. Matt showed up every evening with take-out food. "Eat," he ordered.

One evening, the words she had held back for days spilled out. "It's my fault that he's dead. Dad asked me to have dinner with him that night. If I hadn't been out having a good time, he'd still be alive." Her confession gave her some small relief, but not from the unbearable guilt.

Matt weighed his response for some moments. "You didn't cause the accident. Everything that happens in life can have another outcome, another ending, another possibility."

"*My choice* caused the outcome."

"That's twisted, Ellie, and you know it is."

"It's the truth."

"We don't know the truth about what caused the accident. Dad was a good driver. He drove that highway every day, twice a day. Maybe someone else, another driver, made a bad choice that caused the accident."

Ellie couldn't and wouldn't accept Matt's reasoning. She could not forgive herself. She pushed the uneaten food around on her plate with the fork. Matt sighed, pulled the chair back from the table and gathered the dishes. He tossed Ellie's uneaten dinner in the trash and left the dishes to soak in the sink. "Try to get some sleep. I'll see you tomorrow," he said, planting a kiss on her forehead.

August 22, 2009

A memorial service was held for Ben at a church near Dan's home. Dan was composed, taking charge of all the details. The church was filled with people who knew and admired Ben. The entire newspaper staff sat side by side, red-eyed and grim.

Eulogies were delivered, but Ellie didn't hear the words. Matt sat beside her, pressing her hand in his. Her eyes were riveted on the coffin. *It's a mistake,* she kept thinking. *My father can't be in the coffin.*

At the graveside, there were more words spoken that Ellie didn't hear over the roar in her head. When Ben's coffin was lowered into the grave, she was handed a shovelful of dirt. That was the moment she collapsed in a heap on the grass beside the open grave.

Ellie woke up on a bed in a guest room at Dan's house. The sound of conversations drifted to her from downstairs. Her mind felt detached from her body, and a strange feeling of observing everything from far away made her head spin. She pulled herself up and went into the bathroom. She splashed water on her face and patted it dry with a towel. Then she looked at her ruined face in the mirror, ran her fingers through her curls and walked out of the room.

When she came into the dining room, Dan moved to her side and took her hand. "Feeling better?" he asked. She didn't answer, and he led her to a table set with platters of catered food. "Have something to eat," he told her. Ellie nodded and sat down heavily in a chair, staring into space. Dan left her sitting there.

Matt appeared with a plate of food for her. She took it and set it down idly on the table. "You scared us," Matt said.

Ellie looked at him, uncomprehending. "Why?"

"Because you passed out."

Ellie turned this thought over in her mind. She didn't remember. Matt went to the coffee urn on a sideboard, filled a cup and placed it in Ellie's hand. She sipped the coffee, her eyes settling on the men and women milling around the room. Joan flitted between guests as if she were hosting a celebratory dinner party.

People Ellie and Matt didn't know mumbled awkward condolences and moved on. One by one, newspaper staff came up to them, wiping tears from their eyes, their grief palpable. They had loved and admired Ben, who had treated them more like family than employees.

Finally, it was over. The house emptied of guests and a hollow stillness settled over the dining room. Half-eaten platters of food, empty cups and soiled napkins were the sad remains of the day. Dan turned to Ellie and Matt. "Why don't you both stay with us for a few days," he offered.

"You must stay," Joan said without enthusiasm.

Matt stood. "Thanks, but I need to get home."

"Me too," Ellie said. "I won't be sleeping much, and I can do that in my own bed."

***

Ellie isolated herself in her apartment, losing track of time. Days went by as grief consumed her, dragging her deeper and deeper into a prison of despair. Sleep offered little refuge. Feelings of guilt haunted her dreams. Tormenting thoughts repeated in her mind: *He'd still be alive if I hadn't been selfish. It took seconds for someone you loved to be ripped out of your life…her mother, now her father. One bad choice and she and Matt were orphans.*

She had always been the strong one, looking after Matt, keeping him out of trouble. Now Matt showed up at her apartment every evening and dragged her out of bed. "Get up and shower," he said. "When was the last time you ate?" She didn't answer. "Get dressed. We're going out for dinner," he told her. When she refused, he said, "It's an order, not an invitation."

That night they went to a local Italian restaurant. Matt ordered pizza and beers for them. When the pizza arrived, he dished out a large slice for Ellie. "Eat," he commanded. "You look like crap." Ellie's clothes hung on her. Her face was pale and drawn, her eyes red and puffy. She nibbled on the pizza, but it was tasteless. She studied the new lines that creased Matt's brow and the dark circles beneath his eyes, making him look older than his twenty-five years. "I'm going to find out what happened," he told her.

"What do you mean?" she asked.

"I have questions."

"What questions?"

"I'll tell you when I get the answers."

Ellie didn't press him for more. She knew from experience that Matt would dig up all the facts he could before he told a story. After he dropped Ellie off at her apartment that night, she crawled into bed and fell into a troubled sleep. The doubt that Matt had implied surfaced in her sleep. *What if it wasn't an accident?*

Chapter 12

Monday, September 21, 2009

After meeting for breakfast at a local diner, Ellie and Matt walked into the newsroom at 8:30 a.m. Matt squeezed her hand. "You'll be okay. You're stronger than you think." Ellie couldn't think beyond getting through this first day as she slipped quietly into her cubicle. She turned on her computer and concentrated on catching up on current news.

Staffers began arriving. One by one, they greeted Ellie and Matt with tears in their eyes. Greg Burrows, who had been charged with running the newspaper while Dan was busy reorganizing, came into Ellie's cubicle. "We miss Ben more than you can imagine," he said. Ellie nodded, not trusting herself to speak. "There's an editorial meeting at 10:00," he said on his way out. She sighed and turned back to her computer.

At 10:00 a.m., Ellie and Matt walked into the conference room together. Reporters and other staffers were already seated around the table. An abnormal silence replaced the usual buzz of conversation before an editorial meeting. Most of the staff, except for Greg, had not yet met the new publisher. Ellie sat next to Matt at the far end of the long table, her face pale and drawn. Matt stared into space, the stress of the last few weeks etched in new lines on his brow.

All eyes followed Dan as he entered the room. His shirt sleeves were rolled up, revealing a gold watch on his wrist. He sat at the head of the table, his face impassive as his eyes swept over his employees. "Good morning," he began. "I believe that I'm speaking for all of us when I say that Ben's death is a tragedy. This is a difficult time for you and me. You probably don't know this, but my father, Max, started the Virginia Star and left it to Ben and *me*. Ben was the newspaper guru, while my career has been in medicine and hospital administration."

Dan poured water in a glass from a pitcher on the table. He sipped the water and continued. "I'm assuming the role of publisher now." His gaze rested on Ellie and Matt. Tears welled in Ellie's eyes, but Matt looked down, his jaw set. "The Virginia Star will continue to be the best newspaper in the county. That's why we need a new vision, one that meets the changing needs of our readers. Our audience isn't looking for investigative reporting or news they already get from *The New York Times* and *The Washington Post*. They want *local news* about people, businesses and events right here in their neighborhood."

Staffers shifted in their seats. Ellie met Matt's worried eyes. Dan continued, "We'll be doing feature stories on local celebrities and people of interest. We're going to expand our arts and leisure section with more reviews of films, theater and local restaurants. The Star has a high demographic readership and we'll offer a new expanded travel section."

Dan stood and opened the door. "I want to introduce a new member of the staff," he said, ushering in a man in his late twenties, dressed in an expensive suit and tie. "This is Paul White, our new advertising director." Carol, who was the advertising manager for the Star for the past eight years, was startled, her face draining of color.

Turning to Paul, Dan said, "Tell us about yourself, Paul."

Paul smiled smugly at the staffers, who stared back stone-faced. "I'm a graduate of Georgetown University, and I worked in New York City for several ad agencies and publications. I know how to use advertising to increase profits for this newspaper and for local businesses. I have a great track record, and…"

"Thank you, Paul," Dan cut him off. "We'll hear more about ad campaigns in the weeks to come. When we expand local news coverage, we'll be able to sell more ad space and increase our revenue, which is what we're in business for. Some of you will be getting new assignments. But in the meantime, I'm counting on all of you to do your part as we reorganize. Now, let's get back to work. We have a newspaper to get out."

The staffers filed out, grim-faced and silent. Ellie and Matt struggled behind. "Ellie, Matt, stay a few minutes," Dan said. They took seats beside Dan. "Bring me up to date on your assignments," Dan said.

Ellie began, "I'm working on an article about disease transmission from organ and tissue transplants. After Bob Reynolds' death…"

Dan interrupted. "There won't be any additional stories on this subject. There's no reader interest in this."

"But it's a *local* story, and there's so much more…" she started to protest before he cut her off.

"You'll be covering local politics," Dan said. Ellie's surprise at the harshness in his voice left her speechless.

Matt drummed on the table with his fingers. "What about you, Matt?" Dan asked.

"You already know that I'm investigating Red Ridge. It *is* a Virginia prison and a *local* story," he said.

"You've already written a feature article."

"I'm just getting started with the list of abuses there. I interviewed a prisoner who's giving me valuable information."

"I had Greg conduct an informal poll of our readership. There isn't sufficient interest in the subject for us to continue," Dan said. "You'll be assigned to local business reporting."

Matt clenched his fists, his lips pressed tight. "One more thing," Dan continued. "You're *not* authorized to tell Greg to publish an announcement in the Star without my approval. Asking for witnesses to Ben's accident to contact you was inappropriate. The accident is a police matter. Don't do it again."

Matt's eyes flashed with anger. "Give all your files on Red Ridge to Greg for archiving," Dan ordered.

"No," Matt shouted. "They're my files, my research."

"You work for the newspaper, and the files belong to us, not to you personally."

Matt sprung from his chair, lunged across the table and grabbed Dan by his shirt collar. "Fuck you, Dan."

"Matt!" Ellie pulled him back.

Dan shifted in the chair, adjusting his shirt collar. The color rose in his cheeks. "Take a few days off," he snapped. "Then we'll discuss your new assignment."

Matt stormed out, slamming the door so hard that the sound reverberated through the room. Dan removed his glasses, rubbing his twitching right eye.

"Matt hasn't been himself since…" Ellie said.

"I miss Ben too. But his death is no excuse for Matt's behavior."

"Give him some time," she implored.

"There isn't anything I wouldn't do for you and Matt. You're my family."

Ellie stared at her uncle, who suddenly seemed like a man she no longer knew. Her father's death had changed him too, she reasoned.

"I gave up my medical directorship at the hospital to run this newspaper,"

Dan said.

"Why?"

"The Virginia Star has been in the family for fifty-eight years. I want to keep it that way, and that means I need to run it."

"Your father isn't here judging you."

The truth of her words made him pause. "I feel an obligation to do this, and I *want* to be publisher."

"Your job as medical director of a major hospital *must* be more important to you."

"Someone else can manage that well enough. I'll still confer with them on certain hospital decisions as an adviser. I grew up with the Virginia Star in my blood and I'm going to run it now."

Ellie gathered her papers, feeling a shift in her relationship with Dan. Something had changed. A new hardness had replaced the understanding uncle she had taken for granted. "I'll talk to Greg about my new assignment," she told him on her way out, hiding her disappointment.

Chapter 13

Wednesday, September 23, 2009

Matt walked up to the information desk at the Fairfax County Police Department. "I have an appointment with Detective Malone," he told the officer on duty.

"Second floor," the officer said, pointing to a stairwell. Matt climbed the steps to the main office, where uniformed and plain-clothes detectives sat at desks arranged around the floor. The sounds of ringing phones and buzzing fax machines filled the room with background noise. The smell of stale coffee and leftover food hung in the air.

Matt found Malone at his desk in the center of the office. Malone stood and held out his hand when Matt approached. "I'm sorry for your loss," he said with practiced sympathy in his voice.

Matt nodded. "Thanks."

"How can I help you?"

"I read the police report on my father's accident. I have some questions."

Malone scanned the police report spread out on his desk. "The accident details are all here—photographs, diagrams that the investigating officer drew, witness's statement. What more can I tell you?"

"It's the cause of the accident I'm questioning. According to the report, the accident was my father's fault. But nothing in the report is conclusive."

"After examining the evidence at the scene of the accident, the investigating officer concluded that your father was at fault because he was speeding at sixty miles per hour around a curve in the road that had a twenty-mile-per-hour limit. Your father lost control of the car, stepped on the brake pedal and skidded into the guardrail. If he was going that fast, the car could easily have crashed through the guardrail. These are the facts," Malone said with conviction.

Matt drew in a breath. "I'm puzzled because my father drove this highway every day. He wasn't a reckless driver. I drove that stretch of road with him many times, and he wouldn't have been speeding around that curve in the road. It doesn't make sense."

Malone pointed to photographs of the skid marks on the road. "These tire marks are evidence of the speed of the car before it skidded and crashed through the guardrail."

"Skid marks indicate that my father stepped on the brake. Isn't that correct?"

"What's your point?"

"Something happened that made my father step on the brake."

"He was going too fast, and he lost control. Brakes don't right things when you lose control," Malone insisted.

Matt pulled a photograph out of his briefcase and slid it across Malone's desk. "This is a photo of a tire remnant I found on the road a few days after the accident. I had a forensic expert examine it."

Malone studied the photo for some moments. "This doesn't prove anything."

"The frayed fiber ends indicate that the tire was torn apart by force...by a blowout. If something caused a blowout, wouldn't that explain the accident?"

Malone shrugged. "Possibly. But we don't know if the tire remnant you found on the road came from your father's car."

"I confirmed that it did. My father purchased four new tires only two weeks before the accident. The tire shop positively identified the tire remnant as coming from the same kind of tires my father had purchased."

Malone scratched his head. "Thousands of cars have the same tires. If there was a blowout, which I'm not saying happened, it could have been caused by a nail in the road, a defect in the tire...who knows?"

"I'd like to examine the wreckage."

"The car was consumed by fire. It's been compacted by this time."

"Compacted? You destroyed evidence?"

"I don't care for your tone of voice, Mr. Andrews. We did *not* destroy evidence. Everything was photographed and documented. Your father's insurance company investigated and came to the same conclusion we did. I believe you have a copy of the insurance report. You had ample time to file a request to examine the wreckage before it was disposed of." Malone closed the file folder on his desk and stood. "I don't have any more information to give you, Mr. Andrews. I think you need to accept the facts in the police report and get on with your life."

Matt didn't respond to Malone's abrupt dismissal. He pushed his chair out, turned and walked across the noisy office to the exit. He took note of a police officer across the room—a large burly man with closely-cropped brown hair—following him with his eyes. *A pit bull*, Matt thought, as he walked to his car in the parking lot.

Before starting his car, Matt reached for his phone and punched in a number. After three rings, he heard, "Ralph Citron here."

"Ralph, this is Matt Andrews. I got your name from a police accident report. I understand that you were a witness to my father's accident on the Beltway a few weeks ago."

"I told the police everything I saw."

"I read your statement in the report. But I'm doing some further investigating, and I'd like to meet you...wherever you say."

"I don't think I can tell you more than you already know. But if you think I can help, I can meet you at Mackie's Bar and Grill at 7:00 tonight. It's on King Street."

"I know the place. See you then...and thank you." Matt hung up, excited by the prospect of interviewing an eyewitness.

***

Matt walked into Mackie's Bar and Grill a few minutes before 7:00 p.m. Men and women were seated around the circular bar. Noisy chatter filled the dimly-lit room, and the smell of beer and peanuts filled the air. Matt scanned the tables, and his eyes settled on a young man with light brown hair seated alone in the rear, nursing a beer. Matt made his way to the table. "Ralph Citron?" he asked.

"Yes." Ralph held out his hand. He had a strong handshake and a friendly smile. Matt pulled up a chair.

"I appreciate your meeting me," Matt said.

"Sorry about your father. My wife and I have a subscription to the Virginia Star. I admired the editorials and stories your father published."

"Thank you."

"I was shocked when I learned that the accident I saw was the one that killed your father. I was on my way home from work when I saw flames and smoke coming from the ravine off the highway. A few days later, when I read the news about the accident, I realized that I had seen the aftermath."

A waiter approached the table. "What can I get you?" he asked.

"I'll have a Heineken," Matt said. "And another beer for my guest. Put it on my check." He turned back to Ralph. "Can you tell me exactly what you saw?"

"I was driving along the Beltway and saw the fire as I approached a curve in the road. It's a nasty curve, and everyone slows down there. When I saw the flames shooting up, I pulled over to the side of the road and got out of my car. The railing was broken and, when I looked down at the ravine, I saw a car engulfed in fire. There was so much smoke that I couldn't see anyone inside or outside the car."

"What did you do?"

"I called 911 on my cell and waited till the emergency vehicles arrived."

"You were the only witness listed on the police report. Did anyone else stop?"

"A couple of cars stopped but then took off. When I first pulled over, there was a black SUV parked alongside the broken railing and a man looking down at the accident. I asked him what happened, and he just shrugged. When I asked if he called in the accident, he said he hadn't. That's when I called 911. I thought it was strange."

"How so?"

"The man had a phone in his hand, and he took some pictures of the burning car. I told him I was going to wait for the police to arrive. He said he couldn't get involved. Then he got in his SUV and drove off."

"What did he look like?"

"Big man with short brown hair. Looked like a Marine."

"How was he dressed?"

"Ordinary clothes...dark shirt, khakis."

The waiter arrived with their beers. "Would you like to order some food?" Matt asked.

"Thanks, but my wife's expecting me for dinner."

"What happened after the SUV left?"

"I waited till the police and fire trucks arrived. They took a statement from me."

"There was nothing in the report about the SUV," Matt said.

"I mentioned the SUV to the investigating officer, but I guess the police don't put information in a report that they can't confirm," Ralph said.

"Do you remember the make of the SUV?"

"I think it was a Ford Explorer. Can't be sure."

They finished their beers. "Did you happen to see the license plate on the

SUV or part of it?" Matt asked.

"I think it was a Virginia plate. I would have noticed if it was an out-of-state plate. I thought the guy was strange. Didn't comment about the accident at all."

Matt took a business card out of his wallet and handed it to Ralph. "You've been very helpful. Please call me if you remember anything else... anything at all."

"Good luck with your investigation." Ralph shook Matt's hand and walked away.

Matt finished his beer and paid the bill. He didn't notice the man sitting at the bar who had been watching him and Ralph the entire time.

Chapter 14

Thursday, September 24, 2009

It was late morning, after rush hour, when Matt slowed his car and pulled off the highway onto the shoulder. He stopped near the site of Ben's accident, turned off the engine and stepped out of the car. The guardrail had been replaced since he last examined the site, after the accident. Looking down at the steep embankment, Matt could see tire tracks in the grass, the burned remains of shrubbery, and the damaged tree trunk below where Ben's car had made its fatal impact.

In one swift movement, Matt jumped over the guardrail and traversed the embankment to the bottom. He moved methodically around the site of charred grass, unsure of what he was looking for. Picking up a branch, he poked the debris, sending burned particles into the air. The smell of the incinerated car still lingered in the dust, overwhelming him with nausea. The imagined horror of his father's last moments struck him so suddenly, it took his breath away. He sank down in the grass, dragging air into his lungs until his breathing slowed.

As his eyes rested on the scene around him, a small shiny object poked from beneath the ashes. He fished out the object with the branch, brushed off the dirt and examined the small, twisted cone-shaped bit of metal. Unsure of what it was, he slipped it in his pocket. He spent another half hour sifting through the ashes and debris, hoping to find something more. Finally, he gave up, made his way up the embankment and climbed over the guardrail.

When he turned to where he had parked his car, it was no longer there. "What the fuck!" he said aloud. He pulled out his cell phone and called the Virginia Highway Police. "I want to report a missing Dodge Charger," he said. He gave the operator his location and license plate number and waited for a response.

"The abandoned Dodge was towed to the Arlington Vehicle Retrieval location. You can claim it there for $300 in cash," the operator told him and hung up before Matt could protest. He stamped his feet in frustration. Then he called Ellie.

Forty-five minutes later, Ellie pulled her car onto the highway shoulder where Matt waited. He opened the door and got in. "You want to tell me what you're doing here?" Ellie asked.

"Right now, I need to claim my car. Did you bring cash?"

"I did. Start talking."

"There's nothing to tell. I wanted to examine the accident site."

"And?"

"I found a piece of metal that I'm going to take to a forensic lab."

"Where is this going, Matt?"

"I don't know. What I do know is that Dad was a careful driver, and the police haven't given us a satisfactory explanation for the accident."

"You think someone wanted to kill him?"

"Dad wrote a lot of things in the Star that pissed off powerful people."

"Newspapers all over the country expose things people want to bury. The messengers aren't murdered," she said.

Half an hour later, Ellie pulled into the Arlington Vehicle Retrieval lot. Matt went to the cashier's booth and paid the $300 fine. He received a receipt and the location of his car in the lot. He waved to Ellie, who rolled down her car window. "Everything okay?" she asked.

"You don't need to hang around. Thanks for picking me up."

"Let me know what the forensic lab finds." She closed the car window, her brow creased with worry lines.

***

By the time Matt walked into the reception room of the forensic laboratory in Arlington, it was 4:00 p.m. Jim Harris, a forensic scientist Matt had consulted in the past, came out to greet him. Jim was a ballistics expert favored by defense attorneys in criminal trials.

A white lab coat hung loosely on Jim's lanky frame, and a day's growth of stubble covered his face. "Good to see you, Matt. So sorry about your father."

"Thanks," Matt said.

"What have you got for me?"

Matt reached into his pocket and pulled out the metal fragment. "I hope you can tell me what this is...or was."

Jim studied the fragment for a few moments. "Come into the lab and I'll have a look under the microscope." He led the way through one of several doors to a large room with three stainless steel tables, microscopes, scales, intricate measuring equipment, computers and a digital camera. The walls displayed charts with photographs of firearms, ammunition and their measurements.

Jim sat at one of the steel tables and placed the metal fragment under a microscope. "You can sit," he told Matt, pointing to a chair beside him. Some moments passed while Jim studied the fragment. "This is part of a .40 caliber bullet," he said, looking into Matt's widening eyes.

"How can you be sure?"

"The stamps and markings on the cartridge fragment identify it."

"And the weapon it was fired from?"

"Probably a Glock 22."

"Who would most likely carry a Glock?"

"Anyone who could get one. It's one of the top guns police and military carry."

Matt drew in a breath. "Would you be able to identify the weapon it was fired from?"

"If I *had* the weapon. Do you have it?"

"Not yet."

"Where did you find the cartridge?"

"At the site of my father's car crash."

"Anything else you can tell me?"

"The police sent the car to a wrecker, and it's been compacted. I have photos of a blown tire fragment from the scene of the accident. That's all I have."

Jim raked his fingers through his thick brown hair. "You think someone shot at your father's car?"

"You haven't lost your touch for conclusions, Jim."

"Without the weapon, you can't prove anything."

"I'm working on it."

Jim placed the bullet fragment in a plastic evidence bag and handed it to Matt.

"Can you send me a written report on your findings?" Matt asked.

"I'll put a report in the mail tomorrow."

"Send me your bill, Jim."

***

Matt drove through the dark streets of Alexandria, heading toward his apartment. Everything he had seen and learned today was running through his mind, posing more questions. The pungent smell of take-out chicken in black bean sauce escaped the paper bag on the seat beside him. He hadn't eaten since breakfast and couldn't wait to dig in with chopsticks.

The sound of a siren shattered the night silence, pulling Matt back from his thoughts. Headlights flashed in his rearview mirror. A police car, with its siren blaring, was close behind him.

Matt's heart quickened as he pulled over to the curb. The police cruiser pulled in behind him, and a uniformed officer got out and walked to Matt's car. Matt opened his car window. "Driver's license and registration," the officer barked.

"Did I do something?" Matt asked.

"Driver's license and registration," the officer's voice rose. Matt pulled his wallet out of his back pocket and took out his license. He opened the glove compartment and shuffled through papers until he found the registration. The officer took Matt's documents and went back to the cruiser. Some moments passed before he returned, accompanied by his partner, who Matt recognized. There was no mistaking the thick-set man with a military-style haircut and sneer. He was the police officer who had been watching him at the police station yesterday. "Open your trunk," the officer ordered.

"Do you have a search warrant?"

"Don't need one when a suspect is seen leaving the scene of a crime. Step out of your car and put your hands on you head."

"Crime? What are you talking about?" Matt's heartbeat thundered in his ears as he stepped out of the car. The officer reached beneath the dashboard and popped the trunk open.

His partner walked to the back of Matt's car, rummaging through the contents of the trunk. He returned, carrying a bulging white plastic bag. "Look what I found?" he smirked. Matt's eyes went wild, and he lunged for him. Both officers grabbed Matt and wrestled him to the ground, pushing his face onto the sidewalk.

"You have the right to remain silent..." Matt heard his rights being read to him through a roar in his head that sounded like the ocean. They forced Matt's hands behind his back, handcuffed him and dragged him to the patrol car.

"You son-of-a-bitch! You just planted that," Matt shouted.

"Shut the fuck up, you piece of shit," the partner said, shoving Matt roughly into the back seat of the cruiser.

Chapter 15

Friday, September 25, 2009

Matt sat on a cold bench in the holding cell at the Fairfax County Jail, resting his head on his hands. It was 6:00 a.m., and he hadn't slept since he was arrested, fingerprinted, photographed and booked for drug possession. His eyes felt gritty and his head throbbed painfully. His pleas to make a phone call were ignored. His cell phone and wallet were being held till his release, if that should happen.

He dreaded calling Ellie. It brought back memories of his arrest when he was sixteen for marijuana possession. Three of his wild teenage friends had been arrested with him. Ellie was away at college then, but she came back to Virginia to be with him. "How could you do this to Dad...to me, after we talked about your future?" she had accused. She didn't understand how he felt after their mother left. In his child's mind, he believed he had done something to drive her away.

Dan had helped Ben find a seasoned lawyer to defend Matt. Though Dan lived in Texas then, he reached out to influential connections in the legal community. In the end, Matt was sentenced to parole for one year. But his friends weren't so lucky. They spent a year in a juvenile detention center. These memories came flooding back to him now, along with an uneasy feeling that he wasn't going to be so fortunate this time. Maybe it was a premonition, but his thoughts set his stomach churning and his head pounding.

A police officer approached the cell. "Andrews, you can make a phone call now." He unlocked the cell. Matt followed him to the public telephone.

"Hello," Ellie answered, her words heavy with sleep.

"Ellie, I need a lawyer. I'm in jail."

"What? What happened?" She bolted out of bed.

"The cops planted drugs in my car last night." The desperation in his voice jolted her senses. There was no time to offer words of comfort before the call was cut off.

***

Ellie got to the newsroom by 8:00 a.m. and slipped quietly into her office, watching the clock and waiting for Dan's arrival. She didn't remember getting dressed and driving to the office. Her thoughts were consumed with visions of Matt sitting in a jail cell. *Dan would know what to do. He would know the best lawyers,* she thought.

At 8:30, Dan arrived and went directly to his office. Ellie waited until his door closed before hurrying to his office. She turned the doorknob and burst in. Dan looked up, startled.

"Matt's in jail." Her words spilled out in a breathless torrent.

"Slow down, Ellie. What happened?"

She sank into a chair beside his desk, her legs feeling suddenly weak. "The police planted drugs on him."

"How?"

"He needs a lawyer." She tried to slow her breathing as Dan punched in a number on his phone.

"Ellie, go back to your office and try to calm down. I'll call you when I set things up with Bill Curtis. He's a busy lawyer and it may take time to reach him."

Ellie went back to her cubicle and sat down heavily. She reached for the coffee sitting on her desk with trembling fingers. The coffee was cold, but she wouldn't risk a trip to the kitchen for a refill. The staff would read her face and know something was wrong. She busied herself searching databases on her computer for information about Bill Curtis. He had an impressive resume as a defense attorney. He won 95% of the cases he defended.

Ellie jumped when the phone finally rang and she heard Dan's voice. "This afternoon, 2:00 p.m., in the Fairfax County District Court. Curtis will meet with Matt and discuss the indictment."

"Indictment?" A sudden chill filled her with foreboding.

"Drug possession is serious," he said.

Ellie hung up, put her head down on the desk and closed her eyes, her mind racing as fast as her heart. The spinning in her head made her dizzy. *This can't be happening. Am I imagining this?*

***

Matt stood when Ellie was escorted into his cell. "Matt," Ellie said softly, hugging him. When she stepped back, she noted the dark circles beneath his eyes, the strain on his face. "We got you a great lawyer...Bill Curtis. I checked him out, and his reputation and experience are exceptional," Ellie said.

"Who's we?"

"Dan knows Curtis personally. And, he's one of the best defense lawyers in Virginia, if not the best."

"I don't want him defending me."

"Why not?"

"I don't want a lawyer that Dan selected."

"Are you nuts?"

"I can't explain how I feel, but I'll take my chances with a public defense lawyer or someone I choose."

"You're not thinking straight now. If you don't trust Dan's judgment, you can trust mine. I researched Curtis' record, and I couldn't have chosen anyone more competent myself." Matt didn't answer, which usually meant that he was adamant about his decision. "At least meet him," Ellie said. "Hear what he has to say before you do something you'll regret. He'll be here in a few minutes."

"I'll meet him," Matt said, "But that's all."

"Promise me you'll consider him. And Dan's paying the legal fees, which is no small thing."

Their conversation was interrupted when a police officer appeared at the cell door. "Your lawyer's here, Andrews."

Matt was escorted to a small room next to the courtroom where defendants met privately with their lawyers. Curtis was a man who exuded confidence. He was dressed impeccably in a dark blue Brooks Brothers suit. He held out his hand to Matt. "Bill Curtis," he said.

Matt shook his hand and nodded. "I should tell you up front, so you don't waste your time, that I decided not to retain you as my lawyer."

Curtis pulled out a chair and sat at the conference table. He continued, nonplussed by Matt's dismissal. "Your uncle, Dan, retained me. So, for today at least, I'll be present to represent you at the arraignment."

Matt sat across from him. "Okay, just for the arraignment," Matt agreed.

"Are you planning on defending yourself at your trial?" Curtis asked.

"There won't be a trial because the charges are trumped up and they have no proof of anything. The judge will dismiss."

"I read the indictment. The police produced evidence recovered from your car—enough cocaine to land you in a penitentiary for ten years."

"The police planted the drugs."

"Do you think you'll have an easy time proving that?"

"How would *you* prove it?"

"Witnesses, circumstances. I have a lot of experience as a defense attorney and a record for winning cases."

"Do you believe that I'm innocent?"

Curtis was silent for some moments. "I don't have to believe you're innocent to defend you."

"I admire your honesty."

A court clerk knocked and opened the door. "Proceedings in the courtroom begin in ten minutes," he announced.

The District Court was a large room with dark wood-paneled walls, tall windows along the right side, and rows of empty benches. At the front of the room was a raised bench with a chair reserved for the judge. A large American flag hung from a pole behind the bench.

Matt and Bill Curtis walked through the double doors in the rear to the front of the courtroom and sat at a table reserved for the defense. Ellie sat on a bench behind them. She reached over and squeezed Matt's shoulder. Curtis turned to look at her. "My sister, Ellie," Matt told him. Curtis shook Ellie's hand and smiled.

Other lawyers, handling cases before the court this day, entered the courtroom. Several men and women approached the table and greeted Curtis, shaking his hand. He knew all the judges in the Fairfax County Courts, as well as state prosecutors, the mayor, the governor, legislators and everyone who was important in Virginia politics.

The magistrate judge entered the courtroom from a side door, and the buzz of conversations settled into silence. The magistrate was a large man in his fifties, balding and paunchy. He took a seat at the bench and read the legal documents spread in front of him. Then he nodded to a court officer who announced Matt's case number and directed him to stand.

Matt stood as the magistrate read the indictment against him. "Matthew Andrews was arrested yesterday evening and was found to be in possession of 700 grams of cocaine, a Schedule II drug. Matthew Andrews, you are accused of a Class 5 felony, possession of a Schedule II drug with intent to sell, which is a criminal charge punishable by commitment to the State penitentiary.

How do you plead?"

Curtis stood and whispered in Matt's ear. "Not guilty, Your Honor," Matt said, his legs feeling like they were about to buckle.

The magistrate's eyes narrowed, and he looked at Matt contemptuously. "Considering the weight of evidence, bail is set at $500,000. Mr. Andrews will be remanded to the Fairfax County Jail until bail is posted. This case will be sent to the circuit court for review and possible trial." The sound of the magistrate's gavel echoed through the courtroom, sending a chill through Ellie.

Curtis turned to Matt. "We'll post bail and have you out by tomorrow afternoon."

Two uniformed court officers moved toward Matt. They pulled his hands behind him and snapped on handcuffs. The fear in Matt's eyes and the bewilderment on his face as he turned to Ellie would haunt her through the tense weeks ahead.

Chapter 16

Thursday, October 8, 2009

Matt stared blankly at the TV screen in his living room. It was what he did every day since his release from jail twelve days ago and confinement to his apartment. He reached for a can of beer on the coffee table. There wasn't enough alcohol in the beer to relieve his mounting anxiety. He listened to Ellie chopping salad in the kitchen. She showed up half an hour ago, looked at his twelve-day growth of beard and uncombed hair and told him, "You look like a derelict."

Bill Curtis had phoned early in the morning. "I have important news to discuss with you. Can I come over later this afternoon?"

"Can't you tell me over the phone?" Matt asked.

"I need a face-to-face with you."

"Okay," Matt agreed, unable to tell from the tone of Bill's voice whether it was good news or bad. If the news was good, Bill probably would have told him on the phone, he reasoned. He squeezed the empty beer can now, reducing it to a crushed disk.

When Ellie heard the doorbell at 4:30, she dried her hands on a dish towel and went to the door. Curtis stepped in, carrying a bulging briefcase. "Matt, Ellie," he nodded and pulled a chair over to the sofa. Opening his briefcase, he took out a stack of papers. "The Grand Jury handed down its decision today," he said. Matt's stomach churned.

"The jury examined the evidence in the indictment and interviewed the arresting officers. They ruled that you committed a crime and should stand trial," he said matter-of-factly, as though he were talking about a stranger.

Matt sucked in his breath. "I'm not surprised," he said.

"A trial will prove your innocence," Ellie said.

"You're in denial, Ellie. It's obvious that I'm being railroaded for a trumped-up crime."

"It's *your* word against the police. Who do you think a jury will believe?" Curtis asked.

"Isn't it *your* job to convince them?" Matt snapped. "Or is this case more than you bargained for?"

Curtis ignored Matt's sarcasm. "There's another option. I met with the prosecutor, and she's open to a plea."

"No way," Matt shouted. "I'll never plead guilty to a crime I didn't commit."

"It's a reasonable offer…a three-year sentence if you take the plea."

"You're nuts! Get the fuck out of my sight because you don't want to defend me. You just want an easy payday."

"If that's what you think, you should find another lawyer." Curtis snapped his briefcase shut.

"Whoa. Let's all calm down," Ellie said. "Matt, you need to think this over rationally. Bill has a reputation for winning difficult cases."

Matt turned to Ellie, his face crimson with rage. "Whose side are you on?"

"I don't need a payday from your case," Curtis said. "I'm trying to get you the best deal possible, considering the damning evidence. Three years beats ten, which is what you'll face if a jury convicts you."

"I'll never plead guilty. If I accept a plea, it'll ruin my life…my reputation as a journalist. I'll never work again."

"Think this over before you make a final decision. I learned that Judge Robert Maxwell will be presiding if you go to trial," Curtis said.

Matt shuddered. Maxwell's reputation for favoring prosecutors and the harsh sentences he doled out were well known. Matt had seen him in action when covering the trial of a man accused of armed robbery. The accused man was an unemployed father of three young children whose wife had left them. The gun used in the robbery wasn't loaded. Though the jury found him guilty, they recommended parole so the man could care for his children. Matt still remembered the sneer on Maxwell's face when he delivered the sentence: "I'm sentencing you to five years in the state penitentiary, to commence today." Afterward, Matt learned that the man's children were placed in foster care. Three years into his sentence, the man committed suicide.

"Let me know when you've retained another lawyer so I can send all the documents," Curtis said. "Your trial date is set for Monday, November 9th.

You and your new attorney have four weeks to prepare your defense and select a jury." He reached for his briefcase and stood.

"Don't go," Ellie pleaded. She turned to Matt. "Be reasonable."

Matt had spent days researching the credentials of Virginia criminal trial lawyers and their court records. Bill Curtis topped the list with the most wins. He turned to Curtis. "What can you promise me when I go to trial?" Matt asked.

"If you insist on going to trial, your only chance to win is with a professionally-selected jury," Curtis said.

"How will you do that?"

"I know an expert psychologist with a specialty in evaluating prospective jurors. Based on her analyses of their backgrounds and answers to key questions, we can hopefully get a balanced jury with some who are open-minded and flexible."

"I know how this goes…if the prosecution rejects our selections," Matt said.

"They can't reject everyone we choose. All we need is one juror who is sympathetic. It's our best chance to win. And we'll line up good character witnesses to support you," Curtis said.

"Okay," Matt said.

"We start jury selection Monday morning. I'll let you know what time to show up at court." He closed his briefcase.

Chapter 17

Monday, November 9, 2009

Gray light poured in through the courtroom windows, chilling the air and spreading gloom. Ellie pulled her suit jacket tighter around her body. Dan sat beside her on the bench. He took her hand in his and squeezed gently. Her eyes settled on Matt, seated in front of them at the defendant's table. The weeks leading up to this day had taken a brutal toll on him, and his navy suit hung on him like wet laundry.

The prosecutor and her assistant were reading papers spread out on the prosecutor's table when the jury was ushered in. Last week, Curtis had brought in a specialist for jury selection to weed out jurors who did not appear sympathetic to Matt. Ellie and Matt had objected to several jurors who the specialist recommended. But Curtis had insisted, "Trust her. She knows what she's doing and she never lets me down." Curtis' words did not reassure Ellie now as she studied the faces of the twelve jurors.

The public and press filed in, filling the benches in the courtroom. A court reporter entered through a side door and sat at a table near the judge's bench, readying herself to record the trial proceedings. As the courtroom filled with observers, conversations grew louder.

The bailiff stepped forward and announced, "All rise. The Fairfax County Circuit Court, Criminal Division is now in session, the Honorable Judge Robert Maxwell presiding."

Judge Maxwell, a heavyset man in his fifties, came in through a side door, wearing a formal black robe. He took a seat on the judge's bench. A hush fell over the crowd as Maxwell peered down at the packed courtroom. His thinning gray hair was combed over a growing bald spot at the top of his head, and his small pale eyes appeared swallowed in his jowly face. "Everyone but the jury may be seated. Bailiff, please swear in the jury," Maxwell ordered.

After the jury was sworn in and seated, the bailiff declared, "Today's case is The State of Virginia versus Matthew Andrews." Ellie clasped her hands in her lap to still their trembling.

"Are counsel ready to proceed?" Maxwell asked.

"Ready, Your Honor," the state prosecutor said.

Curtis stood. "Ready, Your Honor."

Ellie's eyes were on the jurors as Alice Cummings, the state prosecutor, delivered her opening statement. She was a tall handsome woman, dressed impeccably in a tailored black suit. She had been working as a trial lawyer for the Virginia District Attorney's office for over ten years, and she rarely lost a case in criminal court. Her words were delivered with confidence and conviction: "In the People's case against Matthew Andrews, we will present reliable testimony and hard evidence to prove that the defendant had the motive and the means to commit the crime he is accused of. You will hear the defense tell you that the state's case rests on circumstantial evidence. But this is simply a tactic. I trust that the members of the jury will weigh the evidence we present and see that there is no choice but to find the defendant guilty on all counts."

The prosecutor's accusations clouded Ellie's thoughts as she listened to Curtis' impassioned opening statement: "My client, Matthew Andrews, is an award-winning reporter for the Virginia Star newspaper. His investigative reporting has helped make lives better in our community for people like you. There are always two sides to every story. The state will not tell you the whole story because they want you to believe only their side. The state's charges are misguided. Matthew Andrews had no motive and no means to commit the crime he has been charged with. After hearing witnesses, you will have the opportunity to prevent the conviction of an innocent man. I have confidence that every one of you will apply the law correctly and fairly, and find my client not guilty."

"Are the People ready to proceed?" Maxwell asked.

"We are, Your Honor," Alice Cummings said.

"Call your first witness," Maxwell said.

"Your Honor, the People call Kevin Moore to the stand."

Kevin Moore, dressed in his police uniform, walked to the witness stand and was sworn in by the bailiff.

Cummings began her questioning. "Mr. Moore, please tell the court how long you have served as a law enforcement officer in Fairfax County."

"Eighteen years," Moore bragged.

"And tell the court what happened on the night of September 24th on a local street in Alexandria."

"Me and my partner, Patrick Duffy, were patrolling the streets near a house where there was a drug raid. We apprehended a man in a Dodge Charger who was fleeing the scene."

"Is the man you apprehended in this courtroom?" Cummings asked.

"Yes. There he is." Moore pointed his finger at Matt.

Ellie's face paled. *Why hadn't Curtis objected to the officer's accusation? What proof did the police have for stopping a random car on the street?* She turned to look at Dan for affirmation of her thoughts, but his expression was calm, unreadable.

"Tell us exactly what transpired on the street that night...the facts only," Cummings said.

Matt glared at Moore as he gave a step-by-step account of how he and his partner had pulled Matt over, opened the trunk of his car, found a bag of cocaine and arrested him. "The suspect resisted arrest and became violent," Moore added.

"Objection, Your Honor. There's no proof that my client was violent," Curtis said.

Alarm bells were sounding inside Ellie's head. *Why was Curtis questioning whether Matt was violent instead of the illegal search itself?*

"Overruled," Maxwell said.

Cummings smiled. Then she held up a bag of cocaine and waved it in front of the jury. "The People enter the confiscated drugs retrieved from the defendant's car as exhibit number one of evidence. The People have no further questions for Mr. Moore."

"The Defense may cross-examine the witness," Maxwell said.

Curtis walked to the witness box. "Mr. Moore, isn't it true that you and your partner, Patrick Duffy, were part of the team that raided a house near the site where the defendant was driving on the night of September 24th?" Curtis asked.

"Yes, we were part of the team," Moore said.

"And isn't it true that you did not make any arrests at the scene where you found the drugs because the house was empty?"

"Yes, but the criminals had already fled," Moore said.

"Were you and your partner given the task to apprehend the criminals who had fled from that drug house?"

"So what?" Moore asked.

"I ask the questions, Mr. Moore. You answer them. And remember that you're under oath," Curtis said.

"It's our job to catch criminals. We apprehended Matthew Andrews fleeing the scene," Moore sneered.

"Did you pull over and search any other vehicles in the vicinity of the drug house that night?"

"We didn't have to because we caught the criminal with the evidence." Moore smirked.

"Mr. Moore, I want to remind you that you are a witness here and it's not your job to pass judgment on the defendant or give your opinion. Were you under any pressure from the Drug Task Force to make an arrest after the house raid?"

"Objection, Your Honor. Counsel is badgering the witness," Cummings shouted.

"Overruled. The witness will answer the question," Maxwell said.

"We found drugs in the car and made the arrest," Moore said.

"No further questions for the witness at this time," Curtis said.

Ellie's anxiety mounted. *Why didn't Curtis continue pressing Moore about the demands made by the Drug Task Force? Did he drop the ball or did he say enough to sow the seeds of doubt in the minds of the jurors?*

Patrick Duffy took the witness stand next. He was shorter and less muscular than Kevin Moore but equally intimidating. He too wore a police uniform and polished boots. He corroborated everything his partner had testified to in a booming voice. Alice Cummings asked, "Is the man you stopped in a Dodge Charger on the night of September 24th in this courtroom?"

"Yes," Duffy shouted, pointing to Matt at the defendant's table. Matt grasped his knees to stop them from shaking. The sneer on Duffy's face and the contempt in his voice startled Ellie. If she were a juror, she would question the motives of such a man. *But what did this jury think?*

"I have no further questions for the witness," Cummings said.

Duffy stuck to his testimony when Curtis cross-examined him.

Maxwell rapped his gavel. "The court will recess until tomorrow morning at 9:00 a.m.," he announced.

Ellie turned to Dan. "I need to speak to Bill Curtis."

"Let him do his job, Ellie. He knows what he's doing," Dan insisted.

Dan's words didn't reassure Ellie. She spent the rest of the day researching public records. She was shocked by what she discovered. She phoned Curtis in the evening. "Bill, Duffy and Moore were accused of planting evidence on defendants' property in four cases. And there was a police brutality case against them several years ago."

"Being accused isn't the same as being convicted," Curtis said.

"When Matt's car was towed from the highway on the day of his arrest, it was Moore and Duffy who reported it abandoned and had it towed," Ellie reminded him.

"I'm aware of all of this, Ellie. In any case, I'm saving this information for when I recall them for further questioning so the jury will remember. You need to trust my judgment."

Ellie hung up, uneasy about trusting anyone when Matt's life was on the line.

Chapter 18

Tuesday, November 10, 2009

As Ellie sat in the courtroom, she replayed her conversation with Curtis last night and questioned why he and his legal staff hadn't discovered the police brutality case against Moore and Duffy. *Were they sloppy or careless or something else?*

At 9:00 a.m., the bailiff called the court into session and Judge Maxwell took his seat on the bench. Curtis presented first. "The defense recalls Kevin Moore to the witness stand." Moore scowled at Curtis as he was sworn in. "Mr. Moore, isn't it true that you and your partner, Patrick Duffy, were tried for police brutality in 1991 in Burns vs. the Fairfax County Police Department?"

Moore's face flushed. "We were exonerated," he shouted.

Alice Cummings sprang to her feet. "Objection, Your Honor. The witness is not on trial here. This information is irrelevant and prejudicing to the jury."

"Sustained," Maxwell snapped. "The jury will disregard the question, and the witness will not answer questions about this matter."

"Mr. Moore, you and your partner, Patrick Duffy, had Matthew Andrews' car towed from a local highway to the Arlington Vehicle Retrieval lot earlier on the day of his arrest on September 24th. Is that correct?" Curtis asked.

"The car was abandoned," Moore said.

"Answer the question, Mr. Moore. Yes or no?"

"Yes. We had it towed," Moore spat.

"Matthew Andrews had not, in fact, abandoned his car. He was investigating the site of an accident which had caused his father's death," Curtis said.

"Objection, Your Honor. This is irrelevant," Cummings said.

"Where are you going with this questioning, counselor?" the judge asked.

"The defense wishes to point out that Matthew Andrews was not in possession of his car for many hours prior to the time of his arrest that evening, time enough for drugs to have been placed in his car," Curtis argued.

"Objection, Your Honor. This is conjecture," Cummings argued.

"Sustained," the Judge said. "The jury will disregard Mr. Curtis' last statement."

"I have no further questions for the witness," Curtis said.

Ellie exhaled slowly, relieved that Curtis had planted some seeds of doubt about the arresting officers and what could have happened that day. But as she studied the impassive faces of the jurors, she wondered if this information had changed minds already made up.

The trial dragged on for the rest of the morning with the prosecution calling witnesses who testified about the personal character of each of the arresting officers and their unimpeachable records. Curtis called witnesses who testified about Matt's record as a reporter and his reputation for speaking truth to power and championing ordinary people.

During the recess, Matt and Ellie met with Curtis in a conference room. "I'm calling Dan to testify this afternoon," Curtis said.

"No! I don't want him testifying," Matt said.

"He's a well-known respected doctor and medical director. Everyone in the community knows him and will believe his testimony."

Matt's face reddened. "No way!"

"Matt would feel more comfortable if Dan doesn't testify," Ellie said.

"Why the hell not?" Curtis asked.

"There's a lot of friction between Matt and Dan. They don't always get along, so maybe it would be best if he doesn't testify," Ellie said.

"Trust me. Dan is the best character witness you have right now. His reputation is impeccable."

Ellie was silent for some moments, her eyes on Matt's clenched jaw. "Bill, would you give us a few minutes alone?"

Curtis stepped out of the room, and Ellie turned to Matt. "Maybe Bill is right. You do need a character witness like Dan, someone whose reputation is not questioned, who the public trusts." She let her words hang in the space between them. Matt glared at her as though she were his enemy. "Put aside your personal feelings and do what's best for your case," she said.

"How can you think his testimony will help me?"

"I just do," she insisted.

"Dan shouldn't even be in the courtroom," Matt said.

"You can't let feelings guide your judgment, not when the rest of your life is at stake."

The court was back in session by 2:00 p.m., and Curtis called Dan to the witness stand. "Dr. Andrews, tell the court how well you know your nephew, Matthew Andrews."

"As a youngster, Matt spent many summer vacations at my home in Texas. I got to know him. He was a nice kid, polite. Liked camping and fishing with me."

"What about now, as an adult?" Curtis asked.

"He's a talented journalist and an asset to the Virginia Star."

"Tell us about your current role at the newspaper since the tragic death of your brother, Ben Andrews?"

"I've assumed the role of publisher."

"Has your brother's death changed Matt's performance as a journalist?"

"Not at all. He continues to meet the highest standards of journalism."

"No further questions," Your Honor.

Alice Cummings stepped up to cross-examine Dan. "Dr. Andrews, isn't it true that Matthew Andrews was arrested as a juvenile for marijuana possession?"

Curtis jumped up, shouting, "Objection, Your Honor! Irrelevant and illegal. Juvenile records are sealed and cannot be introduced in this trial."

Conversations erupted throughout the courtroom. "Order!" Maxwell called out, rapping his gavel.

"Your Honor, I request that this case be declared a mistrial and dismissed. The prosecution has prejudiced the jury, and Matthew Andrews cannot be guaranteed a fair trial now," Curtis pleaded.

"Counselors, approach the bench," Maxwell ordered.

Ellie's eyes were rivetted on Curtis and Cummings as they pleaded before the judge. She took deep breaths to slow her rapid breathing and heartbeat. Maxwell's ruling in the next few moments could end this nightmare.

Curtis and Cummings turned and walked back to their seats. Maxwell addressed the jury, his voice stern. "The jury will disregard the prosecutor's last statement, and it will not be admitted into evidence in this trial." Turning to Cummings, he said, "Counselor, proceed with your cross-examination of the witness."

"No further questions, Your Honor," Cummings said, a faint smile crossing her lips.

A chill swept over Ellie. She pressed her hands together to still their trembling as her eyes settled on Matt's slumped shoulders. She didn't see his face, which had drained of color.

Curtis called his next witness, the proprietor of a local take-out restaurant where Matt had gone to pick up dinner on the night of his arrest. "Mr. Low, can you identify the person in this courtroom who picked up a meal at your restaurant on the night of Thursday, September 24th?" Low pointed to Matt and smiled. "Mr. Low, do you know the defendant, Matthew Andrews?"

"Yes, he orders food from my restaurant often," Low said.

"Did you notice anything different about Mr. Andrews that night? Did he seem nervous, in a hurry?"

"No. He was same as always. Friendly, very nice young man."

"So, you prepared his order and handed it to him. He paid for it and left. Did he rush out? Did he seem to be in a great hurry?"

"No. He was not in a hurry."

"I have no further questions, Your Honor."

"The prosecution may cross-examine the witness," Maxwell said.

"The prosecution has no questions, Your Honor," Cummings said.

"The court will recess until tomorrow morning at 9:00 a.m." Maxwell struck his gavel, ending another grueling day in court.

Ellie raced out of the courtroom to catch up with Curtis as he hurried to the exit. "Bill," she called out. He turned to her, his face unreadable. "Matt was right. It wasn't a good idea for Dan to testify. How will you ever undo the damage?"

"Why don't you let me figure this out? I believe I have more experience in this arena than you do." His words were clipped.

"That's exactly why you should have known the prosecution could use Matt's juvenile arrest against him," she accused.

"Maxwell should have declared a mistrial."

Ellie felt angry tears well behind her eyes. "But he didn't. The jury is prejudiced now."

"It's not over by any means. We're going to win this," Curtis insisted, but his words sounded hollow.

"Can we have a forensic expert examine Matt's car?"

"We can. It's been impounded as evidence, and we have the right to examine it. What do you expect to discover?"

"I don't know," Ellie said. "But I'd like to bring in Jim Harris, a forensic expert who Matt and I know well."

"Okay, I'll file a request with the court. Go ahead and contact him."

When Ellie got home, she phoned Jim Harris. He agreed to meet her and Curtis the next morning to inspect Matt's car. Then she spent the rest of the day researching cases Bill Curtis and his law firm had defended. He was currently the defense lawyer for the Virginia General Hospital in a malpractice case against them for the wrongful death of Bob Reynolds, the football star. He also defended the hospital in other malpractice lawsuits. Ellie berated herself for not uncovering these cases earlier, for trusting Dan's judgment.

Chapter 19

Wednesday, November 11, 2009

Ellie's head throbbed painfully as she watched the jury file into the courtroom. The bailiff called the court into session, and Judge Maxwell took his seat on the bench. It seemed that the trial was racing ahead like a runaway train and she was helpless to stop it.

Curtis stood. "The defense calls Jim Harris to the stand." Jim walked to the witness stand and was sworn in. "Mr. Harris, please tell the court about your job."

"I'm a forensic analyst with an independent laboratory in Arlington," Jim said.

"And how long have you been doing this?"

"Fifteen years."

"When you examined Matthew Andrews' Dodge Charger, which is impounded at the Arlington Vehicle Retrieval lot, what were your findings?"

"I saw evidence of tampering with the lock on the trunk. There were many scratch marks around the keyhole. That indicates that a small, needle-like tool was used. It's a commonly-used tool to slip a lock," Jim explained.

Curtis placed two posters with enlarged photographs of the scratched car lock on an exhibit stand. "I'm introducing two photographs, exhibit C, of the Dodge Charger's trunk with enlargements of the scratches—proof that the lock was tampered with and forced open," he said. He moved the exhibit in front of the jury box and turned his attention back to Jim Harris. "So, in your expert judgment, someone could have forced open the trunk of the car and placed the drugs there at any time during that day, including when Mr. Andrews' car was towed from the highway earlier in the day?"

"It's entirely possible," Jim said.

Cummings stood. "Objection, Your Honor. Defense is leading the witness."

"Sustained," Maxwell said. "Defense will question the witness, not draw conclusions."

"Mr. Harris, did you find evidence of drugs in the front or back passenger areas of the car?"

"No. There were no traces of drugs in those areas of the car," Jim said.

"Thank you, Mr. Harris. I have no further questions."

"The prosecutor may cross-examine the witness," Maxwell said.

Alice Cummings walked slowly to the witness stand, her high-heeled shoes clacking on the marble floor. She smiled at Jim. "Mr. Harris, you testified that you found evidence that the lock on Mr. Andrews' car was tampered with. Is it possible that the lock could have been tampered with days, even weeks, before the car was towed to the Arlington Vehicle Retrieval lot?"

"It's possible," Jim said.

"So, you're saying that with all your expertise, you can't really pinpoint the exact time when the lock was tampered with?"

"That would not be possible," Jim said.

"Mr. Harris, did you find evidence of cocaine in the trunk of Mr. Andrews' car?"

"There were traces there, but..."

"Yes or no, Mr. Harris. Did you or did you not find traces of cocaine inside the trunk?"

"Yes."

Cummings smiled. "Thank you, Mr. Harris. No further questions."

"The witness may step down," Maxwell said. He turned to Curtis. "Does the defense have other witnesses?"

"No, Your Honor. The defense rests," Curtis said.

"Does the State have other witnesses?" Maxwell asked.

"Your Honor, the People rest," Cummings said.

"The court will adjourn until 1:00 p.m., and we will hear closing arguments." Maxwell rose and left the courtroom.

Jim Harris approached Ellie, a pained look on his face. "I'm sorry, Ellie," he said.

"It's not your fault. Thank you for testifying," she said.

Ellie, Matt and Curtis gathered in a private room to prepare for the closing argument. They ordered lunch from a nearby diner, but the sandwiches sat untouched on the table and the coffee grew cold. Matt was grim-faced and withdrawn. Ellie clenched and unclenched her hands beneath the table. Her earlier headache threatened to morph into a migraine.

Matt turned to Curtis. "I want to testify."

"I don't recommend it," Curtis said. "Alice Cummings is experienced at trapping defendants into saying something damning."

"I'm my best defense. I know I'll be convincing."

"You saw what Cummings did to Jim's testimony...even with the photographs as proof," Curtis said.

"Maybe Bill's right, Matt. Your testimony could be turned against you," Ellie said.

Matt's shoulders slumped. He looked at Ellie, his eyes filled with disappointment. Ellie cringed, feeling like she had somehow betrayed him. "Then there's nothing more to say, is there?" Matt said.

"We presented excellent character witnesses," Curtis said. "The prosecutor failed to establish a motive for the crime you're accused of or a convincing argument. I believe that we proved reasonable doubt exists. You need to have faith that the jury will agree." His words did not reassure Matt or Ellie.

When the trial resumed at 1:00 p.m., Alice Cummings stood before the jury box to present the State's closing argument. "Ladies and gentlemen, the State has presented incontestable evidence that a crime was committed on the night of September 24, 2009 by the defendant, Matthew Andrews."

Cummings walked to the evidence table, picked up the bag of cocaine and walked back to face the jury. She held the bag up before the jurors for some moments. "You can see the evidence with your own eyes. A State forensic expert identified this as cocaine. Even the defense's own forensic expert identified traces of cocaine in Matthew Andrews' car. The weight of evidence is irrefutable. You have no doubt seen victims of cocaine addiction in your own communities, among your friends, maybe even in your own families. The quantity of drugs founds in Matthew Andrews' car, 700 grams, could only have been for resale. You have heard the testimony of the arresting officers, whose service is beyond reproach. They testified that the defendant was fleeing the scene of a drug raid, that he resisted arrest when he was stopped and searched. An innocent man would not resist arrest. He would go willingly to prove his innocence."

Cummings paused to let her last statement hang in the silent courtroom. The anger on the jurors' faces made Matt wince. Cummings continued, "The defense argued that the police engaged in a warrantless search, but it is not against Virginia State law for police to conduct searches when they suspect a crime was committed. The defense would have you believe that the drugs found in the defendant's car were planted there. There's no proof of that. What possible motive could there be to plant drugs in a reporter's car. It's absurd. Matthew Andrews committed a crime, a felony punishable by ten years in prison. Ladies and gentlemen, in the interest of justice, the People of this State ask you to find the defendant guilty as charged." Cummings straightened her shoulders, strode back to the prosecutor's table and took her seat.

"Defense, you may proceed with your closing argument," Judge Maxwell said.

Bill Curtis stood. "Thank you, Your Honor." He walked to the jury box. "Ladies and gentlemen, you have heard a lot of testimony these past few days, but the State has proved nothing. I would like to recall for you some important information that the State overlooked, rejected or misinterpreted. First and foremost, what possible motive could Matthew Andrews have for committing the crime he's charged with? Surely it isn't monetary gain. He comes from a relatively well-off family. He is employed by a reputable Virginia newspaper and is an award-winning reporter. He has always been a champion of the disadvantaged. There's no question that Matthew Andrews would never entertain the idea of dispensing illegal drugs.

"The only thing Matthew Andrews is guilty of is being in the wrong place at the wrong time. The police officers who stopped him on the night of September 24th needed to arrest a suspect because they failed to make an arrest in a drug raid nearby. Simply because Matthew Andrews was driving in the vicinity of the drug raid does not make him guilty. My client should never have been stopped by the police at all. They had no cause to search his car. They had no search warrant. They were, in fact, violating Matthew Andrews' Fourth Amendment rights under the U.S. Constitution—protection against unreasonable search and seizure.

"When the trunk of my client's car was opened, he had no way of seeing what the police officer was doing. It is entirely possible that the drugs were planted in Mr. Andrews' car so that the officers could make an arrest. The evidence that the prosecutor showed you is purely circumstantial. We have no way of knowing how the drugs came to be found in Mr. Andrews' car, or where they came from. The police confiscate drugs regularly. There are documented cases of Virginia police planting drugs in order to make arrests. This is one such case. The prosecutor failed to produce any witnesses at the scene of the arrest. That in itself should make you question the events on the day of the arrest."

Ellie studied the jurors' faces. Her eyes settled on a middle-aged woman who had signaled agreement with Curtis when he argued that the police officers were pressured to make an arrest. It was only a small nod of the woman's head, but it was enough to stir her optimism. Matt needed at least one juror who questioned the motives of the police and cast doubt on his guilt.

Curtis continued, "If Mr. Andrews had been fleeing the scene of a crime, as Ms. Cummings would have you believe, would he have stopped to pick up a take-out dinner? Is that the behavior of a criminal? Of course not. He would have gone directly home to hide the drugs. Driving along a Virginia street that happened to be in the vicinity of a drug raid does not constitute a crime. He was driving home at a normal speed after an ordinary workday. You'll recall that our expert forensic witness testified that the lock on Mr. Andrews' car was tampered with. The car had been towed from the highway earlier on the day of his arrest by the same two police officers—Kevin Moore and Patrick Duffy—who also claim to have found the drugs in Mr. Andrews' car. Any reasonable person would find this questionable."

Curtis paused to allow his last words to cast doubt before his final plea. "I could poke many more holes in the State's case against Matthew Andrews, but it would take all day. Matthew Andrews has been wrongfully accused of a crime he did not commit. There is more than reasonable doubt that he committed a crime. Ladies and gentlemen, there is only one just verdict you can deliver. Not guilty."

Ellie exhaled, aware that she had been holding her breath. Curtis' closing argument was impressive, more impressive than the slick prosecutor's. But the bag of cocaine that Cummings had dangled before the jurors would stick in their minds.

Curtis took his seat at the defense table. Judge Maxwell turned to the jury. "Members of the jury, you have heard all the testimony in this case. Now it is up to you to consider the facts and the evidence. Your decision must be based on facts, not on feelings. Do not consider evidence or testimony that was stricken from the record. You must all agree on a verdict. If you find the defendant guilty, he must be found guilty beyond a reasonable doubt. Your verdict must be unanimous." Maxwell continued, giving the jurors detailed instructions on applying the State's law on cocaine possession to the facts.

"All rise," the bailiff announced. He escorted the jurors out of the court through a side door to a deliberation room where they would reach a verdict and seal Matt's fate. Ellie studied the jurors' impassive faces as they filed out.

She shivered as a chill swept over her.

"The defense will be notified when the jury reaches its verdict," Maxwell announced. He rapped the gavel and dismissed the court. Now, all she and Matt could do was wait, agonize and hope.

Chapter 20

Friday, November 13, 2009

All through the day yesterday, Matt and Ellie waited in Matt's apartment in anticipation of the jury's verdict. They watched TV, played Monopoly, Scrabble and card games to pass the time. When there was no word by 8:00 in the evening, Ellie telephoned Curtis. "It's a positive sign," he assured them. "It means the jurors are not in agreement. They need a unanimous decision, and some jurors must believe Matt is innocent."

Ellie ordered pizza for them after Curtis calmed their frazzled nerves. They stayed awake until 3:00 a.m. because neither of them could sleep. Ellie finished half a bottle of wine and Matt downed several beers before they gave in and tried to sleep. "Take my bed," Matt insisted.

"No. I'll sleep on the sofa," Ellie said. She cleaned off the coffee table, tossing the paper plates and uneaten pizza. Then she curled up on the sofa and sank into a troubled sleep, dreaming about her father hurtling toward death in his car.

Exhausted, Matt finally fell asleep at 4:00 a.m. He dreamed about the jurors, having memorized their faces, as though they were imprinted on his brain. He saw them gathered around a table in an otherwise bare room. Their faces were red, swollen with rage. The foreman, at the head of the table, pointed to each juror, and they called out their votes: "Guilty." "Guilty." "Guilty." When he pointed to the last juror at the end of the table, Matt's eyes snapped open and he bolted out of bed. His T-shirt was soaked in perspiration. He sucked in air, drowning in panic.

The sound of the shower woke Ellie now. She dragged herself off the sofa. She was groggy, and her back ached from the unnatural position she had slept in. Early morning light seeped through the blinds, casting shadows on the floor. She tried to shake off a nagging feeling of foreboding as she walked into the small kitchen barefooted and reached for the coffee pot. Yesterday's coffee grinds were still in the basket. She emptied it and scrubbed the carafe. Then she brewed a fresh pot of coffee, set the table and put two slices of bread in the toaster. She should cook a hearty breakfast for Matt, she thought, opening the refrigerator and finding it empty of anything substantial. She found a dish with butter and a jar of blackberry preserves and set them on the table. Neither of them had eaten a decent meal in days, maybe weeks.

Matt came into the kitchen, his hair damp from the shower. "Coffee smells good," he said, reaching for the carafe and filling a mug.

"There isn't much for breakfast. I can go out and get us egg sandwiches," Ellie offered.

"This is fine. I'm not hungry."

Ellie poured coffee for herself and sat at the table across from Matt. She studied his face, where exhaustion and anxiety had carved new creases. All through the day yesterday their mood had vacillated between hope and despair. *When your fate hangs in a precarious balance, is it better to know or not to know?* Ellie wondered.

"Today's Friday the 13th," Matt said.

"So?"

"It's either my lucky day or the worst day of my life."

"The fact that the jury is deliberating longer is a good sign. They apparently don't agree on a verdict. We picked good jurors...some who appeared intelligent enough to question the prosecutor's argument."

"My case should have been dismissed when the prosecutor deliberately introduced sealed juvenile records. The juvenile arrest is rolling around in the jurors' heads. That and the bag of cocaine that cunt kept waving around like a flag are enough to get a guilty conviction."

"The jurors know the police officers aren't squeaky clean. The brutality case brought against them is also inside their heads. Their uniforms didn't convince me of their honesty, and I don't think the jury thought too much of them either. They look like thugs."

"It doesn't matter what *we* think, Ellie."

The phone rang at 9:30, and Ellie jumped up and answered it. When she hung up, she turned to Matt. "The verdict is in. We need to get to the courthouse."

***

Ellie waited in the courtroom for the judge to enter and the jury to be escorted in. Dan sat next to her, his face calm and confident. He took her hand and held it. "You look like you haven't slept in days," he said.

"I'm okay," she lied, trying to contain the panic that squeezed her chest. She withdrew her hand from his, clenching it to still the trembling.

The jurors filed in, taking their seats in the jury box. They looked straight ahead, avoiding eye contact with Matt, who sat next to Curtis, his shoulders slumped.

Judge Maxwell entered and took his seat on the bench. A hush settled over the courtroom. "Will the defendant, Matthew Andrews, and the defense counsel stand," he said. Matt stood next to Curtis, feeling lightheaded and nauseous. Maxwell addressed the jurors. "Members of the jury, have you reached a verdict?"

The jury foreman stood. "Yes, Your Honor. We have."

"Members of the jury, in the case of The State of Virginia vs. Matthew Andrews, what say you?" he asked.

The foreman cleared his throat. "Your Honor, the members of the jury find the defendant guilty on all counts."

Ellie gasped. Talk erupted throughout the courtroom. Maxwell rapped his gavel. "Order," he demanded. He peered down at Matt from the bench. "Matthew Andrews, a jury of your peers has found you guilty on all counts of drug possession as charged. Report to this courthouse for sentencing on Monday, November 16th. Until that time, you are to remain in your home."

Maxwell turned to the jury. "Thank you, ladies and gentlemen of the jury. You're dismissed." He rose and hurried out through a side door. Cameras flashed, and reporters raced out to call in the news about one of their own. Stunned observers turned to each other, talking all at once.

Ellie rushed to Matt's side. She grasped his hand, her eyes brimming with tears. They shared the same thought: *How could this be happening?*

Ellie turned to Curtis, whose face was unreadable. She suppressed an urge to slap him. "I guess your record for winning cases isn't as good as you claim," she said.

Dan, who stood beside her, said, "Bill did the best he could under the circumstances."

Ellie glared at him. *Had she misjudged her uncle too?* "His best wasn't good enough. He wasn't even mediocre," she said.

Curtis' face flushed. "No one could have done a better job of defending Matt. Jury verdicts are unpredictable," Dan said.

"What now?" Matt asked. "Do I go before a firing squad?"

"You haven't been sentenced yet. You could get parole," Curtis said, his words clipped and unconvincing.

"What are the chances?"

"We'll find out on Monday," Curtis said. "There's always an appeal option."

***

Ellie returned to Matt's apartment with him. She wasn't going to leave him alone for the weekend in his state of mind. He spent all day Saturday escaping from reality in sleep. Ellie logged on to her computer and researched statistics on case appeals in Virginia. The depressing reality was that only a small percentage of appeals were granted. And, if Matt were granted an appeal, the verdict could still be upheld. In drug felony cases, the statistics for a successful appeal were frightening. Ellie didn't share the grim numbers with Matt.

Sunday morning, Ellie pulled Matt out of bed and pushed him into the shower. She ordered his favorite take-out foods all day. They watched old comedy films and played card games. Friends called, but Matt declined to see them. Time moved slowly, day stretching into a long night. She could only hope that this nightmare would end with parole for Matt tomorrow.

Chapter 21

Monday, November 16, 2009

Matt and Bill Curtis were seated at the defendant's table when Judge Maxwell entered the courtroom and took his seat on the bench. Maxwell wasted no time. "Will the defendant, Matthew Andrews, and the defense counsel stand." Matt willed himself to stand, his legs threatening to buckle. "By the power vested in me by the State of Virginia, I hereby order you to serve ten years at Red Ridge Prison and pay a fine of $2,500. Sheriff, take the prisoner into custody and remand him to Red Ridge Prison, where his sentence shall commence on this day of November 16, 2009. This court is adjourned." The thud of the gavel finalized Matt's fate.

Ellie gripped the bench, shaken to her core by the harsh sentence. She pushed herself up, moving toward Matt, but the sheriff had already handcuffed him and was leading him out. "Matt!" she called. He turned to look back at her, the shock and despair on his face breaking her heart.

"I'll file an appeal today, Matt," Curtis said.

Ellie didn't remember Dan pulling her into the hallway. His arms supported her as she stumbled. He guided her to a bench. "Put your head down and take deep breaths," he said. She drew in air as a wave of dizziness seized her.

Curtis appeared with a cup of water. She held the cup in trembling hands, taking small sips and willing herself not to pass out. She looked at her uncle, his brow furrowed with concern. *Was it for her or Matt? Was he relieved that Matt could no longer challenge his decisions at the newspaper?*

"You shouldn't think of this verdict as final," Curtis told Ellie.

"Red Ridge! How could Maxwell send him there?" Ellie moaned.

Dan put his arm around Ellie's shoulder, but nothing could still her sobs, not even Curtis' promise, "We'll get Matt transferred out of Red Ridge and start the appeals process."

"How?" she asked. The statistics for successful appeals in Virginia were fresh in her mind. *Were the chances of getting Matt transferred out of Red Ridge just as dismal?*

"Leave that to me," Curtis said. "I've done this many times."

Ellie wanted to believe him. But the despair on Matt's face and the fear in his eyes haunted her. The thought of him in that prison was more than she could bear. *She promised herself long ago, when her mother had left them, to protect Matt. She had promised her father too. She had failed everyone she loved. She had to make things right for Matt now, no matter what it took.*

***

A guard unlocked the door of a solitary confinement cell at Red Ridge Prison and looked into the dimly-lit 7-by 12-foot cell. His eyes rested on the emaciated figure of a man stretched out on a narrow plastic mattress. Purple bruises covered the prisoner's arms and face. "Jeez, Degan, you smell like shit," the guard said, though he knew the prisoner was allowed only one shower in two weeks, without soap.

Rusty looked at the guard, his eyes vacant. "Stand up!" the guard ordered.

Rusty tried to push himself off the mattress. It took several attempts before he stumbled to his feet. His legs wobbled and his collar bones jutted out against the prison uniform. The guard snapped handcuffs on his bony wrists and prodded him into the hallway. "Time to return to paradise," he said. Rusty blinked rapidly in the brightly-lit hallway, his face twitching. The guard led him up several staircases to his former cell block. He unlocked the door to Rusty's cell and removed the cuffs. "Home, sweet home," he said, pushing Rusty inside and locking the door.

Rusty collapsed on the cot, his body trembling. A prisoner in the next cell called out, "Hey, how're you doing?" Rusty couldn't summon the energy to answer. He rubbed his wrists, which had angry red welts from restraints used to strap him to the bed in solitary as punishment for shouting, "Let me out."

***

The prison bus carrying Matt and five other prisoners had hard benches and high windows that didn't allow a view of the Appalachian Mountain terrain.

Leg shackles and handcuffs prevented any movement, though it was hard to imagine any possible escape from the locked door. Matt looked up through the windows at the sky, where a flock of birds flew between the clouds.

It took six hours to reach Red Ridge. The gates opened and the bus pulled inside. When the driver opened the door, two guards, who had accompanied the prisoners, stepped out. "Stand up and move out, fish," one of the guards barked, while the other one waited near the door, wielding a club.

The prisoners hopped down the steps, shuffling to the prison entrance as they were prodded with a club. The metallic clank of the outer door as it closed behind freedom sent a chill through Matt. A dimly-lit receiving room with a red line painted across the center of the floor awaited them. "Line up behind the red line," a guard ordered. Two guards took positions on either side of the lineup.

A side door opened. Four guards, carrying stun guns, marched in and surrounded the prisoner lineup. Matt's head throbbed, the pain growing more intense with each passing minute. His throat was dry and raw. He longed for a drink of cool water and some respite from this hellish day.

The prisoners waited silently as twenty minutes ticked by slowly. The guards prodded them with clubs if they whispered, coughed or fidgeted. Finally, Warden Clayton Parker strode in and faced the prisoners. He stared into the eyes of each prisoner, one by one, without speaking. The hate in his eyes communicated everything they needed to know.

The men hadn't been given food or water all day. One prisoner pitched forward, stepping on the red line. Parker nodded to a guard, who rushed forward and shocked him with a 50,000-volt stun gun. The prisoner screamed, doubled over and fell to the floor. "Get him out of here!" Parker ordered, and the guard dragged the shocked and twitching man out of the room. The other prisoners stiffened as perspiration dripped down their faces and the smell of fear filled the room.

Parker's eyes narrowed, his face filled with contempt. "I am Mr. Parker, the warden. If you break any rules here, you will be punished. So don't mess up!" He nodded to the guards surrounding the lineup and they moved forward, unlocking the men's leg shackles and cuffs.

"Now strip!" Parker ordered. The men hurried to remove their clothing. Some wrapped their arms around their naked bodies. Others covered their genitals with their hands. Matt stood naked and shivering, surrounded by others and feeling more alone than ever.

A door opened at the side of the room, and a team of one male doctor and two female nurses dressed in blue scrubs entered. One nurse held a clipboard, and the other positioned a video camera on a tripod. "Line up in front of the doctor, single file," a guard ordered. The doctor tied a rubber arm band around the first prisoner's upper arm. "Make a fist," the doctor said, plunging a needle into the prisoner's vein and drawing a blood sample. He handed the vial to the nurse with the clipboard. She labeled it with the prisoner's name and ID number, and placed it in a large collection container.

When it was Matt's turn, he asked, "Why are you drawing blood?"

The doctor looked up, surprised to be questioned. "It's routine," he said. "We need to know your blood type, just in case."

"I object," Matt said, pulling his arm away.

Warden Parker stepped up to Matt, his face inches away from him. "You *don't* object to anything here. You do as you're told, whenever you're told. This isn't your fancy newspaper."

After drawing blood samples from the new prisoners, the doctor said, "Now turn around, bend over and spread your buttocks." This ultimate humiliation was recorded on video as the prisoners' anal orifices were probed and searched for drugs, weapons, or anything that could possibly be hidden there. The doctor had donned surgical gloves for this special examination, but only one pair, which he used for all the men.

Matt and the other men were led into an adjoining room where they stepped up to a counter and deposited their street clothing and other belongings. They were issued bright orange prison uniforms and black canvas shoes without laces. They donned the coarse uniforms quickly, grateful to cover their nakedness. The uniforms differed only by the white number on the upper right side. Each printed number was a unique prisoner identification number.

A side door opened, and four guards entered to escort the prisoners to their cells. There were several floors in the prison with blocks of cells that housed over 800 men, and a special solitary confinement wing where even a small infraction could land a prisoner in a cell for twenty-three hours a day.

Matt was led to a cell on an upper floor. The guard opened the cell with a key attached to a large key ring hanging from his belt. The one- and one-half-inch thick steel door slid open with a loud metallic sound. There were no bars here, just solid steel with a five-inch-wide slit to look out or in and a slot for delivering meals. The guard pushed Matt inside, and the door closed with a clang.

Matt nearly dropped the threadbare prison-issue blanket and towel when he saw his cellmate. Rusty Degan's eyes widened when he looked up from where he sat on his bed. "Hey, man, what the fuck you doing here?"

"It's a long story," Matt said. "So, here I am. I'll have plenty of time now to get the rest of my interview with you." Since Matt had last seen him, Rusty looked like he had lost ten pounds. His face was gaunt and pale against his red hair, and his eyes looked wild—the effects of two weeks in solitary confinement. Matt didn't doubt that the warden had personally selected Rusty to be his cellmate, but the warden was mistaken if he saw this as retribution. Rusty was not mean-spirited or threatening.

Rusty pointed across the 11-by 8-foot cell to Matt's bed, a slab of steel bolted to the wall with a thin plastic mattress and pillow. Matt sat down heavily on the cold mattress, and his eyes rested on the stainless-steel toilet and sink. A small steel shelf, referred to as a desk, was bolted to the wall next to the bed. Rusty walked to the toilet and urinated.

An hour later, Matt heard the grating sound of cart wheels outside the cell. A slot in the steel door opened and two food trays were passed through. Matt and Rusty took the trays and sat on their cots. Rusty wolfed down his meal, but Matt just moved the brown gelatinous mass around with the spoon. When he saw something move in the food, he looked closer. Small worms floated in the gravy. "There are worms in the food," Matt said with disgust. "I'm sending this slop back."

Rusty set his food tray down and jumped up. "Don't do that! You'll get into trouble. I will too." The fear in his voice was alarming.

"But..."

"I just spent two weeks in solitary for an argument with an inmate in the rec yard. I'll die if I go back there. Promise you won't complain." The desperation in his voice startled Matt.

"Okay. Calm down." Matt carried his tray to the toilet, dumped the food and flushed.

When the food cart rolled by, Matt and Rusty pushed their empty trays out through the slot. Later, as day turned to night, a loud buzzer signaled the close of the prison day. Matt lay on his cold mattress. The lights dimmed, but not enough to allow him to sleep. He turned to look at Rusty, whose face twitched as he muttered to himself. Rusty soon grew quiet and drifted off, but sleep eluded Matt. His brain filled with horrifying thoughts and the maddening reality that this would be his life for the next ten years. *How would he ever endure this?*

Chapter 22

Wednesday, November 18, 2009

Ellie forced herself to show up at the newsroom today, even though she hadn't slept more than a few hours since Monday. The scene of Matt handcuffed and led away ran through her mind like a bad horror film, turning her into an insomniac. She took off her coat and hung it on a hook in her office. Then she went next door to Matt's office to pack his personal things.

She flinched as her eyes swept across the bare office. Matt's computer was gone, his desk cleaned off, the cubicle stripped of its former life. She opened the file drawers and found them emptied. Pictures, a calendar and tacked-up notes were all gone. Every trace of his existence here had vanished. Ellie's face flushed with anger.

She rushed out, marched across the newsroom to Dan's office and burst in. Dan looked up, the phone next to his ear. "I'll call you back," he said into the phone and hung up. "Ellie, what is it?"

"Where are Matt's things?"

"Sit down and I'll explain."

"No. I won't sit. I want Matt's things."

"This is a place of business. Matt's no longer here. That's the reality. His office will be occupied by a new employee, and we needed to clear it out. There's a carton for you with his personal things," he said matter-of-factly.

"I need access to Matt's computer. I need his files."

"Matt's computer and files are the property of the newspaper. They're in storage." Ellie glared at him. "You'll have to get his computer out of storage. I want it," she demanded.

"You actually don't have the right to ask for these things, Ellie…but I'll see what I can do."

Ellie turned and stormed out.

***

When Ellie arrived at Matt's apartment later in the day, there was yellow police tape across the door. Large black lettering warned, Police Line, Do Not Cross. She pulled off the tape and rummaged in her handbag for the key. After unlocking the door, she stepped into the living room. The book shelves, covering an entire wall, had been emptied and books were strewn across the floor. The desk drawers were open and the contents dumped out. Matt's computer was gone. The file cabinet next to his desk had been emptied. *Were the police looking for drugs or something else?*

Ellie went into the bedroom. The closet door and the dresser drawers were thrown open and clothes were scattered on the floor. She moved on to the kitchen, where the fetid smell of rotting food stung her nostrils. Broken glass crunched beneath her shoes. Open cabinet doors revealed empty shelves. Dishes, glasses and pots were scattered across the floor. A box of cereal sat on the countertop, its contents spilled in the sink.

She opened the refrigerator and tossed the spoiled food into a trash bag. After taking a fresh bottle of water from the refrigerator, she walked to the living room, where she sat down heavily on the sofa and sighed. Her eyes moved across the vandalized room again. As she gazed at the ceiling, a loose tile caught her attention. It jarred her memory, taking her back to her childhood. She saw herself rushing into her parents' house, climbing the stairs to Matt's bedroom, standing on a chair and reaching behind a loose ceiling tile. She had found her mother's car keys, which Matt had hidden in his childish attempt to stop their mother from leaving.

Ellie dragged a chair across the room and positioned it below the loose ceiling tile. She climbed on the chair and poked the tile until it slid back. Reaching inside, her fingers curled around a small package. She yanked it out and jumped off the chair.

Pulling off the package wrapping, she uncovered a plastic DVD case and a folded sheet of paper. She unfolded the paper, smoothing it out. It was a chart with the words *Red Ridge Prison* penned on one side and *The Virginia General Hospital* on the opposite side. They were linked with double arrows.

Anxious to view the DVD, Ellie inserted it in the player and turned it on. The TV screen lit up with the image of a reporter standing outside the Fairfax

County Circuit Court. The courthouse door opened, and two men dressed in business suits and ties stepped out. They were surrounded by lawyers and a cheering crowd. The reporter asked, "How does it feel to be acquitted?" The men smiled but didn't answer. Ellie nearly didn't recognize the two men. When they had testified against Matt, they wore their police uniforms.

The next video segment showed the Virginia General Hospital with a reporter standing front and center. Ellie recalled seeing this broadcast in July, four months ago. It was news about football star Bob Reynolds' death from viral hepatitis contracted during transplant surgery. A huge lawsuit had followed, but Dan had dismissed the case as a rare occurrence.

Another video segment followed, with a TV anchor interviewing an attractive young man. "Our guest tonight is Nick Labelle, an investigator with Human Rights International, an NGO," the anchor said. "Nick, you've been investigating abuses at Red Ridge Prison in Virginia. The story has been in the news recently with an exposé in the Virginia Star newspaper. Tell us about your investigation." A photograph of the ominous facade of Red Ridge popped up, and Ellie shuddered.

"Red Ridge Prison has the highest prisoner death rate in the United States," Nick said. Those were the last words Ellie heard before the screen went dark, words that terrified her.

Every segment of the video was like a jagged piece of a puzzle, sending shocks through her. Dan had been adamant about Matt dropping his investigation of Red Ridge. And he had told her that she wasn't to write anything more about Virginia General. She could understand why he didn't want more stories about the hospital, given his position there. But why did he stop Matt's investigation of Red Ridge?

An overwhelming need to hear Matt's voice made her reach for her cell phone. She punched in a number. After several rings, someone picked up. "Red Ridge Prison," a man said.

"I'd like to speak to Matthew Andrews, an inmate," she said.

"Hold on," he said. Ellie waited for twenty minutes, refusing to hang up. Finally, to her surprise, she heard Matt's voice. "Hello."

"Matt, it's so good to hear your voice. Are you alright?"

"I'm okay." His voice was flat.

"I want to visit, but I had to mail a written request to the warden. I'm waiting for permission."

Matt didn't answer, and she continued. "Curtis is working to get you transferred out of there."

"I'm never getting out of here."

"Curtis already filed an appeal. And I'm going to help him find evidence that you were framed."

"Don't do that! Promise you won't investigate anything." The alarm in his voice startled her.

"Calm down," she whispered into the phone. "Tell me what's going on."

"Don't do anything, Ellie. Just stay safe."

"I'm in your apartment, Matt. The police trashed it and took your computer and your files."

"I'm not surprised."

"I found a DVD and a chart. Tell me what they mean."

She heard Matt's quickened breathing over the phone line. "I have to go. Throw them out. They're trash." The phone went dead, leaving Ellie to wonder if Matt hung up or someone cut them off.

Ellie spent the evening on her computer, researching the Bureau of Justice Statistics data on prisoner deaths. It was alarming to discover the sharp escalation in deaths in the last ten years. In Virginia, inmate deaths had jumped from 265 to 280 in just the last year. She confirmed what Nick had said about the largest number of deaths occurring in Red Ridge. There were too many causes of death listed as unknown, which she found suspicious.

Nick Labelle's name and phone number were listed on the Human Rights International website. Ellie picked up her phone and dialed. "You've reached Nick Labelle. Leave your name and phone number and I'll get back to you," she heard. She hung up, disappointed that he didn't answer, but then realized it was 11:00 p.m.

Chapter 23

Tuesday, December 1, 2009

Nick smiled at the research assistant on the way to his office. "Morning, Amy."

"Hi, Nick. I left the data you asked for on your desk."

"Thanks," he said, opening his office door.

A stack of files sat on his desk. As a senior investigator for Human Rights International (HRI) in Washington, DC, Nick reviewed mountains of data from staff researchers, wrote final reports and made recommendations. He owed his career start to Harry Wilson, a private investigator who he worked for while supporting himself through undergraduate school. He learned valuable investigative and surveillance skills from Harry. Later, he found his calling at HRI, fighting for victims abused by the U.S. criminal justice system.

Nick pushed the reports aside and reached for a letter he had received from Laverne Johnson, an inmate at Red Ridge Prison. Laverne was serving time there for car theft, not an offense that warranted incarceration in a super-max prison. He read Laverne's words again: *"I cussed a guard and was thrown in solitary. No lights. Windows was blacked-out. Couldn't see for 23 days..."* The letter was dated a day after Laverne was released from solitary.

Nick was concerned about Laverne's mental health after the excessive sensory deprivation in solitary. He had phoned the warden and asked to visit Laverne. "Put your request in writing, and the questions you plan on asking," Parker told him.

While Nick waited for permission to visit, Laverne committed suicide. Nick couldn't stop feeling that maybe he could have prevented his death. Laverne's mental illness was documented in his medical file prior to incarceration at Red Ridge. But when Nick investigated his death, his medical history was missing from the prison's records. Laverne's family was suing the prison and the Virginia Department of Corrections.

A tap on Nick's office door interrupted his thoughts. "More reports," Amy said, setting the files on his desk.

"Thanks, Amy. I appreciate your work."

"You're the one who has to make sense of all this." She closed the door on her way out.

Nick looked at the mound of files he had to plow through and sighed. He raked his fingers through his hair, reached for a folder and started reading. Reports released by the Bureau of Justice Statistics showed a significant increase in prisoner deaths in Virginia and throughout the U.S. prison system. Red Ridge had the highest number of inmate deaths from homicides, suicides and delayed medical care. An abnormally large number of cases listed the cause of death as *unknown*. This was reason enough for HRI to open an investigation.

Nick's phone buzzed. "Nick Labelle here," he answered.

"This is Ellie Andrews, Matt Andrews' sister."

"I'm sorry about Matt. His reporting was very important to me...to us."

"His appeal was denied...and the sentence was upheld."

"Oh." He couldn't think of anything adequate to say that would comfort her.

"Matt's lawyer is trying to get him transferred to a low-security facility. Do you think that's possible?"

"Maybe...I hope so."

"I want to visit Matt, but the warden is giving me the runaround."

"I'm not surprised. He doesn't want visitors."

"I'm afraid for Matt...what could happen to him there. I'm hoping you can help me."

"How?"

"Can we meet somewhere?"

"There's a local pub in old town Alexandria—Union Street Public House. I can meet you tonight at 7:00 in the Tap Room."

"I'll be there."

***

Ellie sat at a table in the back of the tavern. She had barely touched the white wine she ordered. Her eyes settled on the long burnished wooden bar, where men and women mingled for happy hour. Enjoying the company of friends was a dim memory now that her days were filled with anxiety.

Rethinking her conversation with Dan earlier in the day ignited her anger again and her jaw clenched. "You must know someone who can get Matt transferred," she had told Dan.

"I've made dozens of calls and talked to people in the penal system. I have some assurances, but no promises. Prisons are overcrowded," Dan had told her.

"What can I tell Matt? I need to give him hope."

"Tell him we're working on it. I know we'll succeed, but it could take months."

She had stormed out of his office, slamming the door. She blamed Dan and Curtis for botching Matt's defense and no longer had confidence that they could help him now.

The door opened at the other end of the Tap Room now, and a young man walked across the tiled floor toward her. She recognized Nick immediately from seeing him in the video segment. He was average height, but there was something powerful about him. He didn't look like a man you would want to cross.

He stopped at Ellie's table. She looked up at him and their eyes met. "Ellie?" he asked, smiling. She held out her hand and he grasped it in a firm handshake. The warmth of his hand lingered in hers after he let go and slipped into the seat beside her.

"Thanks for meeting me," she said. "Matt told me how you helped him when he was investigating Red Ridge."

"It's my job. Matt was instrumental in publicizing the horrendous treatment of prisoners. Thanks to his reporting, we were able to force some reforms."

A waitress stopped at the table. "What can I get you?" she asked Nick.

"Vodka and tonic," he said. Ellie studied Nick's natural good looks and made some instant assessments. Early thirties, strong jaw and honest hazel eyes. A small scar over his right eyebrow. *An accident or something else*, she wondered. "How's Matt doing?" Nick asked.

"Now that he lost his appeal, I can't imagine..." She drew in a breath, holding back tears that sprung suddenly in her eyes.

"It's hard to win an appeal for a felony conviction in Virginia. You would need some really compelling evidence," Nick said.

The waitress returned, setting Nick's drink on the table. Ellie regained her composure. "I'm gathering evidence," she said. "I discovered an escalating number of drug arrests and convictions in Virginia in the past seven years.

Did you know that police department funding is tied to their performance—the number of arrests they make? Matt is now one of their reward statistics."

"That probably explains why one in 214 adults in Virginia is in jail and why the state has one of the highest rates of incarceration in the country," he said.

"I'm hoping you can help me find a way to get Matt transferred to a low-security prison. His lawyer is useless."

"The transfer process can take months or years, if it's even granted. When the super-max prisons were built, there was a rush to fill them. At the same time, the prison system was privatized to generate profits for big business interests. Virginia pays private companies $28,000 a year for each prisoner. Some states pay as much as $60,000. With more than a million and a half people in prison in this country, you can see how it's turned into a billion-dollar business."

"Some conditions improved at Red Ridge after Matt's articles were published," Ellie said.

"Yes, and HRI got more access to interview prisoners." Nick lifted his glass and took a long drink. "Conditions at Red Ridge are still the worst in the country. Inmates are locked two to a cell for most of the day. Toilets are exposed in the cells. There's no privacy. Recreation, education and rehabilitation are nonexistent." He studied Ellie's reaction. "Should I go on?"

Ellie gulped some wine. "Yes."

"If inmates break any of the prison's rules, they go to solitary for weeks or months. There are over two hundred inmates in solitary at any given time, and they stay there for weeks, months, sometimes years. When they're released, they're generally psychotic." Ellie's face paled. "I don't mean to scare you, but..."

"You did."

"If you expect to help Matt, you need to know the facts."

"Where do I start?"

"The warden will throw obstacles at you, but get back in there to see Matt whenever you can. Document everything and, more important, write about it in your newspaper."

"Matt's not telling me what's going on there. He doesn't want me to investigate or write about it. And things have changed at the Virginia Star since my uncle became publisher. He stopped the investigations and reporting on Red Ridge and other prisons."

"That's too bad. But there must be other publications interested."

"I'll find a way to publish the truth."

"I'll file a request to visit Matt," Nick said. "The warden can't deny HRI access. He can stall and make it difficult, but I'll get in there. I'll call tomorrow. You should do the same."

"I appreciate anything you can do."

"I can't promise."

They looked into each other's eyes for some moments. Nick checked his watch and said, "I have another meeting, but I'll be in touch."

The waitress left the bill on the table, and they both reached for it. "This is mine," Ellie said as her fingers brushed against Nick's, igniting a sensation not unlike a soft kiss.

"Well, then I owe you a drink," he said.

"Deal." She watched Nick take long strides to the door, feeling more hopeful than she had in weeks.

Chapter 24

Friday, December 3, 2009

The cell doors opened, and Matt and Rusty stepped into the hallway for the morning head count. Ralph, the prisoner next door, stood alone. A guard moved along the cellblock, checking off inmates' names on a clipboard. He walked up to Ralph. "Where's your new *cellie*?" he asked. Ralph shrugged. The guard looked into Ralph's cell and made a call on his two-way radio.

An order blared over the loudspeaker, "Lock it down!" Matt, Rusty and the other inmates returned to their cells. The doors locked with a metallic clang. From the adjoining cell, they heard footsteps and a loud thump, followed by the sound of a rolling gurney.

Word spread fast when a new inmate arrived. Yesterday, they learned that Ralph's new cellmate was a man convicted of molesting boys. Ralph was a loner who talked to himself. Other inmates avoided him and any prisoners with overt signs of mental illness.

Last night, Matt and Rusty heard screams and thuds coming from the adjacent cell. The guards, who generally didn't tolerate any noise after lights out, didn't respond. Soon it grew quiet, except for Ralph talking softly to himself.

The new inmate was found with his skull smashed and prison linens wrapped around his neck. Ralph was already serving a life sentence for killing his stepfather, who had sexually abused him as a child. The guards put Ralph in restraints now, immobilizing his arms and legs and securing him to his bed. He would remain in restraints for twenty-four hours, and would not be allowed to use the toilet.

Red Ridge dished out punishment liberally, applying its own system of justice. Matt kept a notebook inside a slit in his mattress, where he recorded homicides, suicides and novel methods of abuse by prison guards. No matter where a death occurred in the prison, news traveled instantly, along with the gruesome details. There had been at least two deaths every week since Matt arrived, which confirmed the statistics he had discovered during his investigative reporting.

The lockdown today only lasted for two hours. Afterward, Matt and Rusty were among a small group from their cellblock allowed into the recreation yard. The narrow concrete courtyard was surrounded by two-story-high walls covered with a chain-link grate. Armed guards stationed in watchtowers overlooked the yard. Four prison guards stood behind a red line painted around the perimeter of the courtyard floor, ensuring that no prisoner overstepped the red boundary line.

When Matt first arrived at the prison, Rusty had given him advice, "You got to join a gang for protection, man. You can join mine."

"Thank you, and thank your friends," Matt told him. "I want to remain neutral."

Rusty's gang members sported tiger tattoos, a symbol of power and strength. Some also had teardrop tattoos, signifying murders in their past. Matt feared that gang membership would create more problems for him.

The temperature outside was forty-five degrees, but the men wore only their orange prison uniforms. They were not issued coats, hats or gloves and were expected to remain in the courtyard for the entire recreation period, no matter what the weather. Matt and Rusty stamped their feet to keep them from growing numb. They watched several prisoners tossing a basketball into a single hoop. There was no other equipment here. Small groups of men huddled together, smoking cigarettes and talking.

A prisoner stepped on the red line and a guard rushed toward him with a club and a stun gun. He quickly backed away, and the guard retreated. At the other end of the yard, a gang of three inmates clustered in a tight circle, shuffling their feet. Their necks and muscled arms were covered in tattoos that Matt learned to interpret. The SS bolt on their arms, a symbol of the Aryan Brotherhood, meant that they were either convicted murderers or capable of murder. Tattoos of daggers, spider webs, and skulls adorned their shaved heads and arms, connecting them to other gangs all over the country.

Matt didn't need Rusty to tell him to stay clear of them. Most of the other inmates avoided them. They beckoned to a short slim inmate now, a young man who Matt recognized as one of the newbies who had arrived with him on the prison bus. The gang sent the newbie running to the other end of the yard. He soon raced back to them with a supply of cigarettes, which they took and then pushed him away roughly.

Matt stretched his legs. "I'm going for a jog," he told Rusty. He started jogging around the yard, careful to avoid the boundary line. Taking deep gulps of the cold air, he concentrated on the blue sky and tried to imagine himself in the park near his apartment. The yard was so small that he found himself circling again and again. As he passed the gang of three for the third time, one of them fell into step beside him, knocking into him repeatedly. Another gang member called out, "Here fishy, fishy, fishy." Matt's heart quickened and he picked up his pace, breaking away. New inmates like Matt were called *fish* and were constantly tested and taunted by other prisoners. *Would he ever stop feeling like bait in a shark tank?*

Matt was relieved to hear the loud buzzer signaling the end of the one-hour recreation period. The men moved toward the door, lining up single file. Matt hung back at the end of the line to avoid the gang. They were marched into the mess hall for the afternoon meal. It was a cavernous space with bare concrete walls and guards positioned all around. Prisoners sat on benches attached to long tables to eat the midday meal.

Matt and Rusty picked up trays and moved along a food line in orderly single file. Inmates who worked in the kitchen dished out greasy globs of stew in a watery brown sauce and pasty mashed potatoes. Matt followed Rusty to a table where four of his gang members sat, wolfing down their food. "Hey," Rusty greeted them. One of the men looked up from his plate, nodding a greeting. Matt returned the nod.

Seated at a nearby table was the gang of three from the yard. One of the gang members caught Matt's attention and pursed his lips in a kissing gesture. Matt looked away quickly, his stomach knotting.

They ate in silence until a bell signaled the end of mealtime. Matt picked up his tray and stood with the other inmates. They moved in a line, depositing their trash in a can and stacking the dirty dishes and empty trays on a stand. One prisoner remained seated in the mess hall, eating slowly. Everyone turned to watch a guard with a stun gun rush toward him. The prisoner lifted the tray, stood and walked to the exit. Matt exhaled slowly, aware that he had been holding his breath. He hurried out of the mess hall, following Rusty.

Later in the day, Matt, Rusty and eight other inmates were escorted to the shower. Prisoners at Red Ridge were allowed three showers a week. Soap was a luxury they had to buy at the prison commissary or have it sent to them from friends or family. The communal shower was a large tiled enclosure with shower heads mounted high. The water was controlled from outside by guards who watched the prisoners through observation windows.

The men soaped up as water roared from above their heads. There was no place for modesty, nowhere to hide. Matt soaped his body quickly, anxious to get out. As the water washed over him, he was unaware of the gang of three watching him from the other end of the shower. The threesome moved slowly and deliberately across the shower enclosure. Two guards, observing the scene through a window, turned their backs as the threesome advanced toward Matt.

For a few moments, Matt let the water cascade over him, and he pretended to be in his shower at home. Then he felt his legs pulled from under him, and he fell face down on the shower floor with a loud thud. Two gang members wrestled with him, pinning his arms down as he pushed back and kicked them. Their wet bodies slid against each other, making slapping sounds in the shower. A powerful punch to the side of Matt's head stunned him as he was mercilessly violated. He cried out, but other inmates in the shower turned away as fear spread like the water raining down on them.

When the shower was turned off, the gang released Matt and moved away. He lay there dazed, sprawled across the shower floor on his stomach. "Move out of the shower," a guard shouted from the observation window. Matt lay on the wet floor trembling, too stunned to move. "You, on the floor, get up and move out," he ordered.

Rusty slid across the soapy shower floor to Matt's side, pulling him up. "Do what they say or you'll go to solitary," he said.

Back in his cell, Matt lay on his thin mattress as the lights dimmed. He stared into space, his senses aroused by every sound and movement. He finally slept fitfully for a short time until his own cries woke him. Panic squeezed his chest, and he bolted upright. His sobs woke Rusty. "Hey, man, you okay?" he asked.

Matt's skin glistened with perspiration. His head throbbed. He bolted off the cot, stumbled to the toilet and vomited. Shaking uncontrollably, he lay sprawled on the cold floor. Rusty got up and dragged Matt off the floor, leading him back to his cot and covering him with the blanket.

Chapter 25

Tuesday, December 8, 2009

Matt was in the dayroom near his cellblock when a guard called, "Andrews, you have a phone call." He escorted Matt to the phone.

"Hello," Matt said.

"Matt, thank God they let you come to the phone," Ellie said. "I've been calling for days, trying to get permission to visit you. The warden said you need to agree to my visit in a written letter."

"I don't want you to visit."

"What's wrong?"

"Nothing." His voice was flat.

"Write the agreement letter, Matt. I must see you."

"Okay."

"Promise?" She heard him breathing, but he didn't answer. She asked, "Did you get the package I sent last week?"

"What package?"

"Books, chocolate, toiletries, writing paper and pens."

"Packages are opened and searched."

"You didn't get anything?"

"A few books. Thanks." Those were the last words Ellie heard before they were disconnected.

Matt was escorted back to the dayroom where inmates were allowed to mingle for one hour. They gathered in small groups, playing cards and checkers or talking and smoking. In the center of the room, a corrections officer observed them from a glass security booth—the bubble. Matt pulled up a chair beside Rusty and another inmate and watched them play checkers.

Across the room, a prisoner shouted, "You calling me a cheat?"

"You're a fucking cheat," the other inmate said. The insulted prisoner sprang from the chair, throwing himself at his accuser. They fell on the floor, wrestling and punching each other.

Other inmates rushed to the scene, surrounding the fighters, goading them on, shouting encouragement: "Kill him."

"Take his eyes out."

"Cut off his balls."

Matt stood up, watching the fight unfold. Someone came up behind him, rubbing against his body. Startled, Matt whipped around and looked into the eyes of the man who had raped him. He smirked at Matt before turning away and walking off. Matt's heart thundered in his chest, his breathing quickening. He clenched his fists, stifling the urge to strike back.

The fighters thrashed on the floor as other inmates closed in, tightening the circle around them, their excitement mounting. Matt could see the guard on duty in the bubble talking into a phone, but the guard made no move to leave the booth.

A loud buzzer sounded and, after a long delay, six armed guards rushed in, shouting, "Break it up!" When the inmates ignored the warning, rounds of rubber stinger bullets flew at the men gathered in the circle, stopping the brawl abruptly. One prisoner lay on the ground moaning, his face covered with bloody pock marks from rubber pellets. The other man lay motionless, a knife protruding from his back.

"Everyone down!" a guard ordered. Matt and the other prisoners dropped to the floor. More guards rushed into the dayroom, surrounding the inmates with pointed guns. The men lay on the floor for half an hour until order was restored. The prisoner who had survived the fight was dragged away to solitary, and the other men were marched back to their cells.

Matt's cellblock remained in lockdown for the next two days. There was no documentation of the fight because video surveillance cameras in the dayroom weren't positioned to record anything. This served a double purpose—abuse by the prison staff couldn't be recorded and neither could inmate-on-inmate homicides.

Security measures didn't prevent enterprising prisoners from getting knives and other materials they could fashion into weapons. Packages addressed to inmates arrived daily. They were inspected by guards in a secluded room. Everything was confiscated that could be sold and resold by the guards and the prisoners in an elaborate barter system and black market. Everything was available for a price—knives, razor blades, heavy objects, drugs, alcohol and other items in demand. Cash was slipped into packages addressed to gang members to assure delivery. Everyone profited.

Suicides were another leading cause of death at Red Ridge. A few days ago, Matt learned that a prisoner who had arrived with him on the prison bus, and was enslaved by the gang of three, had swallowed a washcloth and choked to death. There were countless deaths from drug and alcohol overdoses, though the suppliers were rarely found and stopped.

Prisoners who were unlucky enough to have a medical condition could not expect medication or treatment. Last week, in the recreation yard, an inmate had an asthma attack. Matt watched him collapse on the concrete floor, gasping for air. When a fellow prisoner bent over him to help, two guards rushed over, beating both men with clubs and dragging them out of the yard. Later that day, word spread through the cellblocks that the asthmatic prisoner had died.

Matt documented everything he witnessed and learned about abuse and torture at Red Ridge. Hidden inside his mattress were a growing number of reports for Nick Labelle, who had permission to visit him in a few weeks. This gave Matt a sense of purpose, a reason to wake up every morning and live through the day. It became his *raison d'etre*—his reason to be.

Chapter 26

Monday, December 14, 2009

Matt jogged listlessly around the concrete courtyard as lightly falling snow clung to his hair and prison uniform. His fingers were red and stiff, but he welcomed the pain that kept him from focusing on his hellish life. After the phone call from his lawyer two weeks ago, he knew he would have to reach deep inside himself every day to summon the will to survive. Curtis' words played over in his head: "Your appeal was denied. We're going to get you transferred out of Red Ridge, I promise." *Promises were for people who still had hope,* Matt thought.

He ran past the basketball court where four inmates dribbled a ball to keep warm. Huddled together, on the other side of the courtyard, was the vicious gang. Matt felt their eyes on him as he jogged. A prison guard standing watch nodded to the gang with a small movement of his head. The gang broke out of their huddle, catching up with Matt, jogging alongside him. They jostled him. Matt sped up, breaking into a sweat. One of the men stepped in front of him, blocking his path. Matt moved from side to side, trying to escape. A gang member stuck his leg out, tripping Matt and sending him to his knees. He tried to drag himself up as lightning-quick punches and kicks struck his head and body.

Prisoners in the yard stopped their conversations to watch the attack, but no one interceded. A guard shouted, "Break it up!"

Two of the gang members pulled Matt up from the ground, pretending to help him. Matt limped away, relieved that he had escaped the assault with his life. Rusty caught up to him. "What the hell happened?" he asked, his eyes on Matt's bruised face. "You need to go to the infirmary, man."

"No infirmary," Matt said.

A bell rang, signaling the inmates to line up. They fell into a single file, entering the door and marching to the mess hall. Inside, Matt and Rusty picked up trays stacked on a table next to the food line. When Rusty heard Matt's erratic breathing, he turned to him. "You okay?" he asked. Matt nodded and they moved along the food line. He pressed his hand against his side, where a fractured rib impeded his breathing.

They moved on, taking plates of food doled out by prison workers. Matt focused on getting through the meal and returning to his cell so he could lie down. He didn't notice a gang member slip into the line behind him. A sudden searing pain in his back knocked the breath out of him, sending him sinking to his knees. Blood oozed down his back, pooling on the floor. He felt the air being squeezed from his lungs and a strange sensation of falling into an abyss.

A loud warning buzzer sounded. An order blared from the loudspeaker: "Everyone in a seat, now!" Matt lay splayed on his stomach, a sharpened toothbrush protruding from his back. Two guards rushed to him, but neither one checked to see if he was still breathing. The infirmary was summoned.

A guard turned to the prisoners seated at the tables. "What happened here?" he called out. There were many witnesses, but all were silent.

***

As Ellie drove toward Red Ridge, winding her way through the mountain roads, the last phone conversation she had with Matt played over in her head. An unsettling anxiety urged her to step harder on the accelerator.

She arrived in the afternoon and was ushered inside. After a routine search, a guard came up to her. "Miss Andrews, Warden Parker is waiting to see you in his office. I'll take you there."

"I have an appointment to see my brother, Matthew Andrews, not the warden."

"Follow me. The warden will explain."

Ellie followed him to an office. He knocked once, opened the door and motioned for her to enter. Parker sat behind an oversized desk. His shirt sleeves were rolled up, showing off muscular arms. *Intimidating* was the only word that came to Ellie's mind. "I have an appointment to see my brother. Why am I here?" she asked.

"Sit down, Miss Andrews." Parker pointed to a chair facing his desk. He stared at Ellie without speaking for some moments. "Your brother isn't here."

Her hands tightened around the arms of the chair. "Where is he?"

"He's been taken to the hospital."

The color drained from her face. "What happened?"

"The inmates here are unpredictable and violent. Your brother got into a fight with another inmate." Parker sat back in the chair, letting the news hang in a moment of silence. "He was hurt real bad. We transported him to the Virginia General Hospital."

Ellie bolted from the chair and rushed out, slamming the door. She didn't hear Parker's last words, "Don't you worry. That's a fine hospital."

***

Night had fallen by the time Ellie arrived at the hospital. She didn't remember the grueling drive from the prison as she sped along the snow-slicked mountain roads, frantic to reach Matt. Her head swam with self-condemning thoughts. From the time she and Matt were children, she felt responsible for protecting him. Her mother had charged her with this responsibility, and she accepted it, welcomed it. She would never forgive herself if Matt... She couldn't even finish such a thought.

Ellie raced to the ER and was directed to the intensive care unit. She stepped into the elevator that carried her to the ICU floor. An attendant told her to wait outside the ICU. Every few minutes, she went to the nurses' station and asked, "Can I see Matthew Andrews now?"

She was told repeatedly, "I'll let you know, Miss Andrews. Dr. Russell, the attending, will be out to see you."

Half an hour later, a balding man in his mid-forties, dressed in hospital scrubs, walked through the ICU's swinging door. He pulled off his surgical mask as he approached. Ellie stood. "My brother, Matthew Andrews?"

"Your brother suffered massive internal injuries and head trauma," Dr. Russell said, his words as cold as his eyes.

Ellie gasped. "He'll recover?"

"We did everything we could."

"What?"

"Your brother never regained consciousness."

Ellie stared at him in disbelief. She stumbled backward, sliding into the chair, her face ashen. A roaring sound filled her ears. She drew in great gulps of air. *No. He can't be dead. I won't allow it*, repeated over and over in her head.

Russell motioned to an attendant to bring a cup of water. Ellie bolted out of the chair. "You're lying to me!" She pushed past the doctor and ran to the

ICU doors. She pressed against them, but they were locked. "Open up!" She pounded on the doors with her fists.

"It's best that you don't see him," Russell said.

"Let me in!"

Russell swiped the keypad with his ID badge and the doors swung open. The smell of disinfectant permeated the ICU as Russell led her past a row of curtained rooms. He stopped at the last room, drawing aside the curtain. Matt lay motionless on the hospital bed, covered from his neck down with a sheet. Purple bruises covered his swollen face. Tubes inserted in his nostrils to feed him oxygen had not yet been removed.

Ellie took Matt's limp hand in hers. It was still warm. She refused to believe that his eyes wouldn't open in a few moments. "Wake up, Matt. Please wake up." She pressed her lips into the palm of his hand. Great gulping sobs filled the room, and she wondered where they were coming from.

Russell moved to the bed. "You should go now, Miss Andrews."

Ellie looked at him, dazed. "I'm not leaving him."

Russell turned and walked out of the room. A few minutes passed and he returned with two gowned and masked attendants. They rolled the hospital bed away from the wall, leaving the IV connected to Matt's arm. "You can't take him," Ellie said.

"We have to let the hospital do an autopsy now," Russell said.

The word shocked her. "No. I won't allow it! He's had enough abuse."

"It's the law. The cause of death must be established."

"Murder! That was the cause."

The attendants pushed the bed out of the room, moving it along the hallway to the elevator. Ellie followed, her eyes on Matt's chalk-white face, until the elevator door closed behind him.

Chapter 27

Friday, December 18, 2009

Ellie sat on a chair in a corner of the formal dining room in the Andrews' mansion, her hands clasped in her lap, staring into space. She wore a black suit and no makeup to mask her pale face and red-rimmed eyes. People she didn't know milled around the dining room table, filling plates with food set out on overflowing platters. Others gathered in small groups, talking in low voices. Some came up to her, murmuring words of sympathy. She stared at them blankly, unable to respond.

It was five days since Matt's death, but the shock kept Ellie from accepting the truth until today. Seeing the coffin jolted her back to reality. She had been living in a fog since the day she had last seen Matt in the hospital, feeling as though life moved around her in another realm. Today, the finality of his death was so painful, she believed she would not survive.

Dan and Joan had made the funeral arrangements. They sent a limousine to pick her up this morning at her apartment. She remembered hearing screams when Matt's coffin was lowered into the grave. The screams seemed to be coming from a stranger, but they stopped when Dan dragged her away from the grave into a waiting limo.

Joan came up to Ellie now, handing her a plate of food. She smiled at Ellie, a distant cold smile. "You should eat something," she said. Ellie took the plate, but when Joan turned back to her guests, she set it on a table. Her fingers curled around a small plastic container in her jacket pocket—tranquillizers Dan had given her. Last night, she had thought about swallowing all of them at once.

Ellie reached for a bottle of wine on the table and filled a glass. She drank it quickly. It warmed her throat, settling in her empty stomach. She downed a second glass, feeling its welcome anesthetic effect.

A young man walked across the room, stopping in front of her. She looked up into his warm hazel eyes, his familiar face. "Nick," she said. He took her hand and pressed it.

"I'm sorry," he said. "This shouldn't have happened."

"But it did."

"It wasn't your fault."

"If I had gotten to the prison sooner..."

"I could say the same." She looked so ruined, it pained him to gaze at her face. "If there's any way I can help..."

"It's too late."

"Call me. We can talk."

Ellie watched him walk away, her hand still warm from his touch. She poured another glass of wine. When she looked up, Bill Curtis was crossing the room toward her. Her stomach tightened. He stood before her, reaching for her hand, but she drew it away. "I'm so sorry, Ellie," he said.

"How dare you show up here!" Her voice was shrill. An embarrassed silence settled in the room as guests turned to stare.

Curtis' face flushed at the unexpected accusation. "I did everything possible to help Matt."

Ellie's eyes flashed with anger. "Everything? Everything you did got him convicted, sentenced to that hell hole, and murdered."

Curtis turned away, walking across the room to the front door. Dan stopped him as he was leaving. They shook hands, like old friends after playing a chess game.

Ellie poured another glass of wine as the last of the guests said goodbye to Dan and Joan, avoiding her. Exhaustion swept over her as she sipped the wine, longing for it to numb her. A maid wrapped leftover trays of food and wiped up spills. Joan was on her way upstairs. "I have an awful headache," she announced. "I'm going to bed."

Dan took Ellie's hand. "Come sit with me in the living room," he said. She followed him into the adjoining room where a cheerful fire burned in an ornate marble fireplace. A tall Christmas tree, decorated with festive lights for the holiday, spread a scent of fresh pine. It seemed to Ellie like a scene on a Hallmark Christmas card, mocking her grief. "You should stay over tonight," Dan said, sitting beside her on the sofa.

"I need to be at home."

"You insulted Bill. It must have been all the wine you drank."

"Why did you invite him?"

"How could I not invite him? He did whatever was possible to defend Matt."

"His incompetence got Matt convicted. And you chose him. You vouched for him."

"Are you blaming me...and Bill for Matt's death?"

"Matt would be alive now if it wasn't for Bill's botched defense."

"You're not rational if you're blaming us. Take some time off. Maybe go away for a few weeks. You need time to heal."

"I'm going back to work. There are questions I need answered."

"What questions?"

"For starters, what happened at the prison? And why?"

"You can't expect the truth from the prison. You must know that."

"I know how to find information."

"What good will it do? Let go of this, Ellie."

"I'll be in the office on Monday."

"I forbid you to come back for a month."

"Are you firing me?"

"If that's what you need."

"Go to hell, Dan." She stormed out of the room, slamming the front door as she left.

Chapter 28

Monday, December 21, 2009

Ellie opened her eyes slowly, blinking at the sunlight streaming through the bedroom window. Her head hammered with a punishing hangover. She needed aspirin, but the thought of swallowing anything made her stomach roil. She dragged herself off the bed, pushed open the bathroom door and vomited into the toilet until her stomach was empty. Dragging herself up from the cold tile floor, she turned on the tap and splashed water on her face.

Dizziness drove her back to bed. She closed her eyes. Scenes of the lost weekend came flooding back to her. From the moment she stepped into her apartment after the funeral on Friday, grief had wrapped her in a shroud of sorrow so profound it took her breath away. The last thing she remembered from Friday was swallowing Valium with a glass of wine. "Don't mix the tranquilizer with alcohol," Dan had warned when he gave her the pills.

All through Saturday, the phone rang insistently, intruding on Ellie's drugged sleep. The answering machine recorded a stream of messages. Sunday afternoon, her friend, Claire, rang the doorbell. "Go away. I don't want to see anyone," she told her.

"I'm not leaving. I'll wait out here all day if I need to," Claire said.

Ellie opened the door a crack, and Claire pushed her way inside, carrying a pizza box. She set the box on the living room table. "Sit," she ordered, pushing Ellie onto the sofa. She opened the box, selected a slice of pizza and placed it on a paper plate. "Eat," she said.

Ellie took the plate from her. "You only speak in one-word sentences now?"

"Yes," she said.

Sitting beside Ellie, Claire watched her nibble the pizza. "Why'd you come here?" Ellie asked. "I'm not good company."

"That's true. But I'm your friend, and I'm worried about you. And you probably haven't eaten for days."

"The pizza's good. Thanks."

"Have another slice. Then go shower and put on clean clothes. You look like crap."

After Ellie showered and dressed in jeans and a T-shirt, she went back to the living room. Claire had tidied the room and tossed out the empty wine bottles. "You didn't have to do that," Ellie said.

"Let's get out of here, go to a movie," Claire said.

"I'm not ready to go out."

"You can't stay in your apartment forever. I know how much you're hurting, but you need to get back to your life, Ellie."

Tears welled in Ellie's eyes. "What life?"

"The life you want to make for yourself."

"I'm toxic. I make wrong choices...wrong decisions."

"You're blaming yourself for things you couldn't control."

"I shouldn't have trusted Dan and his lawyer to defend Matt. I should have been with my father the night of the accident. They'd still be alive if only…"

"Everyone who lives through tragedy has these kinds of thoughts and feelings—if only I had done this instead of that."

Ellie was silent, mulling over Claire's words, but unable to let go of the guilt and loss that consumed her. After Claire left, Ellie spent the rest of the night drinking wine until she fell into another drugged sleep.

Pushing the events of the lost weekend out of her thoughts now, Ellie got out of bed and stood unsteadily on her bare feet, waiting for the dizziness to pass. She padded to the kitchen.

Opening the refrigerator, she took out a bottle of water and gulped it down with two aspirins. Her hands trembled as she filled the coffee pot with water and measured coffee into the basket. She slid into a kitchen chair, put her head down on the table and waited for the coffee to brew. When it was ready, she filled a mug and went back to the table, carrying a box of dry crackers. As she nibbled on a cracker, her eyes scanned the empty wine bottles on the counter with disgust. Her friend's words came back to her— *"You need to get back to your life."* But she didn't have the will or the energy for that. Not yet.

The doorbell rang. Ellie thought it must be Claire returning to check on her. She went to the door, prepared to scold her friend. But, when she opened the door, it wasn't Claire standing there. It was her mother. She stared at the woman in the doorway as if she were an alien invading her worldly space.

"Hello, Ellie," Laura said. Ellie was stunned into silence. "Can I come in?"

"What…what are you doing here?" Ellie asked, recovering her voice. She stepped back and Laura came inside. They faced each other without speaking for some moments, as though they had forgotten they once knew each other well and were now strangers. *The years had been kind to Laura. She was still an attractive woman who could make heads turn*, Ellie thought.

"You're so beautiful, Ellie." Laura reached out to touch her daughter's face, but Ellie recoiled, pulling away as though her mother's touch would burn her skin.

"Why did you come here?"

Laura flinched at the harshness in Ellie's voice. "When I read about Matt, I was so shocked. I wanted to see you, to tell you how sorry I am for Matt… for you."

Ellie bit her lip. "You, sorry?"

"I wasn't a good mother. But I loved you both."

The painful memory of the day Laura left came flooding back to Ellie. She saw Matt standing beside her, crying. She heard her childish plea as she grasped her mother's hand, *"Don't go, Mom."* She saw her mother drive away, feeling the loss and heartbreak again.

Ellie shook off the memory and turned to Laura. "Mothers don't abandon their children."

Laura looked stricken. "I've been sorry for leaving you every day of my life."

Ellie felt her chest squeeze with rage. She stifled an impulse to slap her. "Not a word, a card, a phone call in fifteen years and you want me to believe you're sorry? You came to the wrong place if you're looking for sympathy. Where were you when Ben was killed? Did you even care?"

"I did care…very much. I didn't think you and Matt wanted to see me then."

"You're right about that. We never wanted to see you again."

Laura took a breath, readying herself for more hurtful words.

"Why *did* you leave my father? It was for some other man, right? Who were you fucking then?"

Laura absorbed Ellie's anger in a long silence. Then she opened her handbag, pulled out a photograph and handed it to Ellie. "I've been with John for the past fifteen years."

Ellie looked at the man in the photograph and stepped back as if she had been punched. She was looking at a ghost—Matt's face, his eyes, his mouth, his expression. She felt the air sucked out of her lungs, and she gasped. "Is this why you came here, to tell me Matt is my half-brother?"

"I thought you should know."

"Why now?" Laura didn't answer. Ellie continued. "Did my father know?"

"Yes," Laura said. "Ben loved Matt unconditionally. He was a good man. It was best that he brought you up."

"You're right. It was for the best that you were out of our lives. Matt worshipped Ben. It would have torn him apart to learn..." Ellie clasped her hands together to still their trembling. "I never want to see or hear from you again."

Laura blinked back tears. She slipped the photograph back in her handbag and snapped it shut. "Maybe one day you'll be able to forgive me."

"Should I forgive you for not loving us? That *is* the truth, isn't it? Do you love the man you left us for? Are you even capable of love?"

Ellie felt a certain satisfaction seeing tears spill down her mother's face, knowing that she had hurt her. She opened the door and Laura stepped into the hallway. "Maybe you'll change your mind one day, Ellie. I would like to see you again."

Ellie closed the door and sank onto the floor, the weight of her anger and sorrow threatening to crush her. Loud uncontrollable sobs came from deep within, going on and on, until exhaustion left her spent, splayed on the floor like a wounded animal.

She sat up finally, drawing in great gulps of air. Then she pulled herself off the floor, opened the door and left the apartment, stumbling down the steps to the street. The cold air stung her cheeks as she ran three blocks to the jogging path in the park. She jogged for an hour without stopping. As she ran, images of her childhood spun through her mind like a tragic film noir. She was consumed by feelings of profound loss, of wanting and needing something that eluded her.

Finally, she stopped running and walked slowly back to her apartment. She went inside and sank onto the sofa. Exhaustion had cooled her anger. Something inside her had changed. A long-buried false conviction that her mother would return because she loved her was shaken loose. Ellie came face to face with the truth now. It was a cruel truth that she had denied her entire life—Laura never loved anyone. She wasn't capable of love.

This undeniable fact shook Ellie to her core, displacing the grief threatening to suffocate her. Confronting it set her free to focus on her singular purpose now—finding those responsible for Matt's death and bringing them to justice. She had work to do and no time to waste.

Chapter 29

Tuesday, December 22, 2009

Today was Ellie's first day in the newsroom since Matt's funeral. She was reading her e-mail when Claire came into her office. "Hey," Claire said. Ellie smiled at her friend. "What happened to taking time off?" she asked.

"Changed my mind. Too much to do," Ellie said

"Let's have lunch later."

"Okay." Ellie turned back to her computer.

Soon after, the managing editor and newsroom colleagues stopped in to see Ellie. When they left, Dan was just arriving for the day. When he saw Ellie, he walked into her cubicle. "What are you doing here? I fired you for a month," he said.

"Catching up on assignments," she said.

"It's too soon, but if you feel better in the office..." His voice trailed off as he walked away, but the look on his face told her that he was angry with her for defying him.

Later in the morning, Ellie phoned the Fairfax County Medical Examiner's office. "I would like a copy of the autopsy report on Matthew Andrews," she said. "I'm his sister, Ellie Andrews."

"We haven't received the autopsy report from the Virginia General Hospital," a clerk told her.

"The hospital? Didn't the chief medical examiner do the autopsy?"

"The autopsy was done at the hospital where your brother died because he was still alive when he was admitted there. In such cases, the hospital pathologist performs the autopsy."

Ellie hung up and hurried to Dan's office. She knocked on the door and walked in, not waiting for an invitation. He looked up from the file he was reading. "What's on your mind?" he asked.

"I just spoke with the medical examiner's office. They told me that the hospital did Matt's autopsy. I want a copy of the report."

"Dr. Russell called me yesterday. The autopsy concluded that Matt's death was a homicide. A stab wound in his back pierced his lung, collapsing it and causing complications that led to his death."

Ellie swallowed hard, the harsh facts stunning her. "When were you going to tell me?"

"Would knowing the details change anything?"

She clenched her fists. "I have a right to know everything."

"You will, but it's best if you recover from the shock first."

Ellie bit her lip, her face coloring. "I'll decide what's best for me. You don't get to dictate what information I'm entitled to have. Call the hospital and tell them I want a copy of the report. Today."

Her fury silenced him. He reached for the phone and punched in a number. "Ellie Andrews will be at the hospital this afternoon for a copy of Matthew Andrews' autopsy report. Please have it ready for her," he said. He hung up and turned to Ellie. "You can pick up a copy at 2:00 this afternoon."

"I'll go on my lunch hour."

"Ellie, I care about you. You know that, don't you?"

She nodded on her way out, regretting her angry tirade. He was, after all, her only family now.

***

Ellie showed her ID to a clerk in the hospital records department. After signing a release form, the clerk gave her an envelope. She took the elevator to the main floor and went to the cafeteria. Sitting at a table in the back, she opened the envelope and poured over the grim facts in the autopsy report.

Documented in precise details were the exact measurements of the stab wound. A photograph of the sharpened toothbrush that had punctured Matt's right lung made her shudder. The dissection of his organs was detailed with descriptions, measurements, weights. The cause of death was listed as pneumo-hemothorax, hypoxia and shock. The manner of death was homicide, an ugly word that itself felt like a wound.

After reading the report for a third time, Ellie thought there had to be more information about Matt's condition when he was transferred from the prison. She went back to the records department. "I need the complete hospital records for Matthew Andrews. I picked up his autopsy report about an hour ago," she told the clerk.

"I remember you," the clerk said. "I'll see if we have the records." She searched her computer screen for a few moments. "We don't have the records. Dr. Russell hasn't sent them over here from his office yet."

"Why would he have the records?"

"Sometimes the attending physician wants to review the records or make additional notations. You can inquire at Dr. Russell's office."

Ellie took the elevator to the administrative unit where chiefs of staff had their private offices. When the door opened, she faced a receptionist's desk. "I'm Ellie Andrews. I need to speak to Dr. Russell," she said.

The receptionist picked up the phone. "Ellie Andrews would like to see you." She hung up, turned to Ellie and pointed to a row of chairs against the wall. "You can have a seat. The doctor will be out shortly."

It was half an hour before Russell appeared. He wore an expensive suit and looked different from when Ellie had seen him in the ICU, dressed in hospital scrubs. There was no mistaking his stern face and cold eyes as he walked toward her. "You have the autopsy report for your brother. Do you have a question, Miss Andrews?" he asked.

"I need to see my brother's medical records and any files that came from the prison when he was transferred."

"Hospital records are confidential. They're the property of the hospital. We don't release them."

"I have the right to see my brother's records."

"It's out of the question," he snapped.

"Then I'll get a court order."

Pressing his lips together, Russell turned away and rang for the elevator. When it arrived, a visitor stepped out. Russell entered and the elevator door closed behind him. Ellie's eyes settled on the double doors leading to the administration offices. As the receptionist turned her attention to the new visitor, Ellie quietly slipped through the doors.

She walked along a hallway lined with private offices, stopping at a door where *Dr. James Russell, Chief of Internal Medicine, Chief of Transplant Unit* was etched on the glass. She turned the doorknob, but it was locked. She pulled her handbag off her shoulder, her press ID tag hanging from the strap, and took out a credit card. Sliding the credit card down next to the lock, Ellie pressed her weight against the door and turned the doorknob. The lock opened with a click, and she exhaled in relief. She was grateful to have learned this technique for unlocking doors when she had lost the key to her apartment.

At the far end of the hallway, two women were leaving an office, talking and laughing. Ellie removed the credit card from the lock and leaned against the wall. She bent her head and rummaged through her handbag, pretending to search for something. The women walked past her, engrossed in conversation. Ellie waited until they exited through the swinging doors. Then she turned the doorknob and stepped inside the office.

She flipped on the light switch and looked around the room. Occupying the center space was an island with a sink, a microscope, some glass slides. A desk with a computer and a phone sat on one side of the office. The far wall was lined with metal file cabinets. She went directly to the files, opening drawer after drawer, thumbing through folders, reading labels. Hearing voices in the hallway, she stopped and shut the light. She had no idea what she would do if she were discovered.

The voices faded and Ellie turned the light back on. She opened other file drawers, then noticed an unmarked cabinet. When she opened it, she found it filled with Red Ridge prisoners' files. *Why were prisoners' records in Russell's office?* Her mind raced as she read the labels on the folders. Her fingers stopped on a file labeled, *Matthew Andrews*. She pulled it out, spreading it open on the counter. As she read the details, her face drained of color.

The sound of men's voices in the hallway stopped her. She closed the folder and put it back in the cabinet. Then she shut the light, opened the door a crack and looked into the hallway. Russell and another man were walking toward her. Ellie's breath caught, and her heart raced as they moved closer. They stopped a few feet away, continuing their conversation. With Russell's back turned away from her, she had to move quickly. Shifting her handbag onto her shoulder, she slipped out of the office. She didn't notice her press ID tag sliding off her handbag strap onto the floor. Turning away from Russell and his colleague, she walked briskly to the other end of the hallway, exhaling in relief, grateful that she hadn't been caught breaking into the office.

Chapter 30

Wednesday, December 23, 2009

Ellie had just settled into her office and turned on her computer when her phone rang. "Come into my office," Dan said, and hung up.

Dan was on the phone when Ellie walked in. He pointed to a chair near his desk and she sat down, puzzling over the stern look on his face. While holding the phone against his ear, he waved Ellie's press ID card in front of her. Her face flushed. He turned on the speakerphone.

"Jim, Ellie's in my office. You're on speaker. Go ahead."

"Miss Andrews, you broke into my office yesterday. I intend to press charges against you for breaking and entering," Russell bellowed.

"I didn't take anything," Ellie said.

"Breaking and entering is a felony."

Ellie took a deep breath. "I needed to see my brother's hospital records. I *did* ask you and you refused."

"You have to file a legal request for records."

"That would have taken too long."

"Reporters aren't exempt from following regulations."

"I think we can settle this amicably," Dan said. He turned to Ellie. "What do you say to a truce, Ellie?"

"I apologize," she said. "I'll submit a formal request for my brother's records."

"You're very lucky, Miss Andrews, that your uncle is a personal friend. The gloves will be off if anything like this happens again. Do you understand?"

"I do."

Dan placed the phone back in the cradle. "What on earth were you thinking, breaking into Russell's office?"

"I know it was wrong, but I *did* read something in Matt's file that was disturbing. The prison did blood- and antigen-typing on Matt. Why would they do that?"

"It's probably routine testing for all prisoners. There are accidents, fights between prisoners who may need medical attention. In emergency cases, they need that information."

"The information didn't save Matt, did it? I have questions I need answered by the warden at Red Ridge. Can you set up a meeting with him?"

"It's not likely. Warden Parker won't allow our reporters into the prison. And we're not writing any new stories now, so we have no reason to go there."

"Isn't Matt's death reason enough?"

"You need to put this to rest, Ellie."

She picked up her press ID from Dan's desk and walked out without another word.

When Ellie got back to her office, she put her head down on her desk and closed her eyes. Getting caught breaking into Russell's office was a close call, but she refused to let it stop her. There was more to learn about the circumstances of Matt's death. She reached for her phone and punched in a number. She listened to it ring over and over, and was about to hang up when she heard his voice. "Nick?" she asked.

"How are you, Ellie?"

Her stomach did a small flip at the sound of his voice. "I'm calling to ask a favor."

"What is it?"

"I need to visit Red Ridge to question the warden, maybe take a look inside Matt's cell. I can't get in as a reporter. Is there something you can do?"

"I can request a visit to investigate Matt's death. They can't refuse Human Rights International. When I get a date, you'll come along. I'll do my best to persuade the warden to allow you in."

Ellie hung up, hopeful for the first time since Matt's death, and looking forward to seeing Nick again. Their first meeting flashed in her mind, along with the feeling it ignited when her fingers had accidentally brushed against his. She shrugged off the memory, dismissing it as silly.

Chapter 31

Monday, January 4, 2010

Ellie sat beside Nick in his Jeep Wrangler as he navigated the winding Appalachian road. They had been driving for three hours, talking on and off. A comfortable silence settled between them now. Her thoughts dwelled on the past weeks. Christmas and the New Year's holidays had come and gone in a blur of self-isolation. She shut herself in her apartment, grieving for Matt and her father, nursing anger at her mother, whose sudden appearance continued to shock and haunt her. *Why had Laura come back into her life now, after all the tragedies?* Ellie could not separate the repressed need for her mother's love from her rage.

Nick turned to Ellie. "Don't get your hopes up for getting inside the prison today. The warden's a hard-ass."

"If I can't get into Matt's cell to have a look around, maybe you can."

"What would I be looking for after all these weeks?"

"I don't know," she said, studying his profile. He was good-looking but not head-turning handsome. It was the strength of his character that drew her to him...or something more she wasn't ready to admit. She remembered the accidental touch of their fingers the first time they met, and she wanted to touch him again.

It was late morning when they pulled into the prison parking lot and walked through the gate. They showed their IDs and were searched. Finally, they were escorted to the warden's office. Parker held court behind his desk, motioning to two chairs facing him. "What can I do for you?" he asked, not hiding his hostility.

"I'm here to investigate the death of Matthew Andrews," Nick said.

"Why is Miss Andrews here? She isn't authorized to visit."

"I didn't think you'd mind answering a few questions for Miss Andrews, since Matthew was her brother," Nick said.

Parker glared at them, not speaking for some moments. "What's your question, Miss Andrews?"

"Can you tell me why blood- and tissue-typing were done when my brother was admitted here?"

"That's what we do. I run this prison the way I see fit. I don't have to explain my policies to you."

"Human Rights International is concerned about the rising prisoner death rate here. That's a matter of record," Nick said.

Parker's eyes narrowed. "This is a super-maximum prison for the most dangerous criminals. Outside, these men were a danger to pampered, privileged people like you. Inside, they are a danger to each other!" He pushed his chair out and stood. "This meeting is over."

"I came here to see the cell where my brother spent his last days. That's all I'm asking," Ellie said.

"Why? We sent you his personal effects," Parker said.

"It would mean a lot to Miss Andrews to spend a few minutes in the last place where her brother was alive," Nick said.

"No," Parker said.

"We'll leave as soon as Miss Andrews sees the cell," Nick said.

"You won't be interviewing any prisoners today?"

"Agreed," Nick said.

Parker opened his office door and spoke to the prison guard waiting outside. "Take Miss Andrews to cellblock four and unlock the cell where Matthew Andrews was incarcerated. She has permission to spend five minutes in the cell. Then escort her out of the prison." Turning to Nick, he said, "You can wait in the parking lot."

The guard led Ellie to a cellblock on an upper floor, stopped in front of a cell and took out a ring of keys. The door opened with a noisy clang. Rusty Degan jumped off his cot, a startled look on his face. "Degan, stand away from the visitor," the guard ordered. "She's here to see the cell, not you. Do not talk to Miss Andrews! Do not approach her!"

"Yes, sir." Rusty sat down on his cot. He reached for a notepad and pencil.

The guard stepped outside while Ellie walked slowly around the cell, memorizing the details. She moved to Matt's cot, touching it lightly with her fingertips. The mattress had been removed, and she thought that strange. The shelf next to the cot was empty. Matt's personal belongings had been removed. Rusty followed her with his eyes while scribbling on a notepad. Ellie looked up, and their eyes met. She smiled at him. "Times up," the guard called.

Ellie walked across the cell. As she brushed past Rusty, he pressed a folded paper into her hand. She closed her fingers around it and walked out, the cell door closing behind her.

Rusty patted a small bulge in his mattress where he had sliced it open and hidden Matt's notebook. It was filled with detailed descriptions of violent incidents and damning evidence about abuses inflicted on the prisoners. He would have to wait until it was safe to barter with one of the prisoners who arranged outgoing mail.

Ellie was escorted outside. She walked across the parking lot and climbed into the front seat of the Jeep beside Nick. Pulling the paper out of her pocket, she unfolded it. "Matt's cellmate, Rusty, gave this to me," she said. She read the hastily scribbled note: *'Look at Matt's body.'* She gasped. "What's he trying to tell me?"

"Was there an autopsy?" Nick asked.

"Yes. I have a copy of the hospital's autopsy report, but I don't know if I should trust it. The autopsy should have been done by the chief medical examiner. I'm still trying to get copies of Matt's medical records. What now?"

"You can have his body examined again."

Ellie shuddered. "Can anything be found after all this time?"

"I know a private forensic pathologist who's exceptional. If there's anything, he'll find it."

"No one can know I'm doing this. Not my uncle, Dan. No one."

"Of course."

Ellie sighed. "After all Matt suffered, he can't even rest in peace now."

They drove for the next hour in silence. Nick concentrated on steering along the steep road. Ellie struggled with her decision. *Was she doing the right thing or was Dan right about letting go?* Finally, she broke the silence. "I wonder how Rusty could have gotten any information about Matt inside the prison."

"Prisoners have reliable sources you can't imagine."

Chapter 32

Wednesday, January 6, 2010

Rows of granite tombstones. Bare trees. Gray clouds skittered across the sky, and a stiff wind blew Ellie's hair around her face. Cold seeped through her wool coat, and her toes grew numb inside her boots. Two gravediggers were at work at an open grave. Heavy equipment had already accomplished most of the job of removing the packed frozen earth piled in a mound next to the grave.

Nick held Ellie's hand, the warmth from his skin seeping through her glove. She shuddered when a shovel struck the coffin, a dull thud echoing in the cold silence. Ropes were secured around the heavy oak coffin, and it was hoisted up and set on a gurney. The sight of the coffin was unbearable, unleashing anguish that felt like physical pain. She bit her lip to keep from screaming. Nick watched her face, pressing her hand in his as the coffin was wheeled to a van parked in the roadway and loaded inside.

***

When Marty Sloane, the chief forensic pathologist, walked into the autopsy room at the laboratory, his assistant, Sean Young, had already arranged the body on the black marble autopsy table. Sloane was a seasoned pathologist, often commissioned by private detectives investigating suspicious deaths. He had already read the hospital autopsy report that Ellie had sent over.

The body had been removed from the rubber transport bag and lay face up, covered with a blue cloth. Sloane pulled the cloth off. The large overhead light illuminated Matt's body. A steady stream of water ran from the slanted top of the table to a drain at the bottom.

Both men wore heavy rubber aprons over scrubs. Masks and goggles covered their faces but didn't insulate them from the acrid smell of formaldehyde. Sloane nodded to Sean, and they began the task of cutting the sutures covering the wish-bone-shaped incision along the length of Matt's torso.

Sloane was not surprised to see that the organs had been removed from the body cavity. It was routine not to replace organs after an autopsy. But the sutures along Matt's arms and legs were suspect. They cut the sutures. Sean mumbled from behind his mask, "What the fuck!" PVC pipes had been inserted to replace the bones that had been removed and to give the limbs a normal appearance. They discovered more—skin removed from the chest, back, arms and legs, eyes removed, ligaments and tendons neatly dissected.

As the autopsy proceeded, Sloane recorded his findings on tape, which would be transcribed into a written report for Ellie Andrews. "The missing tissue from the deceased is consistent with organ and tissue harvesting," Sloane recorded.

***

It was late afternoon when Nick finally heard from Marty Sloane. He phoned Ellie. "I'll pick you up and we'll go to the lab together," Nick told her.

"I can go alone. You've already done enough."

"I'll be there in half an hour," he insisted and hung up.

Now Ellie sat on a bench beside Nick in the white-tiled corridor outside the autopsy room. Nick turned to her and their eyes met. "Thank you," she said. He took her hand. She didn't know why this small gesture made her eyes well with tears.

The lab door swung open and Sloane stepped out, pulling off his face mask as he walked toward them. Ellie sprang to her feet. Sean Young watched them from behind the lab window. He saw the ruined look on Ellie's face as Sloane spoke to her. Nick caught her as she swayed, leading her to the bench. Sloane hurried to the water fountain and returned with a cup of water. Ellie sipped the water, regaining her composure.

"Did your brother sign an organ donor card? Did you give permission to donate organs and tissue at the hospital?" Sloane asked.

"I didn't. Why?"

"I found deep incisions in your brother's groin and abdomen that are consistent with organ harvesting."

"Incisions?" She drew in a breath.

"Incisions are made so that cold fluids can be injected to preserve the organs for harvesting."

Ellie clasped her hand over her mouth to stifle a scream.

"A donor's permission would explain the missing bones and tissue," he said.

"Can we get a detailed report? And we need to keep this confidential," Nick said.

"Of course," Sloane said.

"How can you be sure after all these weeks?" Ellie asked.

"Your brother's body was well preserved for many reasons. It was embalmed. He was buried in an oak coffin, and the temperature has been cold."

"Embalmed?" she asked.

"There was a small incision above the navel. That's where embalming chemicals are injected."

"Don't organs die immediately?"

"Organs are viable for a short time…if there's oxygen."

The memory of holding Matt's still-warm hand as he lay in the hospital bed came flooding back to Ellie. She remembered the oxygen tubes in his nose as he was wheeled away. And the IV had not been disconnected. But he was so still, his face deathly pale.

"Check your brother's driver's license. He may have elected to be an organ donor. That would explain everything," Sloane said.

"Thanks for your work, Marty," Nick said. Ellie nodded, too overwhelmed to speak, her head spinning with the new revelations. *Matt could return to his resting place*, she thought, *but she would not rest until she found the truth.*

Chapter 33

Thursday, January 7, 2010

Dan looked up when Ellie knocked on his office door and walked in. "You look tired," he said, noting the dark circles beneath her eyes. "What's on your mind?"

Ellie took a breath. "I had Matt's body exhumed, and an independent autopsy done."

Dan's eyes widened. "Why?"

"I wasn't satisfied with the hospital's autopsy report. And there were questionable things in Matt's prison medical record."

"Why didn't you come to me?"

"I did. When Dr. Russell dismissed my concerns, I had to go further."

"And now…are you satisfied?"

"The pathologist found Matt's organs and other tissue missing."

There was a long silence before he answered. "I'm sure there's a logical explanation." He reached for the phone and tapped in a number. "Jim, Ellie's in my office. She has questions about the hospital autopsy done on Matt Andrews. She had a private lab do another autopsy. Can you explain to her why Matt's organs are missing?" He turned on the speakerphone.

"Miss Andrews, organs are routinely removed for examination during an autopsy. Then they're discarded as medical waste." Russell's voice rang with irritation.

"There were incisions in my brother's groin and abdomen. Isn't that done to preserve organs for harvesting?"

"It's done to preserve organs for examination," Russell snapped. "Autopsies can be delayed, and decomposition is immediate."

"Why was his skin removed, his corneas, bones?" She didn't hide the outrage in her voice.

Russell cleared his throat. "Our pathologists are meticulous. They remove different tissue for examination, particularly in cases of prisoner attacks."

"That's an understandable explanation. Don't you agree, Ellie?" Dan asked.

Ellie ignored Dan, persisting with her questions. "You said that Matt's organs were disposed of as medical waste. How do you dispose of medical waste?"

"We use a private company," Russell said.

"What company?"

"I can't give you that information. It's hospital policy."

Dan watched Ellie's face color. "We understand, Jim," Dan said. "Thanks for taking the time to explain." He hung up and turned to Ellie. "Are you satisfied? You could have saved yourself the anguish and expense. It may seem ghoulish to you, but it's easier to discard body parts after an autopsy than to replace them."

"Can you get me the name of the medical waste company?" Ellie asked.

Dan sighed. "No. That's proprietary information. This has turned into an obsession for you. Nothing you're doing will bring Matt back. It's tearing you apart."

Ellie was in no mood for a lecture. She stood and marched out of the office. If she was obsessed with investigating Matt's death, so be it.

***

Alone in her apartment in the evening, Ellie had little appetite for dinner. She took a yogurt and a bottle of water from the refrigerator and went into the dining room, where Matt's files and personal papers were stacked on the table. A computer disk slipped out of one of the folders, and she made a mental note to look at it later. After searching several files, she found Matt's driver's license. She reached for her phone. "Nick, it's Ellie. I have Matt's driver's license. He wasn't an organ donor."

"What will you do now?" he asked.

"Find out what happened and why."

"If I can help…"

"You've done so much already."

"I wouldn't have wanted you to do this alone."

Ellie tried to think of something more she could say to keep him on the phone. His voice soothed her. "Thanks," she said and hung up.

She went to the kitchen, filled a kettle with water and waited for it to boil. After brewing a mug of tea, she settled on the sofa in the living room, wishing Nick were sitting beside her. He seemed so strong, and she needed that now. Not that she needed anyone to lean on. She could take care of herself. She always had, even before her mother had left. And yet, she couldn't deny that she was attracted to Nick. He intruded on her thoughts too often.

Ellie set the half-finished mug of tea on the coffee table and leaned back against the sofa. She hadn't slept at all last night. Her eyelids felt heavy, and they soon closed in spite of her efforts to stay awake.

The sound of a heart beating grew louder. Ellie pushed open the doors of an operating room and stepped inside. Red Ridge prisoners in orange uniforms, Warden Parker, Dr. Russell, and nurses were pressed together around an operating table. A bright overhead light illuminated a naked patient strapped to the table, spread-eagle. The patient writhed, trying to break free. Ellie moved closer to the table to see the patient's face. Matt looked up at her, his eyes wide with terror. Warden Parker shouted, "Strip him!" The prisoners moved like zombies, surrounding Matt, tearing at his flesh, stripping off layers of skin and muscle. When their ghoulish task was complete, they backed away from the table, their uniforms and hands covered with blood and bits of skin.

Matt's body lay on the table, opened like a peeled fruit, exposing his organs. His heart pumped furiously inside his chest. The beating sound grew louder in Ellie's ears.

Ellie screamed and bolted from the sofa. Beads of perspiration covered her face. She ran to the kitchen and turned on the faucet, splashing cold water on her face. Gripping the edge of the sink, she sucked in great gulps of air. When her breathing finally slowed, she dried her face with a towel. Then she uncorked a bottle of wine, filled a glass and downed it.

After regaining her composure, Ellie went to her computer and searched for medical waste removal companies near the Virginia General Hospital. There were several in Virginia, in nearby Maryland and Washington, DC. Too many others were listed throughout the country. There was one foolproof way to find the company that serviced the hospital.

Chapter 34

Friday, January 8, 2010

Ellie arrived at the Virginia General Hospital at 8:00 a.m., after leaving a message for Dan that she would not be in the office today. She circled the hospital's perimeter in her car, looking for dumpsters. When she spotted several in a remote corner at the rear of the hospital, she parked nearby and turned off the engine. One dumpster had a biohazard symbol painted on it. Ellie opened the glove compartment, took out binoculars and got a close look at the padlocked dumpster.

An hour passed. When other cars started pulling into the parking lot, Ellie sank down in the car seat, hiding from view. Men and women, dressed in hospital scrubs, entered the hospital through the rear door after swiping their employee ID cards on the keypad. More time passed. Ellie's eyelids felt heavy and started closing. She shook herself awake, wishing she had brought along a thermos of coffee. Then she heard the rumble of a heavy vehicle.

A black van backed up to the biohazard dumpster. A burly man, dressed in work clothes and thick gloves, got out of the van and opened the back doors. He unlocked the padlock on the dumpster with a key, removed large, black plastic bags and tossed them into the van. After closing the van doors, he went to the hospital door, pressed the call button and spoke into the intercom. Moments later, the door opened and a man in a white lab coat handed him a red insulated container. The driver carried the container back to the van, placed it on the front seat and drove out of the parking lot.

Ellie started her car and followed the van along local streets to the Beltway, keeping a distance between them. The van sped up on the highway, changing lanes frequently, and Ellie had to step hard on the accelerator to keep up. As traffic picked up, cars and trucks blocked her view. Her muscles tensed as she moved in and out of lanes, tracking the van. Road signs told her that she had passed the city limit. When the van abruptly exited the highway onto another road, she turned sharply, nearly missing the exit. She hung back, following slowly along a two-lane road. Several more turns took her to a remote side road flanked by trees.

In the distance, Ellie watched the van pull into a private driveway that led to a sprawling, two-story white building. She parked along the side of the road and waited a few minutes before following. Then she drove slowly along the gravel driveway, grateful for the abundant foliage as she maneuvered behind thick shrubbery.

She watched the driver park in front of the building, announcing himself with a blaring horn. Moments later, the entry door opened, and a security guard took the red container from the driver and closed the door.

When the driver returned to the van, he headed to the rear of the building. Ellie followed at a safe distance, pulling her car in behind some trees. She watched the driver unload the medical waste bags from the hospital and toss them into an incinerator. After pushing a lever on the incinerator, he climbed back in the van and drove off. The incinerator rumbled into action and, in moments, spewed thick smoke into the still air. Ellie gagged as a sickening noxious smell spread in the air, seeping into the car. She drove to the front of the property, hiding behind a row of tall hedges.

Ellie sat in her car for hours, observing the front entrance through her binoculars. Except for two deliveries of supplies, nothing happened. She dozed off several times and woke with a start, hoping she had not missed seeing something important. She didn't know how much longer she could stay alert.

Finally, at 4:00 p.m., the front door opened, and employees, some dressed in scrubs, others in street clothes, walked to the parking lot. When the lot was nearly empty, Ellie got out of her car and went to the front door. Peering through a narrow side window, she saw a long corridor leading to a desk manned by an armed security guard.

Ellie was examining the keypad near the door when the sound of an approaching car sent her scurrying back to her car. A Mercedes pulled into the driveway. She looked through her binoculars at a tall slim man dressed in an expensive suit. He went to the door and tapped numbers on the keypad. Ellie read the numbers through her binoculars and memorized them. The door opened, and the man disappeared inside. Then she waited impatiently for him to leave. Time passed. The sky dimmed and the sun set.

Ellie kept her eyes on the door as night settled around her. She worried that she wouldn't find her way back to the highway when she was ready to leave. The door opened at last, and the well-dressed man stepped out, carrying a thick briefcase, which he put in the trunk of his car. When he drove off, Ellie got out of her car and stumbled through the darkness to the back of the building.

The keypad on the back door looked the same as the one on the front door. Ellie peered through a narrow side window into a hallway and was relieved to see it empty. She pressed the numbers she had memorized. The door opened with a click, and she exhaled with relief. Her first good luck of the day, she thought, stepping inside.

She walked down the corridor, passing empty offices, and stopped at a door labeled, *Medical Storage Bank, Authorized Personnel Only*. The sudden sound of footsteps startled her. She turned the doorknob and slipped inside.

The dimly-lit, stark white room smelled of disinfectant and something else Ellie couldn't identify, which made her eyes water. Cold, near freezing, wrapped itself around her. Storage chests lined the room. She shivered as she moved to a freezer and unhooked the latch. Reaching inside, she pulled out a container filled with something transparent floating in liquid. Printed on the label was *Cornea*. She shuddered, dropping the container back into the freezer. She forced herself to open other freezers. There were hundreds of containers labeled with names of veins, tendons, arteries, bones, skin. A battlefield of body parts surrounded her. The containers were numbered. She guessed that the numbers were identifiers, and she copied them quickly onto a notepad.

Her fingers stiffened from the cold. She opened the door a crack, peering into the hallway. Hearing voices, she closed the door quickly and waited. "Good night," she heard through the door, hoping that was the last of the employees leaving for the day. She waited, opening and closing her numb fingers. Finally, it grew quiet. When she opened the door again, the hallway was empty.

Stepping out of the storage bank, Ellie moved along the corridor, looking into empty offices through glass doors. She tried the doors, but they were locked. At the end of the hallway, she found an unlocked door and went inside. It was a nondescript office with a desk, a computer, a phone and file cabinets. She booted up the computer and tried to gain access, but *Access Denied* appeared on the screen. Riffling through files and papers on the desk, she found an office directory. Embossed on the cover was *Virginia Organ Procurement Agency (OPA)*. Brian Payne, Director, was the first name on the list of executives. She turned off the computer and walked out.

At the end of the hallway was a door leading to a stairwell. Ellie opened the door and climbed the stairs to the second floor. The office doors on this floor were embossed with the names of company executives. She stopped at Brian Payne's office and turned the doorknob. She wasn't surprised to find it locked, but it was a simple lock. She pulled a credit card out of her handbag and deftly slipped it in next to the lock until she heard a click.

It was dark in the office except for moonlight streaming through the window. She couldn't risk turning the light on, and she pulled a small penlight out of her handbag. Scanning the room with the light, she noted the plush carpeting and expensive furnishings. A row of file cabinets lined one wall. She tugged the handles, but the cabinets were locked. Moving to the desk, she opened the drawers, searching for a master key that wasn't there. A paper clip would have to do, and she pulled one apart and picked at the master lock until it opened.

Using the penlight, Ellie scanned the files. She opened a drawer labeled, *Red Ridge Prison*, and thumbed through the folders. Her fingers stopped on a file labeled, *Matthew Andrews*. She pulled it out and laid it open on the desk. Matt's prison ID number was printed on every page. She pulled other files from the cabinet. They all had unique ID numbers. She copied the prisoners' names and ID numbers until the sound of footsteps stopped her.

A flashlight beamed light through the glass door. Ellie pushed the file drawer in but not all the way. She huddled under the desk as the security guard turned the doorknob. He stepped inside and turned on the overhead light. Ellie could feel her heart pumping wildly as the guard walked to the open file drawer. She could see his shoes and gray uniform. She held her breath, praying he wouldn't look under the desk. He reached out to examine the partially open file drawer when the squawk of his intercom radio stopped him. "Right away," he said, and hurried out.

Ellie scrambled out from under the desk and stepped into the hallway. She ran to the stairway and rushed down the steps to the first level. When she opened the stairway door and looked into the corridor, the security guard was studying a monitor at his station. *It's now or never*, she thought, as she sprinted down the hallway to the back door. The guard leaped out of his chair, bolting after her. "Stop!" he shouted.

She reached the door and tugged at the doorknob. It was locked. The guard's footsteps grew louder as he moved closer. A button at the side of the door caught Ellie's eye, and she pounded on it. The door would not open. She could hear the guard panting as he gained on her. He reached out, grabbing hold of Ellie's leg, sending her sprawling on her stomach. "Got you," he shouted.

Ellie kicked her leg back, her boot landing against his face with a thud. He cried out in pain. She scrambled off the floor, pounding on the door button with her fist. The door opened as the guard stumbled to his feet, blood dripping from his nose. Ellie bolted into the darkness, diving behind the bushes as the guard ran along the driveway in pursuit.

She could hear her heart thudding as she picked her way to the front of the building, where she had hidden her car. Her hands were covered with scratches. Bits of twigs and leaves clung to her jacket and stuck in her hair. When she reached the car, her breath was coming so fast, she thought she would pass out. She started the car and pulled onto the gravel road, the tires screeching as she sped away. Through the rearview mirror, she saw the guard running along the path, his gun aimed at her car.

After several wrong turns, Ellie found the highway and headed south toward home. After some time, her breathing slowed to normal, but she couldn't shake off the noxious smell from the storage bank that lingered in her nose. In her mind, she saw the containers with human body parts again—bone, tendons, veins, skin. She shivered at the visual memory. Questions flooded her mind—*Where did the tissue come from? Where was it going? What did the numbers on the containers mean…and the numbers on the prisoners' files?*

As Ellie drove on, she realized that if she had been caught inside the tissue bank, she could have been arrested for trespassing or worse. The surveillance cameras inside were well hidden and had escaped her notice.

Chapter 35

Friday, January 8, 2010

Ellie pressed the buzzer on the front door of Nick's apartment building. "Yes?" Nick's voice traveled through the intercom.

"It's Ellie."

A few moments later, Nick stood in the doorway, dressed in jeans and a T-shirt. "What are you doing here?" His eyes swept over her, taking in the bits of soil and twigs stuck to her clothing and her disheveled hair. Taking her hands, he pulled her inside.

She followed him up a flight of steps to his apartment. He closed the door and turned to her with worried eyes. "What happened?"

"I found a building where body parts are stored...It's a business." Her words spilled out in a torrent, and she realized how crazy she must sound.

"Whoa. Slow down." He looked at her wild eyes and her pale face and led her to the sofa. She sank into the soft leather. Nick helped her off with her jacket. "Take some deep breaths," he said. "I'll get you a drink." He disappeared into a small galley kitchen that was visible from where she sat.

The living room was warm and welcoming, lit by soft indirect lighting along the ceiling. A lamp illuminated a corner desk stacked with books and papers. The computer was on, its screen spreading light. She had interrupted his work, even at this late hour.

Nick returned with two glasses of brandy. "Drink," he said, placing a glass in her hand. The brandy burned her throat as she swallowed. She felt its heat warming her empty stomach. A Mozart symphony reached her ears, playing softly from somewhere in the apartment. The brandy and the music were magically soothing. "Want to tell me why you look like you walked through a forest?" he asked.

Ellie drew in a deep breath. "I followed a medical waste van from the hospital to a building that stores body parts." She wrung her hands and continued. "I went inside and..."

Nick stopped her. "You went inside? You rang the doorbell and were invited in?"

"I found the door code and opened the door."

"Oh?"

"Okay," she said, impatiently. "I watched the door through binoculars while someone entered the door code."

"So, you broke into the building."

"You make this sound like *I'm* a criminal."

"You were breaking and entering a building that was locked. We don't know that anyone was doing anything illegal in there."

"You don't believe me! You didn't see what *I* saw." She pulled herself up from the sofa. "I'll be on my way."

"Sit down, Ellie. It's not that I don't believe you, but you need proof to make an accusation." He took her hands and examined the scratches covered with dried blood. "I'll get some alcohol for your hands."

Ellie sat back on the sofa, feeling like a child who had been caught with chocolate on her face. She looked around the tastefully decorated room. The large open space was divided into living room, office and dining room by the arrangement of the contemporary furniture. A colorful woven rug in a rich red and beige covered the polished oak floor. Framed posters of opera performances at the Kennedy Center and art exhibits at the National Gallery hung on the walls. It surprised her that there were no family photographs, no pictures of Nick with girlfriends or with anyone.

Nick carried a bottle of alcohol and a bag of cotton balls into the living room and set them on the coffee table. He gently swabbed the scratches on Ellie's hands. She winced, but he continued until all the small cuts were cleaned. "Thanks," she whispered, feeling like she was thanking him for a sensual experience.

"Tell me exactly what you saw."

"I walked into a storage room filled with freezer chests. There were body parts stored inside—skin, bones, corneas, veins, arteries. The containers were numbered, and I copied the numbers."

"That doesn't prove anything."

"There's more," she said. "I found files from Red Ridge with prisoners' names. Matt's file was among them. The files had ID numbers that I recorded.

I think they were all dead prisoners' files." She pulled her notebook out of her handbag and tore out the pages with her notes. Placing the pages side by side on the coffee table, she compared them.

The color drained from her face. "Oh my God! The prisoners' IDs match the numbers on the containers. They're killing prisoners and stealing their body parts. That's why Matt's organs and tissue were missing."

Nick examined the two sets of numbers. "Who exactly are you accusing?"

"The Virginia Organ Procurement Agency, a tissue bank. Others are involved."

Nick went to his computer to look up the tissue bank. After a few minutes of searching, he said, "The Virginia OPA is a licensed organ procurement agency." He went back to the table and studied Ellie's notes again. "Some of the numbers match. But this doesn't prove that anyone's stealing body parts."

"I have more evidence." Ellie rummaged through her handbag and pulled out Matt's flowchart and DVD. "I found this in Matt's apartment." She spread the chart out on the table. "The Virginia General Hospital is connected to the tissue bank and the prison. Matt suspected they were all involved. That's why he drew this chart."

Nick loaded the DVD in his player. They watched the segments Matt had recorded—two plain clothes policemen standing in front of the courthouse and declaring their innocence, and the Virginia General Hospital implicated in causing an athlete's death from a kidney transplant. When the video ended, Nick turned to Ellie, a puzzled look on his face. "This doesn't prove that the hospital or the tissue bank are doing anything illegal."

"If I find out where the organs and tissue go from the tissue bank, will that convince you?"

"You're making a criminal accusation, and you need more proof."

"What about Matt's cellmate, Rusty Degan? He told me to look at Matt's body. I need to talk to him again."

Nick poured more brandy in their glasses. "You're playing a dangerous game, Ellie. You'll get hurt, or worse."

His words made her face crumple. She looked like a small child about to cry because she was scolded. Nick took her hands in his. His touch was warm and comforting. "It's late. Why don't you stay here tonight? You can have the bedroom. I'll sleep on the sofa," he said.

Relief washed over her. "I'll take the sofa," she said. "I doubt that I'll sleep."

Nick went into the bedroom and returned with a pillow, linens and a blanket. He offered a large shirt. "You'll be more comfortable sleeping in this." He dimmed the lights and headed for his bedroom. "Get some rest. We'll figure out the next step in the morning."

Ellie found the bathroom and stepped into the shower. The hot water calmed her, but she couldn't shake off the shocking discoveries she had made. After drying off and slipping on Nick's shirt, she returned to the living room and curled up on the sofa. Her eyes closed from exhaustion, but sleep eluded her. The day's events unraveled like a horror film behind her eyes—rows of freezers, stacks of containers with body parts, the security guard chasing her.

Moonlight poured in through the window, casting shadows on the walls. Ellie lay on her back, staring at the ceiling. She turned from side to side, then onto her stomach. Finally, she threw off the blanket and got up. She paced around the living room, her eyes settling on an open file on the coffee table. Like her, Nick brought his work home with him. She moved to the bedroom door. Her hand curled around the doorknob. She hesitated, then turned the knob and stood in the doorway, telling herself that she just wanted to see Nick for a moment, to reassure herself that she was safe.

Nick sat up in bed. "Hey," he said. He patted the bed, inviting her to sit. She moved slowly, her bare feet sinking into the carpet, and sat facing him. He turned her around and massaged the back of her neck and shoulders. "Relax," he said. His touch was firm but gentle, stirring a deep longing in her. She turned to him, searching his eyes. They were filled with desire that matched hers. She reached out, touching the scar above his eye with her fingertips.

"How did that happen?" she asked.

"It's a long story."

"I'm a good listener."

Nick studied her face as if he were judging whether he could trust her enough to reveal anything about himself. "My father was killed in an auto accident when I was thirteen. My mother remarried two years later, to a wealthy home builder. My stepfather had a lot of rules."

The episode that resulted in his scar came rushing back to him now. He saw himself walking into his house late one evening. It was 11:30, half an hour past his stepfather's imposed curfew. Nick closed the door quietly, but his stepfather bounded down the steps from the bedrooms and struck him with his fist. Blood...so much blood gushed from the wound above his eye.

Nick pushed the painful memory from his mind now and said, "My stepfather had a mean temper and zero tolerance for me. End of story."

Ellie didn't press him for the longer story he wasn't ready to tell her. She brushed the scar again with her finger. He pulled her into his arms. His kiss was sweet, filled with promise. She didn't pull away, and he covered her face and neck with soft kisses that made her shiver, unleashing a passion she couldn't stop. She clung to him with an urgency that surprised her. They pulled off their scant bed clothes, anxious to feel each other's skin, to satisfy this new thirst.

Afterward, they slept in each other's arms, beneath the tangled blanket. It was the first peaceful sleep Ellie had had since Matt's arrest months ago. She pushed the horrific events of the past to the back of her mind. Tonight she was wanted and safe. She could pretend that she was living a normal life.

Chapter 36

Saturday, January 9, 2010

Ellie woke early. She turned to look at Nick, still asleep beside her. She wanted to reach out and touch him, press her lips against his. But visions of everyone she had loved came flooding into her head—her mother, her father, Matt. She shook off her thoughts and went into the bathroom to shower.

She was dressed and had brewed a pot of coffee when Nick came into the kitchen. She held her cell phone to her ear as her eyes settled on Nick's bare chest. A shiver went through her, and she turned her back on him. "Thank you," she said into the phone. "I'll be there this afternoon."

Nick came up behind her, circling her in his arms. His lips brushed the back of her neck. She caught her breath and slipped out of his embrace. "I have an appointment to visit Rusty Degan today. Do you want to drive to the prison with me?"

Nick searched her face, but she looked away. He waited, expecting more. "I'm sorry about last night," she said at last.

"Sorry?"

"For being out of control."

"Is that what you were?" The hurt in his eyes made her heart ache.

"I enjoyed being with you. Don't think it's anything more."

He stiffened. "You're afraid I might think that you care?"

She couldn't meet his eyes. "Yes," she whispered.

His jaw tightened. "You came on to me!"

"I can't get involved with anyone now."

Nick turned away, storming out of the kitchen. He went into the bathroom, slamming the door.

Ellie stood outside the locked door. "Nick, last night was great," she said. She wouldn't tell him that their lovemaking had rendered any experience in her past meaningless. He didn't answer, and the sound of the shower drowned out the rest of her words.

She waited until she heard him turn off the shower. When the door finally opened and Nick stood in the doorway with a towel wrapped around his waist and beads of water clinging to his chest, she wanted to wrap her arms around him, smother him with kisses and tell him she was sorry. But she said, "You don't have to come with me to the prison. I can get there by myself."

"I'll drive you. I don't think you should go alone. This is strictly business," he added, his words clipped.

As they drove along the mountain road to Red Ridge, Nick stared straight ahead, stone-faced. They drove for hours in tension-filled silence. "I wish you'd talk to me," Ellie said. "You don't understand where I'm coming from."

"Maybe you'll tell me one day," he said.

"I can't have any distractions."

"I'm a distraction?"

Ellie flinched. "Let's not argue."

"You used me."

Ellie didn't deny his accusation. She wanted him to believe this. They drove the rest of the way without speaking. When at last they exited the highway onto an access road, Red Ridge loomed ahead. Nick pulled into the parking area and turned off the engine.

Inside the prison, they showed their IDs. At the entry desk, Ellie said, "We're here to visit Rusty Degan." The guard checked a clipboard for their names.

"He isn't here," the guard said. "He was injured in a fight with another prisoner today and was taken to a hospital."

Ellie and Nick exchanged surprised looks. "What hospital?" Ellie asked.

"The Virginia General Hospital."

They walked out of the prison. It would be at least a five-hour drive to the hospital. Nick started the engine, and they sped away. There was nothing Ellie could say to dispel the dark mood that settled around them. She brooded over her insensitive words to him but told herself it was best for him.

In the distance, an ambulance raced ahead. As they gained on the ambulance, Ellie craned her neck to read the words on the back door. "It's the

Virginia General Hospital ambulance," she said, her voice rising.

The Jeep edged closer, and Ellie strained to see through the back window of the ambulance. "Do you have binoculars?" she asked. Nick reached across her seat and popped open the glove compartment, pulling out state-of-the-art binoculars that he sometimes used for surveillance work.

Ellie looked through the binoculars. A patient lying on a gurney came into sharp focus. An intravenous line snaked from the patient's arm to an IV bag. His face was ashen beneath his red hair. A surgical cloth, covering the lower half of his body, was pulled away. A doctor in a surgical gown, mask and gloves, bent over him. An assistant swabbed the patient's abdomen, coloring the skin with a reddish liquid. He handed the doctor a scalpel. Ellie sucked in her breath as she watched the doctor make an incision in the patient's abdomen. A stream of blood oozed out, and the assistant quickly swabbed it. She gasped. Nick turned to her. "What?" he asked.

"They're operating on Rusty in the ambulance!"

"How do you know it's him?"

"I'm certain. It's hard to see his face, but his red hair is unmistakable." She pressed the binoculars to her eyes and watched the doctor work the scalpel inside the incision. Then he pulled out a kidney-shaped mass covered in bloody fluid. The assistant sprayed it with a liquid, and the surgeon placed it in a metal basin. "They removed Rusty's kidney," Ellie exclaimed. Her heart thudded as the kidney was placed in a large red container with a biohazard symbol.

Then the surgeon looked up through the back window of the ambulance. He saw Ellie spying on him. She dropped the binoculars in her lap as if it burned her hands. "He saw me!"

Ellie didn't see the surgeon reach for his phone. Nick slowed the Jeep and dropped back on the remote stretch of highway. "Are you sure?"

"Yes."

Ellie breathed deeply, trying to slow her heartbeat while Nick drove on. Half an hour later, the sound of a police siren shattered the silence. Through the rearview mirror, Nick could see a police van gaining on them. The ambulance disappeared ahead of them as the police van moved closer, its lights flashing now. "Tighten your seat belt," Nick said, stepping down on the accelerator and speeding ahead.

The van moved closer, tailgating, then rammed into the back of the Jeep, jolting them. Ellie felt her heart pumping wildly and the rush of adrenaline coursing through her veins. Nick's hands tightened around the steering wheel, maneuvering the Jeep along the narrow road. When the van rammed them again, the sound of screeching tires pierced the mountain stillness. Everything was happening too fast. All Ellie could do was react. Nick turned to her. "Hang on," he said.

Nick slowed the Jeep as they rounded a curve in the road, but the van pulled alongside, sideswiping them again and again. The Jeep's tires screeched as they spun out of control, swerving into the railing. Ellie heard a loud crack, then felt the impact as they crashed through the guardrail. The sound of crushing metal filled her ears as they careened down the embankment. Nick wrestled with the steering wheel. Ellie watched their terrifying decent through the windshield as they tumbled toward the dense brush below.

The shrubs cushioned the impact as the Jeep flipped on its side and came to a stop, its wheels spinning in the air like the legs of a trapped insect. Nick unhooked his seat belt and turned to Ellie. She was too stunned to speak or move. Reaching across her, he released her seat belt. He pushed his door open and dragged her out. They stumbled into the surrounding brushwood. Ellie panted, trying to catch her breath, her face ashen as she tried to process whether they were still alive.

Nick sat on the ground, dragging air into his lungs. He looked up at the top of the steep hill where two uniformed policemen were descending the grassy slope with guns drawn. He turned to Ellie. "Stay here."

He crawled across the ground to the Jeep. Reaching into the back seat, he pulled out a length of rope. Then he unscrewed the cap on the gas tank and snaked the rope inside. He took a cigarette lighter out of the glove compartment, flicked it on and ignited the rope. Backing into the undergrowth, he pulled Ellie away as the gasoline exploded with a roar, engulfing the Jeep in flames. Ellie felt the intense heat from the fire on her skin.

When Nick looked back at the two policemen, they had stopped their descent and were observing the burning Jeep. One officer talked into a cell phone. Then they turned away and climbed up to the highway. If Ellie had seen the faces of the officers, she would have recognized them as the two who had arrested Matt and testified against him in court.

Chapter 37

Saturday, January 9, 2010

Nick limped along the mountain road, leaning heavily on Ellie's arm. It wasn't until they started picking their way up the slope to the highway that Nick felt the painful throbbing in his ankle. Blood oozed from a cut on his leg, staining his torn jeans. Ellie's body ached, and bruises on her arms and legs were turning purple.

They stumbled along the deserted highway, their eyes glazed, stunned into silence. Ellie pulled up her coat collar as the sun set and the temperature dipped. Her fingers grew stiff and red, and she pushed her hands into her coat pockets. There was little traffic on this remote stretch of highway, and the few cars that sped past didn't notice Ellie waving at them. It grew darker and colder with every passing minute.

Nick dragged his injured leg. He didn't complain, but the sickly pallor on his face alarmed Ellie. She guided him to the side of the road. "Wait here," she said. "I'll have more luck getting us a ride if I'm alone." Nick nodded, easing himself onto the ground.

Ellie walked ahead. When she heard the sound of an approaching truck, she stepped out, waving frantically. The truck slowed, the sound of its breaks screeching as it came to a stop a few yards ahead of her. She ran to the truck as the door of the cab swung open. "I had an accident down the road. My friend's hurt. Can you give us a lift to a hospital?"

"Get in," the driver said. Ellie waved to Nick, who pulled himself up and hobbled to the truck. She helped him up the step into the cab and climbed in next to him.

***

It was night by the time the truck pulled up to the emergency entrance of the Virginia General Hospital. Ellie jumped down and helped Nick out. "Thank you," she told the driver.

"Good luck," he said, closing the cab door and pulling away.

Nick leaned on Ellie's arm as they walked into the emergency room. He was ushered into an exam room in the ER. Ellie waited outside as Nick's wounds were treated. When the curtain was opened, Nick lay in the hospital bed, his injured leg cleaned, bandaged and propped on a pillow. She sat on the edge of the bed and reached for his hand. He didn't pull away as he looked into her eyes.

Moments later, a doctor arrived. He studied the chart and examined Nick. "It looks like you have a badly sprained ankle. The wound is superficial, but you'll need a tetanus shot," he said. He turned to Ellie, whose hair and coat were covered with twigs and bits of dirt. "Are you okay? You should be examined, too."

"I'm fine," Ellie insisted. "Just shaken up."

"We'll need X-rays to determine if there's a fracture…and maybe other tests," he told Nick. Turning to Ellie, he said, "You can wait outside."

"See you later," she told Nick as he was wheeled out on the mobile bed.

Ellie walked along the ER corridor, passing curtained cubicles. The sounds of coughing, gagging and moaning reached her ears from behind the exam rooms. Up ahead, at the end of the hallway, were double doors labeled, *Hospital Personnel Only*. She made her way to the doors and pushed, but they were locked.

Turning back, Ellie remembered passing a supply room. She walked back and waited in the corridor until the ER personnel nearby were distracted with emergencies. Then she slipped inside the room, where floor-to-ceiling shelves were stacked with medical supplies. She pulled fresh scrubs off a shelf, discarded her soiled coat, and put the scrubs on over her clothing. Raking her fingers through her hair, she picked out bits of debris.

Opening the door a crack, Ellie peeked into the hallway. When no one was in site, she stepped out, moving toward the double doors, uncertain about how she would get through them. Up ahead, two hospital transport personnel were wheeling a patient out of an exam cubicle, heading toward the double doors.

One of the transporters swiped his access card on the keypad and the doors swung open. They pushed the gurney through the doors, and Ellie followed behind them. She nodded to the transporters, turned and walked in the other direction.

Down the hall was a station where nurses and other personnel worked at computers. Ellie walked up to a nurse studying a computer screen. Clearing her throat, she said, "A prisoner from Red Ridge Prison was brought in today. Name's Rusty Degan. Can you tell me where he was taken?"

The nurse looked up at Ellie, then tapped some keys on the computer. "The server's slow today," she said. Ellie nodded, relieved that she wasn't questioned. "Degan's in OR three," the nurse said.

"Thanks." Ellie hurried to the elevator, riding it to the OR floor.

Stepping out of the elevator, she moved along the hallway to OR three. Through a small window on the OR door, she could see doctors and assistants in masks and long gowns surrounding an operating table. She turned the doorknob and walked into a surgical scrub room. Four oversized sinks lined one wall. Shelves held sanitized surgical gowns, masks, caps, gloves and booties. She watched an OR assistant vigorously scrubbing her hands and arms up to her elbows.

Ellie pulled a cap off a shelf and tucked her hair into it. She copied the assistant's moves, stepping on the foot pedal beneath the sink, soaping with antiseptic solution and scrubbing vigorously with a brush. After an orderly helped the assistant into a surgical gown, mask, booties and latex gloves, she backed into the operating room.

Ellie finished scrubbing and the orderly helped her into OR gear. No one seemed to notice her entry through the swinging doors into the windowless, frigid operating room. She moved closer to the table where the patient was laid out, illuminated by a bright overhead light. Doctors in surgical gowns stood elbow to elbow around the table, their faces hidden behind masks and eye goggles. Optic headlights attached to their heads lent an alien cast to the scene.

Ellie moved to the head of the table where she found a space behind the anesthesia cart. The patient's head was covered with a cap, but she recognized Rusty's red hair peeking out from the side of the cap. His face was barely recognizable, with a ventilator protruding from his mouth and tubes in his nose pumping oxygen. The whooshing sound of a respirator and the steady beeping of monitors mingled with the bizarre sound of popular music playing from a radio somewhere in the OR. Ellie inched closer to the table. Rusty's torso was severed from his shoulders to the top of his thighs, his skin and muscles peeled back, exposing his organs. Sudden dizziness and nausea swept over Ellie. She swallowed hard, forcing herself to remain still.

"Turn down the music. It's distracting," a surgeon demanded.

"Get used to it if you want to be part of this harvest team," a doctor nearby said.

Another surgeon, bending over Rusty's torso, said, "I barely had time to get to the hospital for this harvest."

"If you want to be on *my* team, you show up whenever you're called and whenever we have a donor. And don't fucking complain about it," a masked surgeon snapped.

Ellie recognized Dr. Russell's angry voice. She took a step back and pulled the mask higher over her face.

A harvest surgeon reached into Rusty's body, working a scalpel, while others suctioned fluids and clamped vessels. The surgeon dissected Rusty's kidney, held it up and examined it. "Kidney looks good," he said. An assistant rushed forward with a stainless-steel basin to collect the kidney. He covered it with a blue surgical cloth and carried it out of the OR. "Who's getting it?" the surgeon asked.

"A patient on our transplant list is prepped in OR four," Russell said.

The team surgeon nodded and turned back to Rusty's body, reaching inside with his scalpel. "Where's the other kidney?"

"We harvested it in the ambulance," Russell said. "There was an emergency transplant waiting."

"Jesus, you did a harvest in the *ambulance*?" The surgeon asked.

"It was the right decision. We saved a life with the one that was doomed," Russell said.

"Was he brain dead?" Another surgeon asked.

"He was fatally wounded," Russell insisted.

The harvest team doctors met each other's eyes through their goggles but didn't pursue questioning Russell. Whether they believed the patient was brain dead in the ambulance or not, the monitor in the OR showed no brain activity now. Modern medicine was keeping Rusty's heart beating and his organs viable.

As the surgeons continued the harvest, Ellie sidled over to a steel table at the side of the OR where charts were laid out. A chart with Rusty Degan's name listed his organs along with the names of the organ recipients. Ellie's heart quickened as she read the chart. She reached for a pen on the table and copied names from the chart onto her gloved hand. A surgeon, noticing Ellie, called out, "We need all hands over here."

Ellie moved quickly back to the operating table. She mimicked the moves of assistants, replenishing supplies on surgical carts as she listened to the surgeons' conversations.

"We've been getting a lot of organ donors from the prison," a surgeon said.

"The prisoners get into fights. They're violent, and they kill each other," Russell said. "At least some good comes from their deaths," he added.

"I'm surprised the prisoners sign donor cards," a surgeon commented.

"They do," Russell said emphatically.

A surgeon removed a large red slab from Rusty's body and deposited it in a stainless-steel bowl filled with chunks of frozen saline. "Liver looks healthy," he announced. An OR assistant stepped up and flushed the organ with fluid, then placed it in a large red container for transport in a helicopter waiting on the roof of the hospital. He rushed out of the OR with the container. It was the same kind of container Ellie had seen delivered to the organ procurement building.

While the surgeons completed the harvest, Ellie went back to the table where the charts were laid out, hoping she wouldn't be noticed as she scribbled more data from the chart onto her gloved hand.

"Who are you?" Russell shouted.

Ellie looked up. "I'm assisting," she said.

"We have our team. Get out!" he ordered.

Ellie walked quickly across the OR and pushed through the double doors. In the hallway, she looked back into the OR through the glass window. A surgeon removed Rusty's heart and deposited it in a container. An assistant rushed out the door with it. The anesthesiologist turned off the ventilator and a flat line appeared on the heart monitor. Ellie sucked in her breath as a sheet was pulled over Rusty's eviscerated body.

A surgeon looked up and saw Ellie peering through the window. He pulled off his mask and gloves. Ellie recognized Russell in an instant. He looked into her eyes, and his face reddened with rage. He untied his gown, dropped it on the floor, and rushed to the door.

Ellie turned away, hurrying along the hallway to the elevator. She heard Russell's footsteps behind her. She turned a corner, passed a supply room and opened the door. Inside, she pulled off the OR gown, booties and cap and slipped the glove she had written on into her pocket. Dressed in the hospital scrubs she had donned earlier, she opened the door and peeked out. The hallway was empty, and she stepped out, heading for the elevator. Russell walked toward her, calling out, "Have you seen a woman in an OR gown?"

"No," Ellie said, keeping her head down as she moved closer to the elevator. He walked past her. She pressed the down button on the elevator but soon heard footsteps running back toward her. Russell was no longer fooled by her disguise.

Ellie ran to the nearby stairwell and pulled open the heavy door. The door banged closed behind her, and she bolted down the steps two at a time. Russell opened the door, rushing after her. On the next landing, she passed an exit door and tugged it. It was locked. She raced to the next landing as Russell's footsteps grew louder. "Stop," he shouted.

Ellie was panting by the time she reached the next landing. Perspiration dripped down her face, and the sound of her heart thumped in her ears. The door swung open and an intern stepped into the stairwell. Ellie pushed past him into the hallway, slamming the door behind her. Russell reached the landing moments later and collided with the intern. "You idiot!" he shouted.

Ellie found herself on the main level of the hospital. She slowed to a rapid walk and went into a restroom. Inside a stall, she bent over, sucking in air, trying to slow her pounding heart. Images of the gruesome harvest ran through her mind. The smell of antiseptic from the OR lingered in her nose, and she gagged and vomited into the toilet. Beads of cold sweat broke out on her forehead. She drew in deep breaths and closed her eyes, willing herself to calm down. When her heartbeat finally slowed to near normal, she shed the hospital scrubs and stepped out of the stall in her street clothes. Turning on the tap at the sink, she splashed cold water on her face. Then she dried her face with paper towels and ran her fingers through her curls. She felt in her pocket for the latex glove, opened the restroom door and walked to the ER waiting room.

Nick sat in a plastic chair, dozing from exhaustion. His injured leg was thickly bandaged and propped on a chair in front of him. Ellie tapped him lightly on his shoulder. "You okay?"

Nick opened his eyes. "Where've you been? I was ready to call a taxi."

Ellie took his arm and helped him out of the chair. "I'll tell you about it later. Let's get you home."

Chapter 38

Sunday, January 10, 2010

Ellie knocked on Nick's apartment door. There was no answer, and she knocked again. A few minutes passed before she heard footsteps. When the door opened, he stood in the doorway, dressed in a sweat suit, his hair wet from the shower.

"Ellie, what're you doing here?"

"I came to see if you're okay."

"You could have called and asked me." He opened the door wider.

She stepped inside. "Would you have told me the truth?" She followed him as he limped into the kitchen. "Sit down," she said. "I'll make you breakfast."

He pulled out a chair near the kitchen table, sat down and propped his injured leg on another chair. Ellie busied herself brewing coffee and cracking eggs into a bowl she found in the closet. She reached for a paper bag she had brought. "I bought croissants from your neighborhood bakery," she said. "They looked good."

"They *are* good." He smiled for the first time, and Ellie returned his smile.

"I don't suppose you have preserves," she said.

"Why would you think that? Look in the fridge."

"Most men don't think of details like preserves." She moved things around in the refrigerator and retrieved a jar of raspberry preserves.

"I'm not most men."

"You certainly aren't."

A faint smile crossed his lips. "I'm glad we cleared that up."

When they had finished eating the eggs Ellie had scrambled, and the last of the croissants, she said, "You could have been killed because of me." Her words spilled out like a painful confession.

He studied the creases on her brow and her worried eyes. "But I wasn't. My leg will heal, and the Jeep can be replaced."

"I don't want you involved in my investigation any longer."

He read the fear in her eyes...and more. "You've stumbled into something dangerous, Ellie. You shouldn't do this alone."

She was silent, making a decision. "I'll tell you what I discovered yesterday, but you can only give me advice. Understood?"

"Understood."

After describing everything she had seen in the OR, she said, "When I got home from the hospital last night, I researched the names I copied from the OR chart—names of patients who received Rusty's organs. I don't know if these patients were on an organ transplant list, but they were all wealthy people. Eleanor Colton, the wife of Senator Colton, received a kidney transplant yesterday at the Virginia General Hospital."

"That doesn't prove anything illegal is going on."

"I want you to see a video of an interview with Senator Colton after he introduced a bill to the Virginia Legislature. It's on the Internet."

Nick booted up the computer on his desk, and they listened to Colton's speech: "Thousands of Americans die needlessly every year because of a shortage of donated organs for transplants. That's why I'm introducing this bill. We have many healthy donors in our Virginia prison system who can repay part of their debt to society by donating an organ. They could donate a kidney while they're alive, and other organs if they should die in prison. This bill would give county coroners the right to take organs and tissue from deceased prisoners without waiting for family consent. Waiting isn't an option when an organ is only viable for a few hours."

"The bill hasn't passed," Nick said.

"I think Matt's organs and Rusty's were stolen for transplants. The list of organ recipients I got from the OR proves that Rusty's organs were stolen. Now I have to prove that Matt's were, too."

"The chart with the names of recipients doesn't prove the organs were stolen. Maybe there was consent," Nick said.

"I overheard the conversation in the OR. The hospital must have signed organ donor cards, giving permission to take organs after death. I'm certain that Matt didn't sign a donor card. His driver's license did not designate him as a donor."

"Ellie, you have no proof that Matt's organs were used for transplants.

They could have been discarded after the autopsy."

"I have proof that Red Ridge prisoners were blood-typed and antigen-typed, including Matt. That's the kind of information that's essential for organ transplants."

"Maybe Rusty signed an organ donor card," Nick said.

"If Senator Colton got his wish, all prisoners would have been forced to sign donor cards. But a bill isn't a law. Maybe some people didn't want to wait for the bill to become law."

"You're making wild accusations without solid proof."

"There has to be evidence somewhere," she said.

***

After leaving Nick's apartment, Ellie went straight to Matt's apartment. When she opened the door, everything looked the same as the last time she had been there. A thin layer of dust covered the furniture, and a musty smell hung in the air. She opened a window in the living room to let in fresh air. Her eyes settled on the sofa and, for an instant, she expected to see Matt sitting there and grinning at her. The pain of missing him was suffocating.

Her eyes scanned the living room. She looked up at the ceiling where she had found Matt's chart and the video hidden beneath a tile. *Could I have missed something?* she wondered. She dragged a chair across the room, climbed up and pushed the ceiling tile aside. Reaching inside, she swept around the opening with her fingers. Dust was all she retrieved. She jumped down and went to the kitchen for a long-handled brush. Climbing on the chair again, she poked the brush inside the opening. The swishing sound of paper made her heart skip. She raked the paper out with the brush and jumped off the chair.

Unfolding the paper, she laid it out on Matt's desk. It was a spreadsheet Matt had compiled with three years of data on Red Ridge—the number of prisoner deaths, causes of death, hospitals where prisoners were taken, dates of death and autopsy results. Studying the chart, she saw immediately that the number of deaths had increased steadily over the past three years. In every case, the prison reported the cause of death as *unknown* or an *accident*. Injured prisoners were all taken to Virginia General. The autopsy reports confirmed the cause of death declared by the prison. "Thank you, Matt," she whispered.

Chapter 39

Monday, January 11, 2010

The newsroom was relatively quiet when Ellie arrived at 8:00 a.m., except for the fax machines, which hummed steadily. She turned on her computer and scrolled through trending local news. A headline captured her attention: *Senator Colton's wife, Eleanor, received a life-saving kidney from a deceased prisoner.* Engrossed in reading the article, she didn't see Dan walk in until his hand was on her shoulder.

"Are you writing a story about Eleanor Colton?" he asked.

Ellie turned to him. "I found some surprising information about the senator."

"Oh?"

"He introduced legislation that would give county coroners the right to harvest tissue and organs from deceased prisoners *without* family consent."

"I think the senator simply wanted to help critically sick patients who can die waiting for a donor," Dan said.

"Maybe that wasn't his intent."

Dan sighed heavily. "The senator is a friend of mine. His concern was for the 100,000 people in this country who desperately need a life-saving organ."

"Considering that his wife just got a prisoner's kidney, I'm probably not the only one questioning his legislation."

Dan rolled his eyes. "Come into my office. Something important came up that I need to discuss with you." He turned away, and she followed him to his office.

Ellie sat in a chair while Dan drummed his fingers on the top of the desk for some moments. "I got a call from the director of the Virginia Organ

Procurement Agency. You were identified on a videotape inside their facility." His face was impassive as he waited for her response.

Ellie's face flushed. "There's a connection between the Virginia General Hospital and the tissue bank," she said.

"Hospitals all over the country partner with tissue banks. If you had come to me, I would have explained how they work together. Reporters don't have the right to march into private facilities and spy on them."

Ellie took a deep breath, weighing her next words. "The tissue bank has a room full of freezers with human body parts. Where did they come from?"

"The tissue bank is a nonprofit organization. They process donated tissue for patients who need surgical procedures—corneas for people who would be blind without a transplant, leg tendons for people who would not otherwise be able to walk..."

"Inmates at Red Ridge appear to be a primary source for transplant tissue," Ellie said.

Dan bit his lip. "That's simply not true."

She hesitated before admitting, "I have proof. I saw documents."

"You broke into private property. You could be in serious trouble."

"I didn't see another way to get the information." Ellie fidgeted, shifting in the chair while Dan glared at her, his lips pressed together. "The fact is that Red Ridge prisoners supply large quantities of organs and tissue, and I'm questioning how that was arranged," she said.

"No one can be a source for tissue donation unless a signed donor card is on file. Donor permission is always documented by tissue banks and hospitals."

"Matt didn't sign a donor card."

"Matt's organs were not donated to anyone. They were not even viable."

"He was murdered and mutilated."

Dan folded his hands under his chin. "Matt was murdered by prisoners, but he wasn't mutilated during the autopsy," he said softly. "The nature of an autopsy may appear brutal to you or to anyone not in the medical field."

Ellie brushed a sudden tear from her cheek.

"You broke into the tissue bank," Dan continued. "How do you want to handle this?"

"Maybe I can meet with the director and explain."

Dan reached for his phone and tapped in a number. "Brian, it's Dan Andrews...I know, and I apologize. My niece, Ellie, who's a reporter here, got overly curious. She'd like to explain everything to you in person. Would you meet with her, show her the important work you do at the tissue bank?"

Dan turned to Ellie. "Tomorrow morning, 11:00 o'clock?" Ellie nodded. "Thanks. She'll be there." Dan hung up.

Ellie pulled in a breath and stood. As she turned to leave, Dan said, "After you meet with Brian Payne, no more rogue investigations. Agreed?"

Ellie nodded, but Dan's request sounded more like an order.

Chapter 40

Tuesday, January 12, 2010

Ellie walked along the path to the entrance of the Virginia Organ Procurement Agency and pressed the door buzzer. A woman opened the door and asked for her name. A few moments later, a man wearing an expensive gray suit and designer shoes approached.

"Ms. Andrews, I'm glad you could make it today for a tour of our facility," he said, sounding like she had booked a guided tour to Disney World. Ellie guessed that Brian Payne was in his forties. His dark hair was neatly groomed and his nails manicured.

"I'm looking forward to it." Ellie smiled, but Payne pressed his lips together.

"We can start here," he said, opening a door off the main hallway. He led Ellie into a large office where employees worked at computers. Rows of tall file cabinets lined one wall. "This is where we process and verify donor information. We keep files on people who sign up as donors and families who make bequests."

"How do you recruit donors?"

"The Department of Motor Vehicles is our main source. Many people indicate on their drivers' licenses that they will donate organs in case of accidental death. We advertise in various places, encouraging organ and tissue donations."

"And if you don't get enough volunteer donors?"

"In accident cases, most hospitals have their social workers appeal to victims' families. You'd be surprised how generous people are, even in times of grief."

Payne led Ellie out of the office. They moved along the hallway, stopping at a door marked, *Laboratory, Authorized Personnel Only*. A cart stacked with sterile gowns, caps, gloves and face masks stood next to the door. They donned the sterile garments, and Payne unlocked the laboratory door.

Inside, gowned and masked technicians worked at stainless steel tables examining specimens under microscopes and preparing slides. "This is our state-of-the-art lab. Only healthy tissue is accepted. All donor tissue is screened for HIV, STDs and other diseases," Payne said.

Ellie pointed to a huge machine in the center of the lab that hummed steadily. "What's that?" she asked.

"A sterilizer. All tissue is processed through the sterilizer before it goes to storage. It's to prevent any possible transmission of disease from handlers." Ellie had a sudden flashback to a story of an athlete who died from viral hepatitis after a leg tendon transplant.

Outside the laboratory, they discarded their sterile garments in a bin. They walked on, passing a door labeled, M*edical Storage Bank, Authorized Personnel Only*. "What about this room?" Ellie asked.

"After the tissue is sterilized in the laboratory, it's stored in large freezers in this area. When we get a request for donor tissue for surgery, we send it off. But you've already toured our storage bank."

Ellie ignored Payne's sarcasm. "Could I see it now?"

Payne looked at his watch. "Why don't we leave it for after lunch? Our company cafeteria is just down the hall." They walked past an unmarked door, where the frenetic sound of voices leaked into the hallway.

"What's going on in there?" she asked.

"It's a clerical office for data processing. Nothing that would interest you," he insisted, leading her into a brightly-lit cafeteria.

Employees were beginning to drift in and fill the red plastic chairs arranged around white metal tables. Payne handed Ellie a tray from a nearby stand, and they moved along a food bar, selecting dishes. Ellie placed a sandwich and salad platter on her tray, and filled a cup with coffee from the urn. Payne paid the cashier for their lunches, and they found an empty table in the back.

When they were seated, he pried open a can of diet soda, sipped and studied Ellie, who moved the salad around on her plate with a fork. She nibbled the cheese sandwich but had no appetite. "So, how long have you and Dan known each other?" she asked.

"We worked together at the Virginia General Hospital. Your uncle's a good man. He's helped a lot of people through our tissue bank."

"I'm very fond of him." She put her fork down. "Would you excuse me for a few moments? Which way is the restroom?"

"Go to the end of the hall and turn right," he said.

Ellie hurried along the corridor, stopping at the door where unusual chatter could still be heard. Her fingers curled around the doorknob. She turned it slowly and, to her surprise, it opened.

She stepped inside a large office where men and women, wearing telephone headsets, sat in cubicles spaced around the room. They talked into phone mics, while tapping keys on their computers. A giant electronic board, mounted on the front wall, ticked off changing numbers and symbols. Ellie studied the board, her heartbeat quickening as she read a list of body parts—kidneys, livers, hearts, lungs, heart valves, corneas, blood vessels, tendons, ligaments—with escalating prices that changed by the second.

She moved cautiously around the outside of the room, listening to conversations drifting out of the cubicles she passed. "Kidney...$15,000," a man announced. Moments later, $15,000 appeared on the exchange board.

A counteroffer rang out: "I have a twenty-thousand bid for the kidney." The board listed $20,000 for several minutes. A soft bell pinged and the word, SOLD, was posted next to the $20,000 kidney.

"Do we have a liver with a type-A match?" a broker called out.

"I have a match for $40,000," a broker answered.

The bell pinged and the big board posted, *SOLD $40,000 type-A liver.*

Ellie could not take her eyes off the electronic board. She had stumbled into a veritable organ exchange where body parts were sold to the highest bidder. No one appeared to notice her, and she slipped into an empty cubicle and sat down at the computer terminal. The screen was filled with data on organs, blood types, bids, shipment dates, destinations.

In spite of her heart thrumming erratically, Ellie continued reading the screen. She tapped the keyboard and a screen popped up with destinations—kidney to Ohio; liver to New York; heart valve to Dubai. With her attention on these revelations, she didn't notice the man now standing in the doorway.

"Who the hell are you? What are you doing here?" he bellowed. His hands were clenched in fists, his face crimson with rage.

Ellie bolted out of the chair. "I think I'm lost," she said, moving toward the door. "I was on a tour of the tissue bank. Could you tell me where the lady's restroom is? I was headed there." She knew she sounded ridiculous.

"You have to leave right now! The restroom is down the hall," he spat, marching Ellie to the door and pushing her into the hallway. The lock clicked behind her, and she rushed back to the cafeteria, formulating an explanation for her delay.

Payne held his cell phone to his ear. Ellie heard his angry words as she approached. "You idiot," he said into the phone.

"I'm sorry I took so long," she said, taking a seat at the table. "I had to call my office." Payne narrowed his eyes, waiting for her explanation. "I have to cut our lunch short because I must get back to the newsroom," she continued. "Thank you for the tour. We'll be doing a story soon on the tissue bank."

"Not everything you've seen is what it seems. Send me your article draft so I can verify the facts," he said, his offer sounding like a command.

Ellie slipped her handbag over her shoulder and hurried out. In the hallway, a man stepped out of a nearby office and fell into step beside her. "I'll show you the way out," he said. She nodded, and he walked beside her to the exit and opened the door.

After Ellie left, Payne punched the table with his fist. He reached for his cell phone. There was a pained expression on his face as he spoke into the phone. "She saw the trading room."

Chapter 41

Tuesday, January 12, 2010

Ellie sped along the highway, heading back to Alexandria. In her mind, she saw the electronic board at the tissue bank with changing prices for body parts. She could still hear the bidding calls in her ears. The vivid memory squeezed her chest with panic. She pulled over to the side of the road, opened the window and inhaled great gulps of cold air.

When her panic subsided, she reached for her cell phone and called Nick. His voice floated over the wires, but it came from his answering machine. She slammed the phone down on the car seat, closed her eyes and leaned her head back against the seat. Then she redialed. "Pick up the damn phone, Nick," she said aloud.

He answered after the fourth ring. "Nick Labelle here."

"Nick, the Virginia Organ Procurement Agency sells human organs and tissue to the highest bidders."

"Whoa. Slow down, Ellie. Are you okay?"

"You can't imagine what I saw...a brokerage business for body parts."

"What?"

"They threw me out of the office. I stumbled into something I wasn't supposed to see."

"How?"

"It's a long story...I'll tell you later. I need your help to prove the operation's illegal."

"You'll need documents on the donors."

"You don't believe me," she accused.

"Don't get touchy," he said.

"I called you for advice, not a lecture."

"Then why are you turning this into an argument?" She let his question hang unanswered. "I want to help if you'll let me," he said.

"I do...want your help," she mumbled.

"I know a computer security expert. He can find out if the organ donors were voluntary or not. His name is Andy Nolan."

"When can I meet him?"

"I'll call him and get back to you."

Ellie put her head down on the steering wheel, closed her eyes and waited. A few minutes later, her phone rang. "Meet me at Andy's office at 6:00 tonight," Nick said. He gave her the address in Alexandria. "Exit at King Street," he said.

"Nick, thanks. I..." She wanted to say more, but he had already hung up.

***

Dusk had faded to night when Ellie arrived at Andy Nolan's basement office in Alexandria. Nick was already there, seated beside Andy, facing a large state-of-the-art computer. "Meet Ellie Andrews from the Virginia Star," Nick said.

"Hi," Andy said. He had a welcoming smile and intense green eyes.

"Thanks for your help," Ellie said.

"There are no guarantees," he said, turning his attention back to a brightly-lit computer screen. There were multiple computers of various sizes set on tables around the room, running data for his security projects.

The temperature in the room was set at 52 degrees to keep the computers from overheating. Ellie kept her coat on and pulled up a chair next to Andy's computer. In spite of a dark beard, he looked young to her, maybe in his early thirties. He wore his hair in a short ponytail and sported a gold stud in one ear.

"This will probably be a tough system to unlock," Nick said.

"Not for me," Andy said, furiously tapping keys on the computer.

"How do you two know each other?" Ellie asked.

"We met in Sri Lanka back in 2006...during the political and ethnic conflicts there," Nick said. "I was there for Human Rights International, interviewing Sri Lankans in their villages and documenting their stories of human rights violations."

"I worked for a private consulting company then," Andy said. "I was sent there to set up a data coding system to classify and count the violations."

"It was an amazing project. No one thought it was possible, but the system Andy and his team designed helped to identify those responsible for murders, disappearances and abuse of all kinds. Afterwards, people there got some human rights protections," Nick said.

"Do you still work for the private company?" Ellie asked.

Andy studied his computer screen and clicked many keys for some moments. Then he turned back to Ellie. "I've been on my own for a few years, working as an independent consultant. I decide what projects I want to work on and where I want to travel. I also make a lot more money," he said.

Before Nick met him, Andy had been traveling for several years for a private company that recruited him after he graduated from MIT. Andy specialized in discovering vulnerabilities in computer security systems and designing software to repair them. His expertise was in great demand, and the company sent him all over the world—Dubai, South Africa, India, Belgium.

Nick and Andy spent a lot of time together when they were stationed in Sri Lanka. After long, grueling work days, they would go to a local family-owned restaurant for dinner and a few beers. They became fast friends, sharing travel stories. Andy had told him then, "The company I work for makes millions on every project. I do all the work, and they get most of the money."

"So, what are you going to do to change that?" Nick had challenged him.

Andy didn't answer right away. Then he said, "When I get back to the states, I'm setting up my own company."

Andy did start his own company and was very successful. He also married a young woman who had been his classmate at MIT. She now worked alongside him on projects. Andy turned to Nick now. "We didn't tell anyone yet, but Julie is expecting our first child in July," he said.

Nick smiled. "Congratulations. Wow. You're going to be a father."

Andy grinned. "Yeah, this is a really big deal." He turned back to the computer, where new data appeared on the screen and he clicked several keys. *Access Denied* popped onto the screen. "The hospital has a secure system," Andy said.

Another hour passed with Ellie and Nick staring at the screen while Andy pressed keys and multiple *Access Denied* messages appeared. Ellie pushed her hands into her pockets to warm them. Finally, the Virginia General Hospital database system filled the screen.

"I'm in!" Andy announced. "We need to get into the Transplant Department's database now," he said.

"How?" Ellie asked.

"I'm in the main hospital system, so now I need to find the department's password, which is usually stored in the system or transmitted by employees,"

Andy explained.

"That should be easy for you," Nick said.

"It'll take time," he said.

For the next forty-five minutes, Andy concentrated on recovering the department's password while Ellie fidgeted in the chair and watched the hands advance on the wall clock. After more attempts than she could count, the words, *Virginia General Hospital Transplant Department*, came onto the screen.

"Here's your baby!" Andy grinned.

Nick squeezed Andy's shoulder. "You're a genius."

Ellie's eyes were riveted on the computer when a new screen appeared. "Here's the list of donors! Can you access the donors' signature cards?"

Andy tapped more keys. Multiple screens appeared with photographs of donor cards and signatures. Ellie read the names: "Adams, Galbraith, Degan... Rusty Degan! Matt's cellmate. Can you print the documents?" Her heart raced as the printer started up, churning out pages of donor card information.

"Amazing work, Andy," Nick said.

Ellie grabbed the pages from the printer and scanned the names. She hurried to a nearby table where she had left her handbag and rummaged through it. Turning the bag upside down, she spilled the contents onto the table. Her fingers settled on the paper she needed—a list of names she had copied from the tissue bank's files. She spread it open next to the printouts. "Adams, Andrews, Burke, Clark, Degan..." She sucked in her breath, feeling like all the air had been squeezed out of her lungs. "The names of the donors match the names of dead Red Ridge prisoners."

Perspiration gathered beneath Ellie's clothing despite the chill in the room. She felt the eerie presence of Matt and Rusty, as if they stood beside her, looking over her shoulder. Images of their faces floated before her eyes. Feeling light-headed, she staggered backward. Nick was beside her in an instant, gripping her around her waist, keeping her from falling. He led her to a chair.

Andy brought her a bottle of water. "What happened?" he asked.

"I don't know." Ellie gulped the water and took deep breaths. Nick and Andy watched the color return to her cheeks slowly.

"I think we have what we came for," Nick said. "Ellie should probably go home and get some rest."

Regaining her composure, Ellie said, "Thank you, Andy."

After saying their goodbyes, Ellie and Nick left the office. They stopped on the sidewalk outside. "Are you okay? You look pale," he said. "I can drive you home."

"I'm okay," she insisted. "You've been a great friend, Nick. I don't know how I can repay you."

"I don't charge friends," he said. In the dim light of the street lamp, she could see that her words had hurt him. She wouldn't admit to herself that he was so much more than a friend. "Good night, then," he said, turning away.

***

Ellie turned on her computer as soon as she got home. She set up a spreadsheet, first listing the names of Red Ridge prisoners who had died. Next to each name was the prisoner's ID number. A separate column listed the organs and tissue each prisoner allegedly donated. The *Donor Card* category remained blank until she could verify the data.

Armed with the list of dead prisoners and the printout of donor cards from Andy's office, Ellie started making phone calls. "Mrs. Degan, I'm working on an inquiry regarding Rusty's death. Did you sign an organ donor card for Rusty?"

"What are you talking about? I never signed no card," Mrs. Degan's irate voice came over the wires.

"Your son's organs and tissue were removed after his death and donated," Ellie told her.

"What? Are you kidding me?"

"Thank you for the information, Mrs. Degan. I'll be in touch with you again." Ellie hung up and typed an x on the spreadsheet next to Rusty's name in the *Donor Card* column. She went through the list of dead prisoners and their donor cards, repeating her questions to the alleged signees. All the family members she called verified that they had not signed donor cards. As for the cards with prisoners' signatures, she would not be able to validate them unless she had copies of their signatures from other documents. But she had enough documentation to see a pattern of forgery and fraud.

She looked at her watch. It was 11:00 p.m., a little late to call Nick, but she reached for her phone and punched in the number. Listening to his phone ring, she recalled the hurt in his eyes when she called him a '*friend*,' and she felt pangs of remorse.

He answered after the third ring, the sound of his voice sending a shiver through her. "I hope I didn't wake you," she said. "I thought you'd want to know what I found. The donor cards are forged."

"Then this is a criminal conspiracy," he said, surprise in his voice. "It could take a long time to find everyone involved."

"I'll do whatever it takes."

"It's too dangerous. These people will do anything…"

She cut him off. "I'm not afraid."

"You should be."

"Nick, thank you for introducing me to Andy…for everything you've done."

"Be careful, Ellie."

She hung up, feeling calmer than she had for a long time. She thought about how Nick cautioned her to be careful, the concern in his voice, and a smile crossed her lips.

Chapter 42

Wednesday, January 13, 2010

Ellie woke at 5:00 a.m. after a restless night. She was haunted by images of the tissue bank—brokers shouting prices for organs, body parts stored in freezers. She rubbed her eyes, gritty and strained from too little sleep, got out of bed and showered. After dressing, she went to the small kitchen, brewed coffee and toasted a slice of bread. By 6:00 a.m., she locked the apartment door and headed for her car.

The sky was beginning to brighten when she arrived at the newsroom and unlocked the door. She left the lights off in the office and walked across the floor to her cubicle. If she worked fast, she thought, she could probably finish her research by the time staffers arrived.

The newspaper subscribed to LexisNexis, a nationwide search database that Ellie used regularly when she needed to view public records. She logged in with the Virginia Star password, and accessed the electronic archives of federal and state court cases. She typed in the first name on her list of deceased Red Ridge prisoners. The court record came onto the screen with the information she needed: the arresting officer's name, the charges, the presiding judge, the court proceedings and the sentence. As she went through the list of prisoners, she found that they had all been sent to Red Ridge, even when they were arrested and tried in other states.

Ellie raced against the clock, printing out pages and pages of data. Studying the printouts for commonalities would have to wait until later, but the names Kevin Moore, Patrick Murphy and Judge Robert Maxwell caught her attention in too many records. Now she scrambled to complete her research before curious employees arrived. She gathered the papers from the printer and stuffed them into her briefcase.

The wall clock read 8:30 a.m., not much time to search the public archives for death records, but Ellie continued. The printer outside her cubicle hummed, churning out more copies. When she stood to retrieve the last batch of papers, Dan stood motionless in the doorway. "I…didn't hear you come in," she stammered.

"Are these yours?" he asked, handing her a stack of papers.

Ellie drew in a breath. "Yes," she mumbled, taking the copies from him.

"You're working on the prison story again?" It was an accusation, not a question.

"It's personal research. I came in early so it wouldn't interfere with my regular assignments."

Dan's eyes flashed with anger. He turned away, storming across the newsroom to his office. Ellie wondered what consequences she faced for defying him again. She no longer recognized him as the uncle from her childhood…kind and caring.

***

The sun was setting when Ellie rang the doorbell to Nick's apartment, her briefcase in her hand. He opened the door, his eyes widening in surprise. "Hey," he said. His smile made her stomach flutter. "I wasn't expecting you. What's up?"

She followed him inside. "I discovered something that can't wait." She pulled a stack of papers out of her briefcase and set them on the dining room table.

They sat at the table, reading the copies of prisoners' case records.

"Look at the names of the arresting officers," Ellie said. "All the prisoners who were arrested in Virginia were arrested by either Kevin Moore or Patrick Murphy."

Nick read the documents. "Robert Maxwell was the judge passing sentences and sending the men to Red Ridge in *every* Virginia case," he said.

"Let's compare the dates of death with the dates the prisoners arrived at Red Ridge," Ellie said. They spread the papers out on the table. She caught her breath. "There's a pattern here! The prisoners all died within one to three months after arrival. And the Virginia General Hospital is named as the place of death."

"The cause of death is listed as *accident* in every case," Nick said. "That doesn't prove anything because prisons routinely list deaths as *accidents* or *unknown causes* to avoid investigations."

Ellie's mind raced with the implications of this new information. Unable to keep still, she pushed the chair out and paced around the room. When she stopped, she turned to Nick, her face flushed. "The Virginia Justice Department and the medical center are complicit in the deaths of the prisoners," she said. "The police trap men with phony charges. Judge Maxwell sends them to Red Ridge, where they're attacked by other prisoners soon after they arrive. Then they're taken to the Virginia General Hospital, where their organs are harvested and then sold to the highest bidders."

"If this is true, it's a major conspiracy," Nick said.

"The forged documents are proof."

"You'll have to prove that organ transplants were done on the same day that the prisoners died at the hospital. For that, you'll need copies of records from the hospital's transplant department," he said.

"We can get that, can't we?"

"It'll be dangerous."

"I'm not afraid," she said.

"After everything that's happened, you must know that people behind this will do anything to anyone who gets in their way."

"Matt was murdered. I owe it to him to find the evidence he was looking for." Ellie gathered her papers, stuffed them into her briefcase and headed for the door.

Nick followed her. When she reached for the doorknob, he covered her hand with his, his touch electrifying. He placed his hands on her shoulders, turning her to face him. "I didn't say I wouldn't help. We'll need Andy to get into the hospital's computer system again."

***

By 9:00 p.m., Ellie and Nick were seated beside Andy, their eyes on his computer screen as he tapped keys. *Access Denied* displayed on the screen again and again. "Something's wrong," Andy said. "I never have this much trouble."

"Could the hospital have changed its coding?" Nick asked.

"If they suspected that someone unauthorized gained access," Andy said. "A sophisticated system like theirs will detect attempts to hack…successful or failed."

"Keep trying," Ellie said. "If we can get the transplant dates and they match the prisoners' dates of death, we'll have the proof we need."

Andy kept striking keys, and the *Access Denied* message appeared repeatedly. After half an hour of multiple attempts, a screen popped up with strange codes.

"I have to abort!" Andy's voice rang with alarm. "They're trying to trace my IP address." He struck the keys rapidly and the screen blacked out.

"Now what?" Nick asked.

"The hospital definitely detected our first break-in. They programmed a trace, and they'll identify me on another attempt. I can't risk that," Andy said.

Ellie turned to Nick. "I'll have to get the information from files inside the hospital."

"Our best chance is for me to get into the hospital's files. No one there can identify me," Nick said.

"No. I won't put you in danger," Ellie said.

"I have experience finding information in difficult places," Nick said.

"No," Ellie insisted, her voice rising.

"I'll make arrangements," he said.

Chapter 43

Thursday, January 14, 2010

Nick drove a white service van into the hospital parking lot. He wore a blue uniform and a cap with *A&G Electric* emblazoned on it. He turned off the motor, opened a panel behind the driver's seat and stepped into the back, where Ellie waited.

Ellie sat facing a video screen. She was surrounded by high-tech surveillance equipment: cameras, computers, a voice monitor and recording devices. She looked up at Nick. "I'm going with you," she said. "If I wear a cap and dark glasses, no one will recognize me."

"No. You're not." Pointing to the video screen, he said, "You'll see everything I'm doing on the screen. No matter what you see, don't leave the van. Don't come into the hospital!"

Ellie looked at him skeptically. "How'd you get all this equipment?" she asked.

"I have a friend in the FBI who owed me a favor." He reached for a metal toolbox and a head-mounted mini camera that resembled a headlamp electricians use to see in the dark. When he turned to leave, Ellie touched his arm.

"Be careful," she said.

"Do I detect that the lady cares?" he asked. Ellie didn't answer. "Watch the screen and sit tight," he said. He opened the back door and jumped onto the pavement.

Carrying the metal toolbox, Nick walked boldly through the front entrance of the hospital. He marched past the security desk to a bank of elevators. When an elevator arrived and people walked out, Nick stepped inside and pressed the button for the 16th floor. The elevator carried him up, stopping at several floors before arriving at 16. He exited and followed the sign to the Transplant Department.

A receptionist, wearing a headphone, sat at the front desk in the Transplant Department office. Six men and women worked at computer stations spread around the room. Nick approached the receptionist and set his toolbox on the floor. She looked up at him. "Can I help you?" she asked.

Flashing a smile, Nick said, "I'm here to check the circuitry. Can you direct me to the utility room?"

The receptionist returned his smile. "Can I see your work order?" He handed her a paper that she glanced at but didn't read. "The utility room is over there." She pointed to a door across the room.

Nick smiled again. "Thanks. I won't be long."

Inside the utility room, Nick opened an electrical box containing a circuit-breaker panel. The breakers were set in the on position. He studied the labels identifying the areas of the office controlled by each circuit breaker. It was a simple setup compared to some of the circuitry he had to decipher when he had worked for a private investigator. He was often called on to find evidence in office buildings with complex electrical grids that controlled lights, cameras and alarms. He had learned how to disarm them doing undercover work. He heard phones ringing and the buzz of voices in the outer office as he turned off two circuit breakers.

Inside the van, Ellie watched the video screen. From Nick's head-mounted camera, she saw his hand move inside the circuit box. Then the screen went blank and she froze. Moments later, she saw a beam of light coming from a flashlight in Nick's hand.

When Nick opened the utility room door and stepped back into the office, the room was dark and the computers silent. The employees were all talking at once. "What happened?" the receptionist asked.

"Faulty wiring," Nick said. "I'll have to replace it." Turning to the office staff, he said, "Listen up, everyone! I had to turn off the electricity because some connections need to be repaired right away. It should take about half an hour. It would be best if you all left the office. I'll call you as soon as it's up and running."

"I'd better stay," the receptionist said.

"It's way too dark in here to work," Nick said.

"I can't leave the phones unanswered," she said.

An employee interrupted, "Diane, put the answering machine on. It's only for half an hour. We could all use a break." They filed out of the office, chatting happily. The receptionist hesitated at the door, looking back at Nick before closing the door.

Nick hurried back to the utility room and switched on the circuit breakers. The lights came on, and the computers hummed into action. He stepped back into the office with his toolbox and pulled up a chair in front of a computer. Then he began tapping keys, trying to gain access to the department's software program. Twenty minutes passed with no success. Techniques he had learned about accessing computer systems from Andy and from private investigations weren't working now. He watched the hands advance on the wall clock as he tried different combinations on the computer. His uniform grew damp with perspiration.

After trying several more passwords, the word, *Exchange*, popped onto the screen. "Bingo," he mumbled. Opening the toolbox, he pulled out a flash drive and inserted it in the computer port. He glanced at the clock. Twenty-five minutes had passed. He pressed the *enter* key and the computer started copying the program.

Nick watched the copying process register in percentages on the screen...20%, 30%. It seemed to be moving in excruciatingly slow motion. His face grew hot and his throat dry as the numbers advanced on the screen...40%, 50%. He heard the elevator door open in the hallway and the sound of voices. The computer screen displayed 60%, 70%, 80%. Laughter and approaching footsteps grew louder.

In the van, Ellie watched the scene unfold on the screen. The receptionist opened the office door and walked in, followed by the rest of the staff. Nick still sat at the computer station. The receptionist said something to him. Ellie couldn't hear her words, but there was no mistaking the anger on her face. "Nick, get out of there now," Ellie called out.

Nick ignored the receptionist and the staff gathering around, gaping at him. The receptionist reached for the phone on her desk. "Security! There's an intruder in the Transplant office."

Nick watched the computer screen register 100%. He pulled out the flash drive and put it in his pocket. Then he reached for his toolbox, tipped his cap to the receptionist, smiled and walked out.

Ellie wiped perspiration from her brow as she watched Nick race along the hallway with two security guards in pursuit. She saw him round a corner and go into a patient's room before the video screen blanked out. "Nick, where the hell are you?" she called. She reached into her backpack for a baseball cap, put it on and tucked in her hair. Then she donned dark glasses, opened the van door and jumped onto the pavement.

On the 16th floor, two security guards raced along the hallway, searching for the intruder. There was no sign of Nick, only patients' rooms with closed doors. The guards opened doors, looking inside. When they reached the last room in the hallway, Nick, dressed as a doctor in scrubs and a face mask, was reading a patient chart at the bedside. The patient lay motionless, hooked up to a respirator and IV. The patient's eyes moved from Nick to the security guards as monitors near the bed beeped steadily. "Sorry for the intrusion," one of the guards said, closing the door quickly.

When Nick was certain that the guards had moved on to another part of the floor, he walked out of the room and headed for the elevator. He heard the guards running along the hallway and was about to take the stairs when the elevator arrived. He rode the elevator to the main floor, marched across the lobby and walked out the main entrance. Still dressed in hospital scrubs, he crossed the parking lot to the van, opened the back door and climbed in.

Ellie stepped out of the elevator onto the 16th floor and walked toward the patient's room where she had last seen Nick. Two more security guards were now stationed in the hallway. One shouted a warning, "Hey, visiting hours are later. You have to leave."

"The doctor sent for me. My husband's a patient," she said.

The guards approached, surrounding her. "What's the patient's name?" one asked.

Before she could answer, the elevator door opened and Nick stepped into the hallway, still dressed in scrubs. He walked up to Ellie and the security guards. "Mrs. London, I was told you were sent up here," he said.

Turning to the guards, he said, "It's okay. She's here to see me." He placed a guiding hand on Ellie's elbow. "I'll take you to my office," he said. The guards stepped away as Nick took charge, leading Ellie to the elevator.

When the elevator door closed behind them, one of the guards removed a flyer from his pocket. He studied the photograph of the woman in the flyer, seeing the resemblance to the woman who had just stepped into the elevator. Pulling out his two-way radio, he alerted security in the lobby.

Nick pulled off the hospital scrubs in the elevator and left them on the floor. When the door opened in the lobby, Nick and Ellie walked purposefully to the exit, where a guard talked on a two-way radio and scanned the faces of people leaving the hospital. While he was scrutinizing Ellie's photo in the flyer, they slipped out the door among other visitors.

Ellie and Nick crossed the parking lot to the van. Ellie climbed into the back, and Nick settled into the driver's seat and started the engine. As they sped away, he looked at Ellie through the rearview mirror. "We could have been arrested," he said.

"I'm sorry," she said. "I thought you were in trouble."

"Well, you didn't help."

"Did you copy the program?" She held her breath, waiting for his answer.

"I did."

Ellie exhaled, relief washing over her. "Thank you."

Chapter 44

Thursday, January 14, 2010

The sky was darkening outside Ellie's apartment window as she waited for Nick to finish installing the *Exchange* program he had copied from the hospital's transplant department. When at last the program opened on her computer screen, she tensed in anticipation of what they would learn.

Nick turned to her. "Read the names of the dead prisoners on your list to me."

Ellie looked at the paper in front of her. "Matthew Andrews," she began, the sound of his name setting off an ache in her chest.

Nick typed Matt's name on the keyboard, and a screen with details came up. "Doctor pronouncing death...James Russell," he read.

The doctor's name triggered Ellie's memory of Russell with a stethoscope dangling from his neck, telling her Matt was dead. She shook off the painful memory and called out the next name on her list, "Rusty Degan."

Nick read the screen: "Doctor pronouncing death...James Russell."

They went through Ellie's entire list of dead prisoners. "Russell's the doctor in every case," she said. She studied the screen again. "All the inmates have code numbers next to their names." Nick clicked on the number beside Matt's name, and a new screen popped up. "The patients who received Matt's organs had transplants on the day he died, and they had the same blood and antigen types as Matt."

Nick watched Ellie's face drain of color. "Are you okay?" he asked.

"Matt was murdered so his organs could be harvested. So were all the other dead inmates from Red Ridge. The evidence is right here in the hospital's records."

"It doesn't prove they were murdered."

"All the prisoners who had been sentenced to Red Ridge, and later died—supposedly by accident—were a match for some recipient on the day they died. We already know that the organ donor cards are forged."

"It's circumstantial evidence," he said.

"Can you access the billing information?" she asked.

Nick tapped more keys on the computer, and various screens appeared, but not what they were searching for. Ellie shifted impatiently in the chair, searching each screen for conclusive proof of the crime.

A spreadsheet finally came onto the screen that looked promising. "Here's what we're after...the hospital's billing records," Nick said. "Look at this! The tissue bank charges the hospital processing fees for organs and tissue. Since they don't charge directly for the organs and tissue, they're operating within the law because human organs are prohibited from sale. But they can name any price they want to for processing services. And they can also claim to be a nonprofit company."

"From the looks of these numbers, processing fees are earning about $80 million a year or more for them," Ellie said.

Pointing to the screen, Nick said, "Here's how the hospital rakes in money: All transplant organs have a designated dollar value—kidney $30,000, heart $200,000... It doesn't prove that money is actually paid or who's receiving it. The hospital can't legally charge for organs, but they can charge for the surgery and postoperative care, which no doubt includes the price of the organs and tissue."

"Let's look at the spreadsheet again," she said.

Nick accessed the spreadsheet and Ellie studied it for some moments. "We need to see the tissue bank's billing," she said. When the billing data filled the screen, she pointed to dates. "Can you find shipment dates?"

Nick pulled up another screen, and they read the entries. "The tissue bank ships all tissue to the Virginia Transplant Foundation...or they say they do for legal purposes," Nick said.

"The Transplant Foundation then sells the tissue back to the hospital—$3,000 for a heart valve, $2,500 for a cornea, $5,000 for a tendon...Every body part has a price," Ellie said.

"The tissue bank acts as a middleman for the Transplant Foundation and the hospital," he said.

"The money from the illegal sales is funneled to the Transplant Foundation...whatever that is," she said.

A sudden ear-piercing crack startled them as the window behind them shattered. Glass shards flew through the air like missiles, covering their hair, their clothing and their skin in a snowy blanket of sharp crystals. Nick bolted from the chair, pulling Ellie onto the floor. Glass crunched beneath them. Ellie was too shocked to feel the small cuts on her hands, which left red smudges on the floor. Fear sent a rush of adrenaline coursing through her as she tried to process what was happening.

"Stay down!" Nick said. He crawled over the debris on the floor to reach the window. Standing cautiously, he peered through the broken window. Two police officers stood on the roof of the building across the way, holding guns with silencers. Nick watched as one of them lifted his arm and aimed.

A bullet sailed through the broken window, striking the computer. Sparks flew as the computer exploded with a blast, reducing it to chunks of metal and plastic. The acrid smell of melting electronic components filled the air. Ellie coughed, covering her nose and mouth with her hand. Nick inched along the floor to her. "Stay close to me," he said, pulling her to the door. In the hallway, they raced to the back door and slipped outside into the cold night air.

They ran across the parking lot to Ellie's car. Nick took the car keys from her shaking hand and started the engine. They sped away, with a police cruiser close behind them. He stepped hard on the accelerator, making sharp left and right turns as the police pursued them. Ellie clutched the sides of the seat, her heart racing.

The car swerved onto a side street. Nick circled back and forth, making multiple rapid turns that had a dizzying effect on Ellie. He turned to look at her pale face. "We lost them," he said.

"Where did you learn to do that?" she asked.

"Training," he said. He drove on for some time until they reached a neighborhood unfamiliar to Ellie.

"Where are we going?" she asked.

"A safe house. You can stay there until I make other arrangements."

"I'm not going anywhere until I find out who runs the Virginia Transplant Foundation."

Nick turned to her, his jaw set. "It's too dangerous."

"I owe it to Matt."

"You won't find anything if you're dead!" he said, rounding a corner and driving down a dark street.

Nick pulled into the driveway of a modest one-story brick house that looked like all the other houses on the street, and turned off the engine. Ellie followed him to the front door. He unlocked the door and they stepped into a narrow hallway. He flicked on the light in the living room, triggering the memory of his last visit here when he had rescued a teenage girl from a sex trafficking ring.

Ellie sank onto the sofa, sapped of energy. She looked around the simply-furnished room. Two chairs, a coffee table and a desk were the only other furniture. A laptop computer and an untraceable cell phone sat atop the desk. She turned to Nick, a pained look in her eyes. "You could have been hurt, or worse, because of me," she said.

"There's food in the fridge and a comfortable bed in the bedroom," Nick said. "Try to get some rest. I'm going to meet with a friend to get you a new passport and driver's license…and make arrangements."

"Arrangements?"

"To leave the country." When she didn't answer, he said, "Promise you'll stay here."

"I promise," she whispered, too exhausted to argue. Nick leaned toward her, brushing her forehead with a soft kiss before walking to the door. He turned to look back at her with worried eyes before closing the door.

His kiss lingered on her skin like a caress, and she ached with wanting him. Dismissing her feelings, she rose from the sofa and went into the small kitchen. It was clean and organized with a white bistro table and two chairs. A small pantry was stocked with packaged crackers, cereal, tuna fish and canned soup. She opened the refrigerator and took out a bottle of water.

Back in the living room, Ellie gulped the water. Setting the empty bottle on the floor, she curled up on the sofa and closed her eyes, drifting into a troubled sleep within minutes.

Ellie woke with a start, disoriented. When her thoughts came flooding back, everything that had happened today left her trembling. *Who wants to silence me?* ran through her mind.

Her head throbbed, but she heaved herself off the sofa and went to the computer. She booted it up, accessed the Internet and searched for the Virginia Transplant Foundation. The foundation's website filled the screen, and she started reading. A board meeting was scheduled for Friday, January 15, at 10:00 a.m. "Tomorrow," she said aloud.

She continued reading, scrolling through the web pages. Her eyes widened. "You son-of-a-bitch!" She pounded her fist on the desk. Pushing herself off the chair, she paced the room, too agitated by what she had read to keep still. She went back to the desk, found a notepad in a drawer and copied the address of the foundation. When she slipped her hand inside the drawer again, her fingers brushed a cold metal object. She pulled out a small handgun, examined it and dropped it into her handbag.

Chapter 45

Friday, January 15, 2010

Nick parked in the driveway of the safe house and turned off the engine. When he unlocked the front door and stepped inside, it was quiet, too quiet for early morning. "Ellie!" he called. An empty water bottle lay on the floor near the sofa. He opened the bedroom door and saw that the bed had not been slept in. In the bathroom, wet towels hung from the towel rack, and a hairdryer was plugged into the outlet.

"Ellie!" he called, returning to the living room. He thumbed through papers on the desk. The computer screen was dark, but when he tapped a key, it lit up. He read the screen page that Ellie had not closed and hurried out of the house.

***

A taxi pulled up in front of a gray high-rise office building in Franconia, Virginia. Ellie paid the driver and walked through the revolving doors of the imposing stone building with opaque windows.

At the security desk, Ellie flashed her press ID card. "I'm here to interview the Board of Directors of the Transplant Foundation for the Virginia Star Newspaper," she said. "Where is the board meeting taking place?"

The security guard reached for his phone. "Your name? I'll call and tell them you're on your way up," he said.

Ellie flashed one of her practiced reporter smiles. "Please don't do that. I mean...I'm so late already." She looked at her watch dramatically. "I wouldn't want to interrupt the meeting twice."

He returned her smile and pointed to a bank of elevators across the lobby. "Take the elevator to fourteen."

"Thanks." Ellie smiled again and walked to a waiting elevator.

When the elevator door opened on the fourteenth floor, she faced an elaborately-carved oak door. She hesitated, frozen for some moments. Slipping her hand into her jacket pocket, she curled her fingers around the handgun. Inhaling deeply, she opened the door and stepped inside onto plush green carpeting.

Startled by Ellie's entrance, the five men and one woman, seated in high-back leather chairs around a large conference table, turned to stare at her. One by one, Ellie identified them—Judge Robert Maxwell, Warden Clayton Parker, Dr. James Russell, Brian Payne, Eleanor Colton and, at the head of the table, Dan Andrews.

Ellie glared at Dan with naked fury. His eyes met hers with a coldness that made her shudder. "What are you doing here? This is a private meeting," he said.

"What are *you* doing here?"

"You need to leave right now," he ordered.

"Let's discuss your involvement in the human organ trade," she said.

"That's absurd!"

"You earn $650,000 a year as the head of this foundation. I can only imagine what you've done to earn it!"

Dan bolted out of the chair. "You don't understand any of this!"

Ellie pulled the handgun out of her pocket. Eleanor Colton gasped. The other board members stiffened, their eyes riveted on the gun. She walked around the table, waving the gun. Stopping beside Dan, she pressed the gun against his temple. "Sit down, Dan! I'll tell you what I understand."

Dan slid into the chair, perspiration beading on his brow. The board members squirmed in their seats as Ellie confronted them. "You're using prison inmates for spare body parts," she said. "Red Ridge Prison is your holding pen for organ donors. You entrap people, have them sent there, and then murder them for their organs and other body parts."

She pointed the gun at Eleanor Colton and continued. "That's what made it possible for wealthy people like you, Eleanor, to get an organ when you needed one. No need to wait your turn on a transplant list. Matt's cellmate, Rusty Degan, was murdered so you could get the kidney you needed."

Eleanor gripped the arms of the chair. "Rusty Degan died accidentally. The organ match was found for me *only* after he died," she insisted.

"Bullshit! He died on the day you had your kidney transplant because it was arranged. Wasn't it a lucky coincidence that he died in the hospital where you had your transplant?"

"You have no proof," Eleanor said.

"Your husband, the senator, pushed through the legislation to build Red Ridge. That was just the beginning of this criminal enterprise."

"That's ridiculous! No one will believe you," Eleanor said.

Ellie turned to Judge Maxwell. "Maybe I'm imagining that, as a judge, you worked with corrupt Virginia police to make certain Matt was arrested and then tried in your courtroom. And I'm imagining that you sentenced him to Red Ridge." Maxwell's face paled, his eyes darting to Dan for guidance.

Ellie faced Parker, who sat at Dan's right. "As the prison warden, you made sure Matt was attacked and then taken to the Virginia General Hospital, where Dr. Russell was waiting to harvest his organs." Parker's face reddened and his hands clenched into fists. He sprang from the chair, but Dan reached out and pushed him back.

Russell glared at Ellie. "How dare you! I'm a doctor. I save lives," he shouted.

"You remove prisoners' organs and tissue, which you ship to Brian Payne at the tissue bank," Ellie said. Moving beside Payne, she asked, "Isn't that how it works, Brian?" Payne looked at Dan with pleading eyes. Ellie pointed the gun at Payne's head. His face twitched. "Answer the question!" she demanded.

"We... we help people," Payne stammered.

"You sell their body parts to the highest bidders! You do this with all the Red Ridge inmates who are murdered, like my brother. His tissue and bones were in cold storage in the tissue bank."

"You're mistaken. You have no proof," he insisted.

"The numbers on the body parts in the storage freezers matched my brother's prison ID number. The ID numbers of other dead inmates all matched body parts in the tissue bank's freezers. But you already know that," Ellie said.

"The tissue bank only accepts legally-donated organs and tissue," Payne whined.

"I have copies of forged organ donor cards, and affidavits from the families of dead inmates, certifying that their signatures were forged," Ellie said.

She walked around the table to Dan and waved the gun at him. "You're awfully quiet," she said. "Can't explain your way out of this?"

"Why would anyone do the things you imagined?" he asked.

"Money!" she shouted. "Obscene amounts of money from organ brokering is funneled from the tissue bank to your transplant foundation, which owns and operates the tissue bank. The profits are then paid out to all of you in inflated salaries. And you, Dan, are the chairman of this foundation. Your foundation is the laundering operation for your shell game. Matt was uncovering your scheme, and you had him murdered."

Dan crossed his arms across his chest and glared at Ellie defiantly. "If Matt hadn't gone snooping around after Ben's accident, he'd still be alive."

Ellie gasped. "So, my father knew about your ghoulish operation, too? You had your own brother killed?" Her hands trembled. "Soon, the whole world will know."

Dan's face hardened, his eyes narrowed. "No one will believe you, Ellie."

Ellie opened her handbag and pulled out a small cassette recorder. She clicked it on. Dan's damning words poured out: *"If Matt hadn't gone snooping around after Ben's accident, he'd still be alive."*

Ellie turned off the recorder, waved the gun, and backed out of the room. "Now you can all serve time at Red Ridge." The door closed behind her. Dan reached for a phone on the table.

Outside the boardroom, Ellie rang for the elevator, trembling with rage. She tapped her foot impatiently, her eyes on the elevator indicator, stopped on the fifth floor. She heard the sound of voices and footsteps before she saw the two security guards running toward her with guns drawn. Spinning around, she raced to a nearby stairwell.

She tugged open the heavy door and bolted down the steps. When she reached the floor below, she heard the door above open and close with a bang. She ran faster, keeping a floor ahead of the guards. The sound of shots startled her, urging her on. On the next landing, she pulled on the door frantically, but it was locked from the outside. Panting, she drew in deep breaths as her pursuers' footsteps grew louder, closer. Shots rang out again. The sound of her own heart thundered in her ears.

Pushing herself harder, she took the steps two at a time, landing on the next floor. The stairwell door burst open. Nick stood in the doorway. Startled, Ellie stared at him as though he were an apparition. He pulled her into the hallway and slammed the door. "How...?" she gasped.

"Not now," he said, grasping her hand, pulling her along the hallway. They heard more shots as the guards fired at the door from inside the stairwell. The door flew open with a thud and they burst into the hallway.

Nick opened a door to a nearby storage room and pushed Ellie inside, locking the door behind them. Breathing hard, they looked around the small airless room. Floor-to-ceiling shelves held boxes of files. Stacks of papers were piled on a table in the center of the room. A container of cleaning fluid labeled, *flammable*, sat on the floor in a corner. Outside, in the hallway, they heard the security guards opening and closing doors. One of the guards spoke into a phone: "Not yet, but we'll find them."

"Hand me those papers," Nick told Ellie, pointing to the table. He took a cigarette lighter out of his pocket, flicked it on and fed papers into the flame. He scattered the burning papers around the floor, and they quickly ignited other papers. Embers landed on the wooden table, and the dry wood smoldered and caught fire.

"What are you doing?" she asked.

"Shh," he said.

Smoke rose toward the ceiling, setting off the fire alarm. Ellie coughed and pressed her hands over her stinging eyes. Nick motioned to her to crouch on the floor and cover her mouth and nose. The security guards pounded on the storage room door. In the hallway, they heard doors opening, shouting, the sound of people running. Alarms rang out as smoke spread rapidly through the hallway. Panicked employees ran to exit stairwells, gasping and pushing the guards aside.

Nick opened the storage room door and pulled Ellie into the hallway. She sucked in air, coughing and stumbling. Nick held tight to her hand as they merged with the panicked crowd, fleeing down the stairwell. When they reached the lobby, security guards were searching the faces in the crowd. As firefighters rushed in with hoses and axes, Ellie and Nick streamed out the front doors with the terrified employees, hidden in the melee.

Alarms could be heard blaring inside the boardroom. "It's only a drill," Dan told the board members. The door burst open and smoke poured in.

A security guard shouted from the doorway, "Fire! Get out!"

The board members scrambled out of their chairs, rushing to the door as thick black smoke blanketed the room. They coughed and pushed each other aside. The sprinkler system had not stopped the fire from spreading upward from the lower floor. Fire found an easy path through the elevator shaft, which acted like a funnel, feeding it air so it could consume everything in its path.

Dan was the last to get up and move to the door. He covered his mouth and nose with a handkerchief, but the dense acrid smoke stung his eyes, blurring his vision. When he reached the doorway, his shoe caught in the metal lip. No one saw him stumble and fall face down. He clawed at the floor for something to grasp…for some way to pull himself up. He gasped as smoke filled his lungs and blinded his eyes.

Chapter 46

Friday, January 15, 2010

Fire trucks, ambulances and police cars with lights flashing clogged the street in front of the Transplant Foundation headquarters. Dazed and frightened people, fleeing the smoke-filled building, staggered out of the front doors, coughing and rubbing their eyes.

Ellie and Nick hurried away from the building to the far end of the street where Nick had parked. They got into the car, and Nick turned on the engine and pulled out, heading to the Beltway. He gripped the steering wheel and stared straight ahead, the muscles in his face tense. Ellie opened the window and gulped air. She turned to Nick, and sudden tears sprung in her eyes. *He could have died because of me*, she thought.

"Why didn't you stay in the safe house?" His question was an angry reprimand.

"I had to do this. You weren't supposed to follow me...risk your life."

"You could've been killed," he said. She touched his hand, and their eyes met, communicating more than words could say. They drove on in silence.

Ellie was lost in thought when, an hour later, they exited the highway at the Baltimore Washington International Airport. Nick turned into the airport parking lot and pulled into an empty spot. He opened the glove compartment, took out an envelope, and handed it to Ellie. "There's a passport, a driver's license and an airline ticket in the envelope. You have a new name. Someone will meet you at the airport."

She opened the envelope and read the documents. "How long?" she asked.

"Until this blows over."

They stepped out of the car, and Nick took a laptop computer case and a duffel bag from the back seat and handed them to Ellie. "Some things you'll need," he said.

"Will you come with me?"

"It's too dangerous now."

They crossed the parking lot to the terminal. Inside, Ellie waited in a line with other passengers checking in for the flight. Nick had insisted that she wear dark glasses and a cap.

He watched her from a seat in the waiting area, his face hidden behind an open newspaper. When he spotted two policemen searching faces in the crowd, it took only a moment for him to identify them—Kevin Moore and Patrick Murphy. He closed the newspaper and moved quickly to Ellie's side.

"Pick up your bags and follow me," he whispered in her ear. She turned and recognized the two policemen at once. Panic set her heart thudding in her chest. She willed herself to walk at a normal pace while adrenaline coursed through her veins.

It took only minutes for Moore and Murphy to spot them and cut through the lines of passengers. Nick grabbed Ellie's hand, and they ran across the terminal to an escalator, riding it up to the next level. The police were close behind them when they stepped off the escalator and slipped into a moving crowd of passengers. Nick carried Ellie's laptop case and pulled her along, weaving through the crowd. When he turned to look back, the officers were nowhere in sight. He exhaled in momentary relief but knew they had to keep moving or find a place to hide.

When he saw a sign for the women's restroom, he stepped out of the moving crowd. Ellie followed him to the restroom door. "Wait inside till I come back," he said. There was no time for questions, and she went inside.

Nick moved at a fast clip, stopping at a kiosk that sold books. The police were back, searching for a man and a woman, but they passed him by. He left the kiosk and backtracked, turning into a busy shop that sold clothing and luggage. He bought a sweatshirt and cap. Removing his jacket, he slipped on the sweatshirt and cap. Outside the shop, he tossed his jacket into a trash can. At another shop, he purchased a woman's windbreaker jacket, a wool hat and a large duffel bag. He put the windbreaker and hat inside the duffel. On his way out of the shop, his cell phone buzzed. "Yes?" he answered.

"Where are you?" Ellie's words echoed her anxiety.

"Wait inside the doorway. I'll be there in five minutes."

Nick kept his head down and walked briskly along the terminal, weaving between crowds of arriving and departing passengers. Moore and Murphy stood at the side, searching faces in the crowd. His heartbeat quickened, and perspiration gathered beneath the heavy sweatshirt as he passed them. Their eyes were on him, a man in a sweatshirt and cap, walking alone.

He made his way back to Ellie, who waited inside the restroom doorway. She didn't recognize him at first, but then she heard his voice as he whispered, "Ellie." He handed her the new duffel bag and spoke fast. "Put on the clothes in the bag. Transfer everything from your bag to the duffel and toss your old bag in the trash. Go to baggage claim. I'll be waiting near an exit door, facing outside the terminal. Don't look at me or talk to me. Walk out the door," he said, turning away. There was no time for explanations.

Ellie went into a handicap bathroom stall. An ordinary stall would not do for changing clothes and repacking a bag. She zipped up the windbreaker, tucked her hair into the wool hat and packed her belongings in the new duffel. Outside the stall, she set the two bags on the floor next to a sink and washed her hands slowly, waiting for two women nearby to leave. When they left, she tossed the empty bag in the trash can, picked up the new one and walked out.

Keeping her head bowed, Ellie followed the signs to baggage claim. Then she spotted Kevin Moore standing beside the escalator, staring at the passengers getting on. Panic set her heart racing. She turned her head away and stepped onto the escalator, passing just inches away from him. *Where was Murphy?* she worried as the escalator carried her down.

When she reached baggage claim, multiple carousels spun around with luggage from planes that had arrived. Passengers surrounded the carousels, waiting to grab their bags. Then she recognized Murphy standing at the side of the terminal. Ellie tucked a stray curl into her cap and willed herself to stay calm as her stomach churned.

Making her way along the terminal, she kept close to clusters of passengers while searching for Nick. People walked out of the terminal wheeling baggage, but she didn't see him. Too many carousels, too many people, too many doors made it impossible to find him. *What if he wasn't here? What would she do?* She moved on, her stomach tightening, perspiration dampening the wool cap. Then she saw him, facing the last door, talking on his cell phone.

She moved toward him at a normal pace when she wanted to run. His words reached her ears as she passed him on her way out the door. "Charlie, I need a favor," he said. "Can you take another passenger?"

Nick was right behind her when she reached the sidewalk. People gathered at the curbside with their luggage, waiting for cars and taxis. Horns honked, and a man in a yellow vest directed traffic. A Marriott Hotel van pulled up to the curb, and the driver unloaded luggage. Nick touched Ellie's arm lightly. "Don't look back," he whispered.

They walked straight ahead to the parking lot. When they reached the car, Ellie looked back at the terminal, terrified that she would see the police. There were only ordinary people walking to their cars. Nick started the car and pulled out. He turned to her. "We're going to plan B."

"What is plan B?"

"You'll see," he said.

***

It was dusk when they reached the waterfront in Alexandria. Ellie recognized the marina in Old Town Alexandria as soon as they approached. It was one of her favorite hangouts. Her father first took her and Matt here when they were children. They would watch the small ships and private sailboats, and meander through the nearby Torpedo Factory Art Center. Now there was a 90-foot yacht docked at the marina, flying a British flag. Well-dressed passengers climbed the gangplank.

"Wait here," Nick said. She watched him walk along the pier and climb onto the ship, where a man dressed in a dark blue uniform waited on the deck. *The captain*, she thought. They spoke for a few moments, then shook hands. The captain gave Nick a package wrapped in brown paper.

When Nick returned to the car, he handed the package to Ellie. "There's a waitress uniform inside. Put it on and board the ship."

Ellie changed into the service uniform with the yacht's insignia. "How did you arrange this?" she asked.

"I know the captain. You'll be safe," he said.

"Where am I going?"

"Cayman Islands. The captain will help you get settled there."

"How do you know all these people?"

"Are you ready?" he asked. "You need to board now."

The yacht's horn blared a departing signal. They got out of the car and walked along the pier to the water's edge. Ellie set her duffel and computer case down and turned her face to Nick. He bent his head and brushed her lips with a soft kiss. Placing her hands on his face, she drew him closer, kissing him deeply. It was a kiss filled with longing and so much more. Then she picked up her bags and climbed the gangplank.

Nick stood on the pier as the yacht's ropes were untied and the horn sounded. The feel of Ellie's kiss lingered on his lips. Relief, mixed with regret, swept over him as he watched her sail to safety. He waited until the yacht was just a dot on the horizon. When he returned to his car, he didn't notice a black car, parked among other vehicles in the marina lot, where a man in the driver's seat watched through binoculars.

The man set the binoculars on the seat next to him and pulled a cell phone out of his pocket. "I'm sure it's her…No, he didn't board with her. The Whitley is flying a British flag. Meet me in one hour… the usual place. I'll be waiting at the bar. Have the other half in unmarked bills, senator."

Chapter 47

Saturday, January 16, 2010

Joan applied mascara to her lashes and a pale-pink lipstick to her lips. *No blush on my cheeks today*, she decided, pulling a comb through her long blonde hair one more time. Opening her jewelry box, she chose a simple pair of small silver earrings. Then she stood before the full-length mirror, admiring herself in a tailored black dress.

The front doorbell rang, and she opened the bedroom door and started down the steps. "I'll get the door," she called out to Hilda, her maid.

She opened the door to Tom Newton, the newly-divorced U.S. senator from Texas, a longtime friend of her family. He smiled warmly. "I'll get my coat," she said.

He came into the hallway and helped her on with her coat. "You look pale," he said. "I can understand why...the shock of it all."

She smiled, pleased by his comment. "Thanks for coming with me."

"You shouldn't have to do this alone," he said.

"Dr. Russell told me to prepare myself...that Dan is badly burned and it will be upsetting to see him." Her eyes filled with tears.

***

When they arrived at the hospital and Tom parked his Mercedes, he put his hand on Joan's arm. "I'll come in with you," he said.

"He won't want anyone but me."

"It won't be easy. I'll stay close in case you need me," he said. She pressed his hand in hers, and they stepped out of the car.

They waited for the elevator in the hospital lobby and, when it arrived, they rode it to the 10th floor. The door opened onto the Burn Center, where the acrid smell of antiseptics permeated the air. Tom took Joan's hand as they walked to the nurses' station in the center of the floor. "Dan Andrews?" Tom asked the nurse.

"The last room on the right," the nurse directed. "There are gowns, masks and gloves outside the patient's room. You must put them on before entering."

"Of course," Tom said.

They made their way along the hallway, passing rooms where patients lay in state-of-the-art beds that gently moved them to prevent pressure sores. The doors were open so as not to delay emergency care. Monitors beeped steadily, ready to sound an alarm when there were breathing difficulties or cardiac events. They passed a room where a woman with blistered and grotesquely swollen arms and legs lay unmoving on the bed. Joan shuddered as they walked on. In the adjacent room, it was impossible to tell if the patient was a man or woman. Charred brown skin covered half the patient's face, and bandages masked the eyes. A sickening sweet odor drifted into the hallway—the smell of rotting flesh.

Joan clutched her stomach, gripped by a sudden wave of nausea. Tom put a bracing arm around her waist. "This is too much for you," he said.

She steadied herself and took a breath. "I'm okay. I need to do this for Dan."

Tom nodded. He was such a kind and caring man. He understood her because they came from the same place, where their privileged lives sheltered them from ugly distressing events like this. Tom's empathy triggered a memory of her father's words: *"You should be marrying a man like Tom Newton, from our social circle, not an outsider."*

They stopped outside Dan's room. Joan lifted a sterile gown from a cart and put it on. She tucked her hair into a paper cap and pushed her hands into vinyl gloves. "I'll wait out here if you need me," Tom said. She nodded, her eyes welling with tears for herself and what was expected of her.

Inside the room, she felt the warm humid air closing around her like a shroud. Dan lay in a specially-designed hospital bed, swathed in bandages. An oxygen mask covered his mouth and nose. IV tubes dripped antibiotics, other medications, and saline to prevent fluid loss from the burns. Heart- and lung-monitoring devices beeped, registering signals on a bedside screen. A small portion of Dan's face, not wrapped in bandages, looked more like undercooked meat than human flesh. His eyes fluttered open, reflecting intense pain in spite of the morphine coursing through his veins.

Tendrils of Joan's hair peeked out of the cap. She blinked back tears, hoping her mascara wouldn't run. The chemical smell of antiseptics, and something nauseating she couldn't identify, made her gag. She stumbled backward, grasping the hospital bed table to steady herself.

Dan pulled the oxygen mask away from his mouth. "Sit," he said, his voice hoarse, his eyes reading the revulsion on her face. Her Texas family had sheltered her all her life. Dan had always kept unpleasant news from her, too. Even if he survived his burns, he knew she could never tolerate life with a disabled, disfigured husband.

Joan dragged a chair from the side of the room to the bedside. "Dr. Russell said you'll have surgery tomorrow...skin grafts."

Dan didn't answer. His eyes settled on Tom Newton, standing in the doorway like a voyeur. "Why is he here?"

"He's a good friend."

Dan's eyes bore into her, and she shifted uncomfortably in the chair. "I never liked him," he said. "He's always sniffing after you like a dog in heat. Now he's waiting for me to die."

"That's simply not true. And I came to be with you, not talk about Tom. Dr. Russell said you'll recover after the grafts and rehab."

A moan so deep and mournful emerged from Dan's throat that Joan jerked back in the chair. "Go! You don't want to be here," he said.

"I just got here."

"I don't care. I don't want to see you...or anyone."

"I'm your wife. I...I care about you."

"Go home, Joan."

"It's not like you to snap at me," she stammered. She stood, pushing the chair back. "I'll see you tomorrow then, after your surgery."

"Come without Tom," he croaked.

She turned away from the body in the hospital bed that no longer resembled her husband and fled from the room. Tearing off the gown, cap and mask, she tossed them into a basket near the door. Tom took her hand, and they hurried to the elevator.

A wall-mounted television, suspended above Dan's hospital bed, was tuned to a local news station. A news anchor, standing in front of the Virginia General Hospital, was reporting: "Senator Frederick Colten's wife, Eleanor, was admitted to the Virginia General Hospital late last night, following a three-alarm fire at the Virginia Transplant Foundation. While Mrs. Colton was not injured in the fire, she is suffering from kidney failure. Doctors here report that she recently received a kidney transplant at the hospital. The donated kidney was found to be infected with hepatitis B virus. Investigations are underway to determine if the donated kidney was properly screened."

Alarms sounded from the monitors near Dan's bed. Doctors and nurses rushed in with a crash cart. Dan's eyes rolled back as he lost consciousness. The medical team surrounded his bed, attaching a defibrillator to his chest.

Chapter 48

Friday, January 22, 2010

Today's *Washington Post* was spread open on Nick's desk in his office. He read the headline—*Arson Blamed for Fire at the Virginia Transplant Foundation Headquarters*. Bob Larson, a reporter friend at the Post, was all ears when Nick phoned him after the fire. The Transplant Foundation was not on anyone's radar before the fire. The public didn't know who they were and what they did.

"I suggest you investigate where and how the foundation procures organs for transplants," Nick had told Bob.

"I'm listening," Bob said.

"This is off the record. All the information I've been feeding you for months about Human Rights International investigating the rise in prisoners' deaths at Red Ridge is connected to the foundation."

"What do you mean?"

"The foundation is supplied with organs from dead prisoners."

"Is that illegal?"

"You'll have to find out."

"So, you're accusing the Virginia Transplant Foundation of illegally procuring human organs? Are you implying that they're responsible for increased deaths at the prison?"

"I can give you the names of prisoners' family members. I'm sure they'll talk to you *on the record*. You can connect the dots."

As Nick read the full feature article now, there were quotes from deceased prisoners' family members insisting that no permission was given to donate organs. A law firm had been hired to represent the families. They were filing a class action lawsuit against the foundation, its board of directors, its affiliates and Red Ridge Prison. Photographs and resumes of the foundation's board of directors appeared in the article, as well as their six-figure salaries.

Local TV stations ran with the story, broadcasting it for days. TV crews showed up at Senator Colton's home to interview him about his wife, Eleanor, and her role in the foundation. "Please respect our privacy while my wife recovers her health," was all he told them.

Judge Robert Maxwell, filmed leaving his house in Virginia, ducked into a waiting car. Reporters who went to the Virginia General Hospital to interview Dr. Russell were told that he was out of town on business. Warden Parker would not permit visitors at the prison and refused to comment over the phone. And Brian Payne was conveniently out of the country.

Nick wanted to phone Ellie and tell her the news but thought better of it. She would no doubt have seen the story on the Internet. Yet he missed talking to her, seeing her. Even though he had taken every precaution to keep her safe, he was uneasy. *Could he be absolutely certain that she hadn't been seen boarding the yacht?* He brooded over this since the day she left.

***

On Monday morning, Nick turned on the TV in his apartment while he dressed for work. A local cable network reporter announced from the Capitol building in Richmond, Virginia, "We bring you breaking news from the Capitol: The governor issued an executive order early this morning, creating a senate commission to investigate allegations against the Virginia Transplant Foundation, its executive board members and affiliates," he announced. "Hearings will begin in a few days."

Chapter 49

Monday, February 1, 2010

Joan stopped outside Russell's office in the administrative wing of the hospital. Tom Newton was beside her, as he was most days since the fire. "I'll be waiting here for you," Tom said, squeezing her hand. Russell had asked to see her alone, and she was apprehensive now as she knocked on the door.

"Come in," Russell said.

Russell sat at his desk reading medical reports. "Thanks for coming, Joan. Please sit." He motioned to a chair beside his desk.

"What's going on?" she asked.

"I don't have good news. The infection is spreading. Unless we can get more skin for grafts, I don't know how much longer..."

"I don't understand. Why can't you get skin?"

"I've been calling tissue banks all over the country for days, begging for available skin."

"This is unbelievable...unacceptable."

"The truth is that it's more profitable to sell skin for cosmetic procedures than burn treatment."

"We'll pay whatever it costs."

"I'll keep trying, but Dan should be told."

"No. You mustn't tell him." Her voice rose. "What good will it do?"

"I don't believe in lying to patients."

"You must give him hope...please."

"If that's what you want."

When Joan left Russell's office, Tom took her hand, and they walked to the elevator. "Are you alright?" he asked.

She looked into his eyes, and his genuine concern moved her to tears. She wiped her eyes with her fingertips. "It doesn't look good for Dan," she said as they rode the elevator to the Burn Unit.

Outside Dan's room, Joan tied a sterile gown over her clothes. She covered her face with a mask and her hands with vinyl gloves. "I'm here for you," Tom said. She nodded and went into the room.

Since Dan had been admitted to the Burn Unit a little over two weeks ago, he had undergone three skin grafts to replace charred skin on his torso. The oxygen mask that covered his face did little to mitigate the inflammation in his airways caused by smoke inhalation. His lungs produced fluid that had to be drained regularly. His breathing grew more labored every day. The next step was a ventilator or maybe even a tracheotomy tube. His vital signs were checked every half hour. The morphine drip was adjusted, blood was drawn to measure infection, and stronger antibiotics were added to the infusions.

Joan stood beside Dan's bed, though not too close. The smell of rotting flesh made her stomach roil. She swallowed, fighting the urge to retch at the sight of his ruined face. "Darling, I spoke to Dr. Russell, and he said you're coming along nicely. They're going to do another skin graft soon, and you'll feel much better then."

Dan groaned. His gaze moved to Tom Newton, hovering in the doorway.

Joan brushed a stray lock of hair from her cheek. "You can't imagine how hard it's been for me, Dan. When the commission was appointed to investigate the foundation, it caused irreparable damage to your reputation... and mine. How dare anyone accuse you of such things? It's malicious. It's libelous." Dan struggled to breathe, his eyes on Joan as she continued her tirade. "You and I both know how judgmental people are. This scandal will always be remembered when your name comes up in a conversation."

Dan moaned, blinking rapidly.

Joan stepped closer to the bed. "I can't go to the country club for lunch or dinner anymore," she whined. "People stare at me and whisper. Friends make excuses not to see me. They aren't *real* friends. Our friends are in Texas, where we come from. Virginia's an unforgiving place." She paused, waiting for a response from Dan, whose eyes glistened with tears. "We need to sell the house and go back to Texas, where my family and our true friends will welcome us. You'll get excellent care there. Don't you agree?"

"I'm dying, aren't I? Tell me the truth," he demanded, his voice raspy. "That's why you want to go back to Texas...with Tom, who's waiting for me to die." Speaking exhausted him, and he closed his eyes.

"Tom's a friend. You're imagining things that aren't true because you're so sick now. But you *are* getting better."

Dan wanted to shout at her, but he didn't have the energy. "I'm not running away to Texas," he managed to whisper. More than anything, he wanted to live so he could punish Ellie and her partner. He wanted to make it impossible for them to ever work again…or worse.

"I'll start making arrangements," Joan said, ignoring his wishes. "I'll call a realtor today and put the house on the market. You needn't worry about the Virginia Star. We can sell that as well. In the meantime, the managing editor is doing a good job running the newspaper."

Dan made a guttural sound. His heartbeat accelerated, setting off a monitor at the nurses' station. "I'll go so you can rest now," Joan said. "See you tomorrow." She had told Dan what she came to say and there was no need to prolong her visit, which she found torturous.

A nurse rushed in as Joan hurried out of the room, pulling off the gown and mask. The nurse checked Dan's vitals and adjusted the morphine drip. "You need to stay calm," she said, smiling sympathetically.

Dan drifted into a drugged, troubled sleep and woke later to the sound of a familiar voice. His eyes fluttered open, settling on Russell.

"How are you feeling?" Russell asked.

Dan moaned, sucking in a breath behind the oxygen mask.

"You're going to need several more skin grafts, but you'll recover," Russell said.

"I can't breathe," Dan wheezed.

"We're waiting for a shipment of skin for your next graft. You'll feel better afterward."

"When?" His question, filled with desperation, hung in silence for a few moments.

Russell cleared his throat. "Our own tissue bank shipped all of its skin supply to plastic surgeons for cosmetic surgery. It's too late to recall. We have urgent requests out to other tissue banks, but you know how hard it can be to get skin for burn treatment when cosmetic surgery is so profitable." He paused to give Dan a chance to process this news. "I'm optimistic that we'll get a shipment soon," he added.

Dan's eyes brimmed with tears. "You're lying. I'm dying."

"I wouldn't lie to you. We can put you on a ventilator…till the graft tissue arrives."

"No ventilator," Dan rasped.

"I have some good news. Our investigator located the target in Grand

Cayman. There's no threat of further damage. And we're keeping a close watch on her partner, but we have to be careful because of his connections."

A faint smile crossed Dan's lips behind the oxygen mask. He hadn't believed Joan when she said he was getting better, but he was certain that Russell wouldn't lie to him. Maybe, after all the pain and suffering, he would recover after all. He felt a glimmer of hope for the first time since the fire. Perhaps Joan was right about returning to Texas and starting over. He closed his eyes, thinking about all the things he could no longer control—his health, his wife, his future. The irony of being imprisoned in a hospital bed did not escape him, but he was determined to live now, to exact revenge on the person responsible for his suffering. Ellie would be stopped and his taped confession destroyed.

Chapter 50

Monday, February 1, 2010

It had been more than two weeks since Ellie stepped off the yacht onto Grand Cayman. The yacht's captain had arranged an apartment rental for her in a condo near Seven Mile Beach, where she blended in with vacationing tourists. The two-story condo was hidden behind palm trees, red flowering hibiscus and mango trees.

Ellie spent every day recording her story for the world to see. Tears streamed down her face unabated as she wrote, often until 3:00 or 4:00 in the morning. She found herself reliving her visits with Matt in prison—seeing the pain in his eyes, the purple bruises on his face and arms. Anger consumed her as she wrote about the elaborate organ theft conspiracy—the complicity of the legal system, the foundation's money-laundering scheme, her uncle's betrayal. She named names and documented events. Surely there would be justice and punishment when the report was published.

It was a beautiful sunny morning when Ellie typed the last word of her story. She saved two copies on flash drives as Nick had instructed. Slipping the flash drives into her purse, she left the apartment and went to the reception desk in the lobby. "I'd like to rent a safe," she said.

"There's a $50 deposit and $20 a week charge," the receptionist said. "It's $100 if we need to open the safe for you."

Ellie paid the charge with cash, placed one flash drive inside and punched in a combination. Then she went outside to her rental car. When she got into the car, she didn't pay particular attention to a tall thin man, wearing a baseball cap and sunglasses. He appeared to be waiting for someone near the front door.

She drove to the airport, where she rented a locker. After paying the rental fee, she placed the second flash drive inside. Then she selected a combination, memorized it and closed the locker. When she returned to her car, she felt lightheaded—like a weight that had pressed in on her for too long had been lifted. She reached into her pocket, pulled out the disposable phone Nick had given her, and keyed in the only number she was allowed to use. Her heart quickened, anticipating hearing Nick's voice after weeks of silence and solitude.

"Yes?" Nick answered. Ellie caught her breath at the sound of his voice.

"It's done," she said, giving him the combinations for the condo safe and the airport locker.

"You can relax now, enjoy the island."

"When can I release the story?"

"Not yet. We have to wait for the commission's findings."

"Maybe they'll confirm my story," she said.

"Don't count on it. Not with Colton's cronies on the commission."

"Colton? I didn't know. But you're right. I was just hoping…" she said, unable to hide her disappointment.

"It's a temporary delay."

"Will I see you?" she asked.

There was a long silence as Nick processed the longing he heard in her voice. "Maybe soon," he said.

When Ellie got into bed that night, she replayed their conversation over in her head. *He probably never wants to see me again. I've been nothing but trouble for him. I need to stop thinking about him, hearing his voice. He's in danger because of me*, she thought. Knowing it was irrational to blame herself didn't stop her from feeling that she was poisonous to everyone she loved. She drifted into sleep, seeing Nick's face. She dreamed they were making love, felt his hands sliding over her, his body pressed against hers. She felt his lips brush her face, her neck, her breasts. She woke in the morning with his name on her lips and overwhelming longing. Throwing off the cover, she got out of bed, shaking off the dream.

Maybe Nick was right. She should relax and enjoy the island. She showered, slipped into her swimsuit, and took a container of yogurt from the refrigerator for her breakfast. Then she started out for the public beach, a ten-minute walk from the condo.

Stepping onto the beach, Ellie found an empty space among the sunbathers. She spread her beach mat out on the warm sand and walked to the water's edge. The sea was as tranquil as a lake, a beautiful clear turquoise glistening in the sunlight. She dipped her toes in, then splashed in and swam out. When her arms tired, she turned onto her back and floated, letting the currents carry her back to shore. *Why hadn't she done this earlier?*

When she walked out of the ocean, making her way across the sand to her mat, she didn't notice the tall thin man, wearing a baseball cap and sunglasses, who sat some distance behind her, pretending to read a book. He watched her dry herself with a towel and stretch out on the mat.

The ocean had energized her, and now the sun soaked into her skin, relaxing her muscles for the first time in weeks. She dozed, and when she woke, the sun was setting lower in the sky and the beach was emptying of tourists. Ellie jumped up, wrapped the towel around her waist and rolled up the mat. Her stomach grumbled with hunger, and she decided to treat herself to dinner out tonight, instead of picking up a take-out meal.

After returning to the condo, showering and dressing in slacks and a loose shirt, Ellie walked to a local restaurant. She sat at a table, enjoying a glass of wine while she waited for the grilled fish and vegetables she ordered. The chatter of conversations from couples and families drifted through the restaurant, lifting her spirits after weeks of isolation. All the seats at the bar were filled. The man who had surveilled Ellie on the beach sat at the far end of the bar, nursing a beer.

***

Ellie spent her days at the beach now. She left soon after breakfast, stored the room key and important papers in the lobby safe and set off with her beach mat, towel and the snorkel gear she had purchased in George Town. She recognized some of the tourists she had seen on the beach before— single women and men, couples, families, the thin man in the baseball cap who always had a book in front of his face. There was nothing particularly noteworthy about the man, except that he never went into the water. *Not a swimmer*, she thought, donning her snorkel gear near the shoreline.

After observing Ellie for days, the man knew she would be snorkeling out to the coral reef for half an hour or longer. When he could no longer see her form in the ocean, he left his book on the beach chair and strolled along the sand, stopping beside Ellie's mat. He went unnoticed by the sunbathers nearby as he gazed at the ocean, pretending to admire the view. Lifting the edge of Ellie's mat with his toe, he felt for a room key, where she may have hidden it. *She was smart and careful*, he thought...even though he didn't credit women with having any sense and found them abhorrent. Frustrated, he walked back across the sand to his beach chair.

His earlier attempts to get into Ellie's room in the condo had failed. The lobby was too small to walk in unnoticed by the receptionist at the front desk, and the back door was locked. There was no way to climb up to the second floor from outside the building. His name was on a waitlist for a room, but vacancies were infrequent during high season. He would have to bide his time until an opportunity arose.

The man, who went by the alias of Wayne Dorsey, phoned Senator Colton every night at a secure number. Names were never spoken over the phone. Yesterday, Colton told him, "I want results. You're not on vacation." Wayne hung up, angry that he was accused of not doing his job. He was proud of his work. He always delivered, no matter how gruesome the assignment. He thought of himself as a highly-skilled professional.

In the evenings, Wayne stood outside the condo, hidden in the shadows, waiting for Ellie, who frequented a local restaurant for dinner. He followed her there, sat at a table in the back, and pretended to read a book. When Ellie looked around the restaurant at other diners, Wayne appeared to be an ordinary tourist like her, dining alone.

More than two weeks after Wayne had put his name on the condo waitlist, he got a call from the receptionist. "We have a cancellation. If you want the room for a week, you have to take it today." An hour later, he was settled in his room on the second floor. He hung out in the hallway alcove, near an icemaker and vending machines. When Ellie left her room at the other end of the hallway, carrying a beach mat and towel, he went back to his room and waited twenty minutes, making sure she wasn't returning. Then he opened his door, checked the empty hallway, and headed to Ellie's room. Moments later, a door opened and children's voices filled the hallway. Wayne kept walking, passing Ellie's room, perspiration gathering beneath his baseball cap.

The children ran to the stairwell, their parents close behind. When Wayne was certain that the family had left, he walked back to Ellie's room. Opening the door lock was easy for him. He had been breaking into homes and offices since he was a teen. He stepped inside and went directly to the laptop computer on the table.

His orders were to destroy all computer files. After many failed attempts to unlock the computer, a smile crossed his lips when he finally hacked in. But his smile soon faded when he realized that all the files had been deleted. *The bitch was too smart for her own good*, he thought. *She must have made copies on flash drives and hidden them somewhere.* He rifled through the dresser drawers, cabinets, the closet, the bed, the small refrigerator. Frustrated, he wanted to smash the computer, but thought better of it, and carefully replaced everything, leaving no trace that he had been there.

When Ellie returned to her room after swimming and slipped the key in the lock, she didn't hear the familiar click. She turned the doorknob and stepped inside, her heart racing as her eyes swept around the room. She opened and closed the drawers, looked inside the closet and checked the cabinets. Nothing looked like it had been disturbed. *Could she have been that careless and left the door unlocked? Or was she being paranoid?* She showered quickly, unable to shake off the feeling that someone had been in the room.

Though Ellie was looking forward to going out for dinner, she thought better of it tonight and ordered a pizza from a local Italian restaurant. When it arrived, she found that she had little appetite. She opened the refrigerator and took out a bottle of white wine. After uncorking it, she poured a large glass, sat on the sofa and sipped. She poured a second glass and tried to recall how she had locked the door that morning, whether she had jiggled the doorknob as she usually did.

Wayne reported to Colton that evening. "The computer was scrubbed. She must have made copies."

"Do whatever you have to, but get the copies...all of them," Colton ordered.

"The risk just went up," Wayne said.

"So?"

"The price went up, too."

"How much?"

"One mil, deposited in my numbered account. Today."

"Just do it."

Chapter 51

Tuesday, February 9, 2010

After showering and dressing in shorts, a T-shirt and sandals, Ellie went outside, where a mango tree offered ripe fruit to guests. She picked up a freshly-fallen mango and went back upstairs to brew a pot of coffee. After setting a dish with sliced mango and a mug of coffee on the kitchen table, she turned on the TV.

A reporter appeared on the screen, standing in front of the Virginia State Capitol in Richmond. She spoke into a hand-held microphone: "Human Rights International accused the Virginia Transplant Foundation of operating an illegal trade in human organs. The allegations and the public outcry were taken so seriously that the governor appointed a senate commission to investigate. The commission has been holding closed hearings for weeks. We take you now inside the capitol, where the commission is about to announce its findings."

Ellie gripped the arms of the chair, her eyes on the TV as a camera panned the packed hearing room. The commission members sat stiffly at a dais, their faces impassive as chatter inside the room grew louder. The chairman rapped a gavel, silencing the talk.

"This commission has done an exhaustive investigation of allegations against the Virginia Transplant Foundation of illegal trade in human organs. We interviewed dozens of witnesses and read hundreds of pages of documents. We have found that the charges against the Virginia Transplant Foundation, its board members and affiliates, are unfounded," the chairman said.

"The dead can't testify," a woman in the gallery shouted.

"Order," the chairman said. "Officer, escort that woman out."

A court officer pulled the woman out of her seat. "Get your filthy hands off me," she screamed. Reporters and TV cameras recorded the officer pushing the woman out the door.

"Outbursts from the public will not be tolerated," the chairman said. "Witnesses had an opportunity to testify."

A man in the gallery stood. "Not everyone who wanted to testify was called. This is a kangaroo court," he bellowed. All eyes turned to gawk at the protester, whose face flushed with rage.

The sound of the chairman's gavel rang out. "Officer, remove that man," he ordered.

Moments later, the protester was dragged out of the gallery. He shook his fist at the chairman. "They're all guilty, and the commission's covering it up," he shouted, before the door closed behind him.

The commission members shifted uncomfortably in their seats. The TV camera moved slowly around the hearing room, capturing the public's reactions. Ellie gasped when the camera focused on Senator Colton, sitting in the second row of the gallery.

"There was no evidence presented to this commission to support any of the allegations. Erroneous charges are the work of perpetrators trying to do malicious harm and damage the reputations of honorable citizens and reputable organizations. Charges will be brought against the perpetrators, and they will be prosecuted to the full extent of the law," the chairman said.

Conversations erupted. The chairman rapped his gavel. "This commission is dismissed," he said. The commission members stood and hurried out through a back door.

Ellie turned off the TV. Her hands curled into fists. She was not surprised that they dismissed the charges brought by the victims' families. Commissions were usually established to debunk the truth and pacify the public. Nevertheless, the case opened a can of worms, and the foundation's reputation was tarnished. She worried that Nick was in danger now. Surely this was the time to upload her files and expose the truth. There was no way Dan's taped confession could be debunked. Why didn't Nick call and tell her to go ahead?

She paced back and forth in the living room, clenching and unclenching her fists, anger and frustration building inside her. She slipped into sneakers, grabbed her cell phone and fanny pack, and hurried outside.

Ellie jogged along West Bay Road. Her shirt was soon damp with perspiration, clinging to her skin. She longed to hear Nick's voice but feared she would put him in danger if she phoned. The muscles in her legs soon began to ache, and she slowed her pace, wishing she had brought along a bottle of water.

The sound of a runner behind her grew louder. Moments later, a tall thin man jogged alongside her. She turned to look at him. He nodded, then slowed his pace and dropped back. Ellie sensed something familiar about him, though he looked quite ordinary. Then images came back to her—the man on the beach always reading a book, the same man in the restaurant where she went for dinner most nights. *Is he a tourist, a stalker...or worse? Am I imagining things or am I in danger?* she thought.

Ellie slowed her pace and sat down on the grass at the side of the road to catch her breath. The jogger ran past her, dispelling her suspicions. She rested for a few minutes, then pushed herself up and headed for a tiki bar, just ahead, off the main road.

Inside, she walked up to the bar and ordered ice tea. She took the glass to a small table that was open to the outside. Soon after, the jogger came in and took a seat at the bar. *He's following me*, Ellie thought, sipping the tea, her eyes on him. He turned to look at her. Then he got off the bar stool and walked up to her. "You're the reporter from the Virginia Star. Andrews, right?" he asked.

Her hands tightened around the glass of ice tea. "You're mistaken," she said.

"You look just like her," he insisted.

"I'm not."

"I could swear you are."

"You're wrong."

He turned away and went back to the bar. Ellie was certain that he would follow her to the condo. She had been naive to think that she hadn't been tracked to Grand Cayman, that she was safe here. The foundation must know where all their enemies were at all times.

There was only one thing she could do now to buy time. She pulled her cell phone out of her fanny pack and called the local police station. "I want to report a man harassing me at Judd's Tiki Bar on West Bay Road," she said.

Ten minutes later, a Cayman Island patrol car arrived. Two uniformed policemen came into the bar. Ellie waved to them and they walked over to her table. She pointed to the man at the bar. "He's been following me for hours and harassing me," she told them.

"Do you want to press charges?" one of the officers asked.

"I do," she said.

They took her name and the phone number for the condo. Then they walked up to Wayne at the bar, pulled his hands behind his back and cuffed him. Tourists and locals sitting at the bar grew silent and turned to stare.

"Hey, what's going on?" Wayne protested.

"You're under arrest for harassing the woman sitting at the table to your left," one officer said.

"You're mistaken. I'm having a beer," Wayne said. "She's nuts."

"The woman is pressing charges against you, so we're taking you to the station. You can sort it out there." They pulled Wayne off the bar stool.

Passing the table where Ellie sat, Wayne turned to her. "You bitch!" he spat.

"You'll have to come to the station and file a written charge," one officer told Ellie.

"I'll get my car and drive to the station," Ellie said.

When the patrol car pulled away, Ellie left some money on the table, and hurried out. She raced back to the condo, her heart pounding and her head throbbing. When she reached her room, she locked the door and the windows. There was no time to wait for Nick to call. She punched in his number on her phone.

"Ellie, I was about to call and tell you to upload your files."

"I'm being followed. I only just realized that a man's been stalking me since I arrived."

"What happened?" She heard the alarm in his voice.

"The man's tall, slim, in his forties. Wherever I go, he's there. He confronted me in a local bar and asked if I was the Andrews reporter. I called the police and reported that I was being harassed. They showed up and arrested him. But I have to go to the police station and press charges now. What proof can I give them?"

"He'll be locked up for a while. Not long if you don't show up at the station. You need to get away," Nick said.

"Where?"

He heard the desperation in her voice. "Take your computer, the flash drive and your travel documents. Pack a small bag, one that doesn't look like you're checking out. Leave the rental car and call a taxi to take you to the harbor in George Town. There are a few marinas there where you can charter a boat that'll take you to Cayman Brac."

"Cayman Brac?"

"It's far enough away from Grand Cayman to buy you time."

"Nick, I..."

"It's your best chance to lose this guy. You can do this, Ellie."

"What if he follows me?"

"The boat will take three to four hours…enough time to get away."

"If this doesn't work out, you know where the other flash drive is," she said.

"It will," he insisted. "I'll book a condo for you at Brac Caribbean Beach Village. There'll be people around…tourists. It's a popular place on the beach."

"Can't I upload my files right now…just in case I don't get there?"

"There's no time. You need to leave in the next few minutes." He hung up before she could say more. Then he called for a taxi to take him to the Baltimore Washington International Airport.

Chapter 52

Tuesday, February 9, 2010

Dan's condition had deteriorated during the night, and he required emergency surgery to relieve his obstructed airways. A tracheotomy tube extended from a surgical opening in his throat to a ventilator. The tube allowed him to make guttural sounds, not words that could be understood. He faded in and out of consciousness from the morphine. But, when Russell and Joan entered the room and stood beside his bed, he was aware of them.

"I'm here, Dan. Can you hear me, darling?" Joan asked. Dan's eyes fluttered open, moving from Joan to Russell. All he could do was blink.

"I know you didn't want a trach tube, but we almost lost you last night," Russell said.

Dan struggled to speak but could only manage an indiscernible sound. Tears spilled down his cheeks.

"A trach tube is nothing to get upset about. We'll remove it when your airway heals," Russell said. Dan closed his eyes, helpless to protest, certain that he was dying and they were lying to him.

A news broadcast on the TV above Dan's bed caught their attention. Russell pressed the sound control on the remote and raised the volume. The hearing room at the Virginia State Capitol was on the screen, the camera focusing on the chairman of the Virginia Senate Commission.

"This commission has done an exhaustive investigation of the allegations of illegal trade in human organs against the Virginia Transplant Foundation. We have found that the charges against the Virginia Transplant Foundation, its board members and affiliates, are unfounded," the chairman announced.

When the camera moved to a protester in the gallery, Russell turned off the TV. He smiled at Dan. "This is good news. No need to worry now."

"You see, darling, everything's going to work out for you...for us," Joan said.

Dan relaxed. He was exonerated. He let the morphine carry him into blissful sleep.

***

Wayne waited on a cold steel bench in a bare holding cell at the Grand Cayman police station. The clock on the wall outside told him that he had been here for more than an hour. *They can't keep me here much longer if the bitch doesn't show up to press charges,* he reasoned. He clenched his fists as he thought about what he would do to Ellie when he was released.

More time passed, and there was no sign of Ellie. He rattled the bars. "Let me out of this shithole," he shouted. "I have rights. You can't keep me here without charging me."

The arresting officers, who had expected Ellie to arrive and press charges, were discussing their options. They phoned the condo where Ellie was registered several times, but there was no answer in her room. They didn't like the looks of Wayne or his attitude, but legally they couldn't keep him locked up if he wasn't charged with an offense.

Wayne banged on the bars with his fists, working himself into a fury. "You motherfuckers! Let me out of this fucking shithole," he shouted. After another half hour of listening to Wayne's obscenities, one of the arresting officers unlocked the cell. "You're free to go," he told him. "But we'll be watching that you don't harass any other women." Wayne sneered at them, collected his wallet and stormed out.

***

Ellie closed her laptop and slipped it into a carry case. She packed a few necessities in a small duffle bag. Nick's warning to leave immediately and the urgency in his voice had frightened her. She left the room, locking the door behind her, and went to the lobby. "I need my safe please," she told the receptionist. She signed for the safe, opened it and removed the flash drive. Then she locked the safe and returned it for storage. "Can you call a taxi for me?" she asked the receptionist.

Ellie paced back and forth in the lobby as she waited for the taxi, her anxiety mounting as the minutes ticked away. *Where was the taxi? How long would the stalker be detained at the police station when they realized that she wasn't showing up? What if he came back here before she could get away?* As she was contemplating driving to the marina in the rental car, a taxi pulled up. She hurried outside and got into the taxi.

"Where to?" the driver asked.

"The George Town marina," she said. They pulled away, passing a taxi driving toward the condo with Wayne seated in the back.

When the taxi pulled up to the condo, Wayne paid the driver and went into the lobby. "Would you ring Ms. Andrews' room?" he asked the receptionist. "She left a book on the beach, and I'd like to return it to her."

"There's no one here by that name," the receptionist said.

"I thought that was her name," he said. He pulled out his phone and showed her a picture of Ellie.

"She left in a taxi," the receptionist said.

"Where was she going?"

"I wouldn't know...and I don't give out that information," she said, noting that Wayne wasn't carrying a book that he wanted to return.

Wayne left the condo and walked down the road to the taxi station. Inside the office, he told the dispatcher, "One of your drivers picked up a woman at the condo down the road. She dropped her credit card on her way out and she'll be worried. Can you tell me where the taxi was taking her?"

The dispatcher checked his computer screen. "The marina in George Town," he said.

"Can I get a taxi there now?"

"It'll be a few minutes," he said.

Wayne waited outside, pacing back and forth. It took fifteen minutes before an empty taxi showed up. On his way to the marina, he contemplated his next move.

It wasn't until he arrived in George Town that he learned there were several marinas Ellie could have gone to. "Where would I charter a boat to another island?" he asked the taxi driver.

"Maybe Kaibo Marina or South Sound Dock. Depends on what's available this time of year," the driver told him.

"Let's start with the closest one," Wayne said.

The taxi made its way around the dock, stopping at several marinas, where Wayne got out and showed Ellie's photo at the booking office. He wasn't having much luck until he arrived at Kaibo Marina. "She left on a charter boat to Cayman Brac with a few other passengers about half an hour ago," a man in the office said.

Wayne got back in the taxi. "Take me to the airport," he told the driver.

***

Ellie sat in a chair on the deck as the charter boat sailed into open ocean. There was nothing to do but look at the dark water and worry about whether she would get to tell the world the truth. *What if she didn't succeed? Nick would have to. She had to believe that.*

Minutes stretched into hours, and Ellie grew restless. She got off the deck chair and walked the length of the boat, from the starboard side to the port and back again. She passed other passengers—three couples, a family with two young children chasing each other around the deck. The younger child, a blonde girl with a ponytail, bumped into her. "I'm sorry," the child said, startled.

"It's okay," Ellie smiled. The girl returned her smile and ran off. Ellie wondered how it would feel to be on a family vacation with your mother and father. It was an experience she never had, one she sadly missed.

After another hour of sailing, limestone bluffs appeared in the distance, jutting out of the ocean as they neared Cayman Brac. When they docked and the boat was secured with a rope, a crewman helped Ellie climb onto the dock. She headed for one of the taxis waiting nearby.

"I'm going to Caribbean Beach Village," she told the driver, opening the door and taking a seat in the back. They sped along a road where palm trees and brush dotted the landscape and the rugged bluffs rose along the coastline.

When the taxi pulled up to the condo, Ellie paid the driver and went into the rental office. "I have a reservation," she told the man at the desk. She showed him her passport, the one Nick had given her when she left Virginia, with her photo and her name—Amy Walker.

"You'll be in room 104, Miss Walker," he said, handing her the key. "It's on this floor, to the left," he directed.

"Thanks." Ellie took the key and carried her computer case and duffle bag to the room. She looked both ways in the hallway before unlocking the door. There was no one in sight and she went inside, locking the door behind her.

Chapter 53

Tuesday, February 9, 2010

Wayne would have to wait two hours at Owen Roberts International Airport on Grand Cayman for the next Cayman Airways flight to Cayman Brac. He pulled his cell phone out of his pocket and tapped in a number. "There's a two-hour wait for the next flight to Cayman Brac. That's where she's headed by boat," he said.

"Charter a private plane," Colton said.

"If I can get one."

"Get one, whatever it costs. And when you find her, you'd better get all the copies."

"Are you threatening me?"

"If you want what we agreed to, I need all the deliverables."

"The deliverables will cost more now. It's riskier."

"How much?"

"Double."

"Agreed. Just do it."

Wayne hung up. He made some inquiries at the airport and soon found a private charter operation. Half an hour later, he took off for Cayman Brac in a private plane. It was a thirty-minute flight and, when the plane landed at Charles Kirkconnell Airport, he rented a car and drove to the marina.

The charter boat that had left Grand Cayman with Ellie and several other passengers had already docked when Wayne arrived at the marina. Two crewmen were hosing down the deck on the boat when he approached them. He showed them Ellie's photo on his cell phone. "Have you seen this passenger? She lost her credit card and I want to return it," he said.

The men examined Ellie's photo. "She left in a taxi," one of them said, "about fifteen minutes ago."

Wayne went to the nearby taxi stand and showed them Ellie's photo, repeating his lie. He quickly learned where she went.

***

At Caribbean Beach Village, Ellie set her computer on a table and turned it on. She took the flash drive out of her pocket and inserted it in the USB port. While she waited for the computer to boot up, she went to the window, which looked out on the empty roadway. An uneasy feeling made her jittery, and she went back to the computer, anxious to upload the file. *A few taps on the keyboard and her story would be on its way to the world*, she thought.

She pressed the enter key and her file started uploading. She watched the screen register 10%, 20%, 30%. The sound of a car arriving outside sent Ellie to the window. Seeing Wayne step out of a car set adrenaline coursing through her veins. As panic gripped her, she struggled to think clearly. There was no time to finish uploading the file. She had only moments to get out of the room before he found her.

She pulled the flash drive out of the computer and slipped it in her pocket. Leaving through the front door was not an option. She opened the window and climbed out into the bushes. Keeping low behind the brush, she made her way around the property to the pool. Behind the pool was Dave's Bar & Grill, housed in a rustic wooden building.

Ellie went inside. A bar stretched along one side of the restaurant, with tables filling the rest of the space. The smell of grilled fish and spices hung in the warm air. A few tables were occupied, and the bar was doing a brisk business.

Ellie walked up to the bar. "Do you have a computer I can use for about half an hour?" she asked the bartender. "I'll pay for it."

"Sure," he said, pulling a laptop out from beneath the bar. "We'll settle the price when you're done," he said, writing the password on a napkin and sliding it across the bar to her.

Ellie carried the laptop to a table, turned it on and waited for it to boot up. She typed in the password and inserted the flash drive. Then she entered the addresses for U.S. and world media news, identified herself and composed a short message. She pressed the enter key. The Internet connection was maddeningly slow. Her anxiety mounted as she watched the screen register—20%, 30%, 40%, 50%. *How long before he tracks me here—minutes, seconds?* As these thoughts ran through her mind, Wayne walked through the door.

***

Nick's taxi was stuck in traffic on the way to the airport. When he finally arrived, he had missed a direct flight to Cayman Brac. "I can get you on a flight to Grand Cayman in half an hour," the airline representative told him. You can get a connecting flight to Cayman Brac from there."

"I'll do that," he said.

Half an hour later, Nick was on an American Airlines flight, taking off for Grand Cayman. He had tried calling Ellie several time, but she didn't pick up. It wasn't like her not to answer her phone or call back. He could only hope she had arrived safely in Cayman Brac. But he was certain that she was in danger.

Three hours later, Nick's plane taxied across the runway at Grand Cayman. Inside the airport, he booked the next flight to Cayman Brac. There would be an hour wait. He wasn't expecting to be at this airport, but it gave him time to retrieve the second flash drive that Ellie had stored here. He went to the rental lockers and located the one Ellie had reserved. Keying in the combination he had memorized, he opened the locker and removed the flash drive. He slipped it into his pocket, hoping he wouldn't have to be the one uploading the file.

Chapter 54

Tuesday, February 9, 2010

Ellie watched Wayne step through the doorway of Dave's Bar & Grill. He walked toward her, but she kept her attention on the computer screen as her file uploaded to the Internet…60%, 70%. He pulled up a chair beside her, reached across to the keyboard and pressed a key, pausing the action. "Take the flash drive out and slide it over to me," he demanded, his voice low and mean.

"No," she said.

His eyes narrowed. He reached into his pocket and pulled something out. Ellie felt the cold hard metal of a gun barrel pressing against her leg. With Wayne's back to the bar, no one noticed anything unusual about a man and woman sitting at a table.

The bartender looked across the room at Ellie and the man now sitting beside her. They hadn't come in together, and he didn't like the looks of the man. She had seemed nervous when she asked him for the computer. "Everything alright, miss?" he called from the bar.

Wayne pressed the gun harder against Ellie's leg. "I'll kill you and everyone in here," he hissed. "And I'll walk out of here with the flash drive."

"Everything's fine," Ellie answered. *I will finish this for you, Matt,* she thought. She reached her fingers to the keyboard, but instead of releasing the flash drive, she pressed the enter key. The file continued to upload…80%.

Wayne's hand shot out to stop the computer. "You bitch! I'll kill you."

Ellie grabbed a pen, lying on the table next to the computer. In one swift movement, she thrust the pen into Wayne's outstretched hand. He howled in pain and shock, pressing back against the chair and falling onto the floor.

The bartender leaped from behind the bar and rushed to the table. Blood oozed from the puncture wound on Wayne's hand, where the pen was still lodged. His gun had fallen onto the floor, and the bartender snatched it, slipping it into his pocket. He pulled Wayne up from the floor. "I'm calling the police," he said.

"Fuck, you're not," Wayne said, pulling the pen out of his hand with a grunt and covering the wound with a napkin snatched from the table. He was out the door before the bartender could get to his phone.

The bartender turned to Ellie. "Are you okay?"

"I think so," she said, her voice shaky. "Thank you."

"That man's dangerous…probably has more weapons," he said, pulling a cell phone from his pocket and dialing the local police.

Ellie's eyes were rivetted on the computer screen as it registered 100%. People seated around the bar stared at her now, chattering excitedly. She felt suddenly light-headed. Grasping the table to steady herself, she doubled over, gulping air like a drowning swimmer. The bartender pulled out a chair for her. Then he went to the bar and returned with a glass of brandy.

Ellie's hands trembled as she sipped the brandy and tried to slow her runaway pulse. She read the computer screen again, feeling exhilarated and empty at the same time. Her struggle to expose the truth was finally over. It wouldn't take long for the media to vet her story and broadcast it. But revenge was bitter, and justice could not erase her loss.

***

At the Virginia General Hospital, a nurse came into Dan's room in the Burn Unit. She adjusted the IV. Saline, morphine and antibiotics dripped steadily into Dan's veins. Some of the bandages were removed from his grotesquely swollen face. A ventilator pumped oxygen into his lungs and helped him breathe. A nurse dabbed Dan's damaged lips with medication. She checked his vitals and made notations on the chart. "We're expecting a shipment of skin to treat your burns today. Dr. Russell will be in to discuss your next graft with you." Her words gave him little hope.

Dan's eyes grew heavy as the morphine did its work. Sleep was the only escape from his hellish life. The voice of a reporter on the TV screen above his bed startled him, and his eyes fluttered open.

"We interrupt this program to bring you breaking news," the reporter's voice blared. "Evidence supporting allegations of an illegal human organ trade in Virginia was released over the Internet by Ellie Andrews, a reporter for the

Virginia Star. The Virginia Transplant Foundation and its board of directors were operating a human organ theft scheme for years, making hundreds of millions of dollars. Evidence indicates that prisoners at the notorious Red Ridge Prison were the victims who supplied transplant organs and tissue. The Virginia Tissue Bank, another partner in the crime, brokered the stolen organs and tissue to the highest bidders. The Virginia General Hospital was part of the operation, profiting from performing organ harvesting and transplants. The total profits have not yet been calculated, but the number is expected to be shocking. We await a response from state and federal investigators."

Dan struggled for breath, a sickening sputtering sound emanating from the breathing tube. A steady beeping on the monitor tracking his vital signs grew louder, sounding a *code blue* alarm at the nurses' station.

A code team rushed in, wheeling a crash cart. Dan's heart rhythm was erratic, his blood pressure elevated, signaling a dangerous arrhythmia. A nurse opened Dan's hospital gown, exposing his chest. Paddles, attached to a defibrillator, were positioned on his chest. The team stepped back as an assistant activated the defibrillator and an electric current fed through the paddles to Dan's heart. The EKG monitor continued to show an alarming arrhythmia.

"Clear," the doctor ordered. Dan's heart was shocked again. The code team waited, watching the monitor as Dan's heart rhythm appeared to be recovering. When a normal heart rhythm returned, the paddles were removed from his chest. "That was a close call," the doctor said.

The crash cart was rolled out of the room, and the medical team left Dan to rest. Twenty minutes later, another *code blue* was sounded. The code team hurried back to Dan's room with the crash cart in tow. Paddles were quickly positioned on Dan's chest, and his heart was shocked again. Two more shocks followed, but failed to reverse the arrhythmia.

After a fourth shock, a flatline replaced the erratic heart rhythm on the monitor. The doctor continued with many more attempts to revive Dan, but the flatline persisted…irreversible now.

"Asystole," the doctor finally called. He looked at the clock on the wall. "Time of death, 3:45."

Chapter 55

Tuesday, February 9, 2010

Wayne drove the rental car miles past the condo. He detoured down a side road, hid the car in a thicket and turned off the motor. There was no choice but to wait here for a few hours until the police left the condo property. His hand throbbed painfully, but he comforted himself by planning revenge. He would break into the bitch's room in the middle of the night and strangle her—his murder method of choice. A woman who outmaneuvered him would not be tolerated. The buzz of his cell phone interrupted his thoughts.

"Yes?" Wayne answered.

"Abort the job," Colton ordered. "Get out of there."

"I don't want to."

"That's an order...if you want your money."

Wayne hung up. His eyes were wild, his face murderous.

***

Police arrived at Caribbean Beach Village, surrounding the property. They took statements from Ellie, the bartender and witnesses. They searched the grounds and the rooms, but Wayne had already fled. A description of Wayne was broadcast throughout the island, including the airport and marina.

"The island's less than fifteen miles long," an officer told Ellie. "We'll find him."

When Nick's taxi arrived at Caribbean Beach Village, his pulse quickened at the sight of police cruisers, their lights flashing. He feared that he was too late. He paid the driver and headed to Dave's Bar & Grill, where the police were gathered. Bracing himself for the worst, he stepped inside.

Ellie sat at a table, looking more beautiful than ever, her hair in disarray, her eyes on the computer screen. She read the breaking news on the Internet again and again. Her story—the truth—was finally out there for the world. The guilty would be judged. She could only hope that justice would be swift and merciless. She should feel euphoric, but instead she felt empty. With Matt and her father gone, the victory was hollow. And there was no one here to celebrate with.

Her cell phone rang, surprising her. When she answered, Nick's familiar voice drifted over the line, and her heart quickened. "Great news," he said. "We expect arrests."

"Can I come home now?" she asked.

"You can," he said, hearing the urgency in her voice.

"Will I see you?"

"Turn around."

Startled, Ellie turned her head. Nick stood in the doorway, smiling a smile she wanted to drown in. She bolted from the chair and flew into his arms, planting kisses on his face.

"I missed you, too," he said, folding her in his arms.

"How did you...?" she started to ask, but he silenced her with a deep kiss.

"Let's get out of here," he whispered in her ear.

Ellie went back to the table where she had left the computer. She retrieved the flash drive and carried the computer to the bar. "How much do I owe you?" she asked the bartender.

"No charge," he said. Ellie smiled and left a fifty-dollar bill on the bar.

She took Nick's hand and led him to her room. When the door closed behind them, Nick pulled her into his arms. "I was worried about you," he said.

"But *you* were the whistleblower. If anything had happened to you..."

"Is that what you're afraid of?" His eyes held hers, demanding an answer. Ellie looked away. He placed his hands on her face, turning her to look at him. "It's not your fault that Matt and your father were murdered."

"I loved them. And they're gone."

"Is that why you're afraid to love me?"

She let his question hang in silence, not wanting to answer.

"Tell me."

Tears welled in her eyes. "Yes. I'm afraid. I don't want to love you. But I do," she whispered so low he barely heard her.

He cradled Ellie in his arms, kissing her face softly. They made slow sweet love, discovering each other again. They slept afterward, wrapped in each other's arms.

The sun was setting when Ellie woke, thinking she had dreamed their lovemaking. But when she turned to look at Nick lying beside her, she knew it was real. She couldn't deny loving him, though she was afraid. For now, for this moment, she would let herself love and be loved. She would sort out her complicated feelings later.

###

Epilogue

Ellie and Nick returned to Virginia. As the only legal heir to the Andrews' publishing company, Ellie was now the sole owner. The State of Virginia charged members of the Virginia Transplant Foundation with conspiring in the illegal trade in human organs. The foundation was disbanded and its funds seized. The Executive Board members—Judge Robert Maxwell, Dr. James Russell, Brian Payne, Clayton Parker—were tried by a jury and convicted of numerous counts of conspiracy. All received prison terms and were sentenced to Red Ridge Prison. Judge Maxwell was disbarred from the Virginia Bar Association, and James Russell lost his license to practice medicine.

Dan Andrews, now deceased, could not be convicted, but his name would be forever associated with the notorious crime. Joan Andrews fled to Texas to live near her family, never to be heard from again. Eleanor Colton, also deceased, was not convicted.

Ellie pursued legal actions against officers Kevin Moore and Patrick Murphy. After finding notes in Matt's papers about Ralph Citron, a witness to her father's accident, she met with him. Ralph's statement and a tire fragment from Ben's car were used to open a case against Moore, charging him with the attempted murder of Ben Andrews. Moore's Glock 22 was confiscated as evidence. Ellie produced the bullet fragment that Matt had retrieved at the scene of Ben's accident. Ballistic experts proved that markings on the fragment matched Kevin Moore's Glock 22.

Moore accepted a plea bargain from the Virginia District Attorney. After admitting to firing shots at Ben's car, he identified Senator Colton as the man who ordered the assassination. His testimony resulted in a reduced sentence of seven years at Red Ridge Prison, where he served three months before dying in an unexplained accident in the prison laundry room.

Patrick Murphy was brought in for questioning. When told that Moore accepted a plea deal, he accused Moore of setting up Matt Andrews by planting drugs in his car. Felony charges were brought against Murphy. He then negotiated a plea bargain of a reduced sentence in exchange for the names of other accomplices. He named Judge Maxwell and Senator Colton as the men giving the orders. He received parole, but lost his job and any chance at a pension.

Though Senator Colton was not a member of the Virginia Transplant Foundation Board, his wife Eleanor was, and the scandal forced him to resign from the Virginia Senate. Soon after, he was charged with conspiracy to commit murder, based on testimony from Kevin Moore and Patrick Murphy. Two days before his trial was to begin, Colton was found strangled in his home office.

After the legal cases were settled, Ellie negotiated the sale of the Virginia Star to a rival progressive newspaper in Virginia. Nick returned to work for Human Rights International. He would be starting a major investigation in sex trafficking.

Ellie moved to New York City, renting an apartment on West 68th Street. She needed a fresh start and would be working as an independent investigative journalist, a stringer. She and Nick spent weekends together. He traveled to New York or she took the train to Washington. Their bond to each other continued to grow and evolve in unexpected ways.

Author Notes

Throughout the world, the demand for transplantation organs and tissues is far greater than the availability. While the sale of human organs is illegal in the U.S. and other countries, favorable outcomes after organ transplants spawned the growth of a worldwide underground market.

Desperate patients in need of healthy organs often travel to another country for a transplant, and a thriving transplant tourism industry has developed to meet the demand. It is estimated that about 10 percent of all transplants worldwide, 12,000 annually, are illegally purchased. And billions of dollars a year in profits are generated worldwide from illegal organ trafficking.

A living donor can donate one kidney or a portion of a liver. But the demand for these organs exceeds the number of people willing to donate. That explains why there is widespread exploitation of people by organ traffickers in countries with vulnerable populations like India, Sri Lanka, Pakistan, the Philippines, Brazil, Turkey, eastern Europe, Colombia, Egypt and China, where the poor are often coerced, deceived, abused, forced and sometimes abducted.

Unscrupulous traffickers arrange for poor donors to have their organs removed at for-profit private clinics and transplanted into wealthy recipients who travel across borders. On the black market, a liver can cost $98,000 - $137,000 and a kidney $62,000 - $138,000.

China performs more transplants than any other country. In 2019, an independent tribunal found that prison inmates in China, particularly Falun Gong practitioners and other political prisoners, are executed and their organs harvested for wealthy people seeking transplants. Transplant surgeries are done at predominantly military-run hospitals. While the Chinese government denies this, human rights activists and medical professionals gave evidence against China's practice in 2001 to a U.S. Congressional Subcommittee on International Operations and Human Rights.

Human organs are only viable for a limited number of hours after death and must be transplanted shortly after harvesting, but human tissue can be stored for an extended time, which makes harvested human tissue from one deceased donor more profitable than organs.

Transplantable human tissues—bones, tendons, ligaments, corneas, middle ear, skin, heart valves, nerves and veins—are supplied from cadavers and used in over 600 types of medical procedures. With over a million tissue transplants performed in the U.S. every year, demand surpasses supply.

Universities, medical device companies, and surgical equipment companies require a steady supply of cadavers for teaching and research purposes, and willed body donations do not meet the need. Cadavers and body parts are purchased through brokers. Shortages have spurred a profitable underground cadaver trade, with dealers procuring body parts from funeral homes, morgues, cemeteries, crematoriums and autopsy rooms without consent from families. Some of the underground tissue from cadavers is sold to for-profit companies supplying bone and skin products.

According to a report in The Orange County Register (April 2000), all the tissue from one cadaver that can be harvested, processed and sold by a private company or tissue bank is estimated to be worth over $200,000. Companies that process human tissue and make bone and skin products for medical procedures are part of the multi-billion dollar human tissue industry. Some companies are openly traded on the New York Stock Exchange.

The FDA does not provide information about tissue banks or companies that make skin and bone products. They do not release information about the manufacturing processes of bone and skin products. The reality is that the sterility of tissue products is not guaranteed, which sometimes leads to surgical infections. Surgeons themselves are unaware that the products they are using may be infected.

The underground trade in human organs and tissue may one day be only a dark chapter of the history of transplant medicine. Advances in regenerative medicine, using tissue engineering, have produced human organs and tissue in the laboratory. Using 3-D techniques, functional bone, liver, pituitary gland, retinal tissue, stomachs and heart tissue, ear, bone, and muscle structures have been grown for transplants.

Stem cells extracted from placental tissue and amniotic fluid can grow into multiple cell types. In 2006, children and teenagers received transplanted bladders engineered in the laboratory using their own cells and bioprinting. The first synthetically-grown trachea was transplanted in a patient in Sweden in 2011. Laboratory-grown vaginas were successfully transplanted in girls and women to correct missing or underdeveloped organs in 2014. These and other success stories offer hope for saving vulnerable people all over the world from organ traffickers.

About the Author

ELAINE BOSSIK is a novelist, screenwriter and editor. In addition to *Body Merchants*, she is the author of *The Last Victim*, a literary romance novel.

Bossik grew up in Brooklyn, NY. She is a graduate of Brooklyn College (CUNY), where she earned BA and MS degrees. After teaching in the New York City school system for several years, she pursued a new career, first as an advertising copywriter, and then as a medical writer and editor.

Surprising real life events and unpredictable people are the inspiration for Bossik's fiction. She is an avid reader and researcher. She lives in Florida with her husband and family, where she enjoys Florida's wildlife and pens her novels.

For more information, visit www.elainebossik.com.

A Conversation With Elaine Bossik

Where did the idea for Body Merchants come from?

I was drawn to media reports in the 1990s about organ trafficking in this country and globally. The idea for this story began to take shape when evidence emerged about China's elaborate system of executing prisoners and harvesting their organs for wealthy recipients. I asked myself then, *"Could this happen to prisoners in the U.S.?"* This story began as a screenplay, which was developed and written in collaboration with Glenn Bossik, my co-author. The novel is an adaptation of the original screenplay.

Did you plot your entire story before you started writing?

I do plot my stories before I write. I know the beginning, middle and end. This often changes as I begin to write, but I plot the ending so the action can move toward that direction. Sometimes I change the beginning to a different point in time because it improves the story or is more dramatic. I try to be flexible so that the story flows naturally and is believable. With *Body Merchants*, I was following the scenic action in the original screenplay, so I knew the plot very intimately. In a novel, readers depend on the writer's detailed descriptions of a character's actions and emotions so they can see it as clearly as they would in a film.

What kind of research did you do for this book?

I did a great deal of research on the worldwide underground market in human organs and tissue, and the big money organization behind it. I read many books, investigative reports by journalists, and U.S. Congressional testimony about human organ trafficking. I also researched the for-profit prison system in the U.S.—prison conditions and prisoners' accounts, and U.S. Justice Department reports and statistics so that I could write accurate descriptions.

How did your own feelings about what you discovered in your research influence your writing?

I was surprised and often shocked by the information I found. I tried to portray the truth about organ trafficking and U.S. prisons in my story so that readers would also be shocked. Fiction depicts reality in an emotional context. If a reader identifies with a character abused by the prison system, it has more of an impact than reading a non-fiction account of prisoner abuse. The message stays with the reader.

How do you create such believable characters?

I like to model my characters after people I know because it makes them believable. Often a character is a composite of several people. I give my characters the attributes I want them to have so they will clash with each other. When I have two characters with opposite characteristics interacting, it creates drama. For example, if one personality is a gambler and another is thrifty, they will be at odds.

I write detailed profiles for my characters. I know everything about them: physical appearance, family history, psychological profile, flaws, fears, likes and dislikes, dreams and goals. When I understand everything about them, I know how they will react in every situation and what they will say and think. This is essential in creating believable characters.

How did you choose the settings for your novel and write descriptions that make readers feel they are there?

I chose Virginia for the central setting because it's a place I visited several times. I was familiar with Alexandria and Arlington, and also Washington, DC. I set the Virginia Star newspaper office there. Also, I needed a place where a prison could be located, and there happens to be a super-max prison in nearby West Virginia. When my protagonist fled to the Cayman Islands, I did a good deal of research in order to describe it because I had never been there.

I always research my settings so I can name real streets and roads, landmarks, restaurants and physical land descriptions. When I write descriptions, I incorporate as many of the five senses as possible to recreate reality. I particularly used smell descriptions in the hospital scenes because smell is a very powerful sense that people remember and connect with emotionally.

Love and loss are a central part of this story. How do you get the reader to empathize with the grief a character feels after losing a loved one?

Grief is an emotion we all experience in life. Most readers experienced the loss of a loved one — a friend, a family member, a lover, a pet. My novel examines the devastating emotional upheaval of this kind of loss. Ellie and her brother, Matt, experience this as children when Laura, their mother, abandons them. Though Laura didn't die, it was more destructive for her children because children naturally feel that they are somehow responsible for driving a loved one away. Their grief was compounded by guilt. This kind of early trauma influences relationships later in life, which is why Ellie struggles with her feelings for Nick. When Ellie loses her father and then her brother, the two people she loved most in life, her grief nearly destroys her. But her love for them drives her to find the truth behind their deaths.

How did you achieve heightened drama in the climax scene when Ellie confronts all the players in the organ theft scheme?

The drama is achieved because the reader knows the truth before the climactic scene, but doesn't know how the characters will react and what will happen to them. The anticipation of the climax heightens the drama.

What part does jealousy play as a motivating force in the novel?

The antagonist, Dan, is driven by jealousy. It shaped his character early in life when his father favored his brother, Ben. He can never please his father, so he's motivated to outdo his brother, the object of his jealousy. He becomes an overachiever, always needing more in life — more wealth, more recognition as a doctor and a businessman. But his achievements are never enough to assuage his jealousy, and it turns into hate, motivating his destructive actions.

Why is trust and betrayal such a strong theme in the novel?

We all know people who gained our trust and later betrayed it by doing something unforgivable. In the story, Ellie trusts her uncle, Dan, who she's known since she was a child, who demonstrated in many ways that he cared about her and loved her. So, it's a shock when she discovers that he betrayed her.

As a child, Ellie gave her love and absolute devotion to her mother. When her mother abandoned her, she naturally felt betrayed. It's understandable why the adult Ellie couldn't forgive her mother when she turned up later seeking forgiveness.

What do you hope readers will take away as a message from this story?

Jealousy, greed and betrayal have consequences that can ultimately lead to tragedy.

Discussion Questions

1. How does Ellie show that she is an exceptional reporter?
2. Describe the relationship between Ellie and her father, her brother, her uncle.
3. How did Ben demonstrate that he was a good father?
4. Why do you think Matt hides information when he's conducting an investigation?
5. Trust and betrayal are important themes in the story. Why do you think Matt didn't trust Dan? Why does Ellie's trust in Dan slowly erode? What does Ellie want when she discovers his betrayal?
6. Why does Ellie feel responsible for her father's death?
7. Why is Ellie burdened with guilt over Matt's conviction?
8. How did Laura's abandonment of the family shape Ellie's behavior as an adult? Why do you think Ellie is unwilling to forgive her mother?
9. What does Ellie realize about her mother when she understands the truth about her character? How does it change her?
10. Jealousy is a powerful emotion that can lead to hate and motivate crime. What role did jealousy play in influencing Dan's feelings for his family? How did Dan's relationship with his father shape his life and his feelings for Ben? Why was Dan constantly striving to excel and acquire more wealth and recognition? Do you think he cared for Ellie, Matt, Ben?

11. Why can't Ellie commit to a romantic relationship with Nick when she is clearly attracted to him?

12. How does Nick show his loyalty and commitment to Ellie?

13. Why does it take Ellie time to piece together the organ theft scheme and discover those involved? How does she unravel the complicated scheme?

14. How does Ellie show that she's not afraid to take risks to find the truth?

15. How does Ellie show her resourcefulness when she discovers that an assassin followed her to Grand Cayman?

16. How does Ellie show she is fearless when the assassin tries to stop her from releasing her story?

17. What motivates Dan to keep struggling to survive his injuries?

18. What does Dan's wife, Joan, reveal about her character when she confronts Dan's serious injuries?

19. When Dan is severely burned, his survival depends on a lifesaving skin graft, but skin is in short supply. Why does this demonstrate irony?

20. Are outcomes in the story a result of fate or choice? Why does Ellie feel that the choices she made determined the fate of her father and brother?

21. How did the choices Ben made contribute to his death? How did the choices Matt made lead to his arrest and imprisonment?

22. How did the choices Dan made cause his ultimate downfall?

23. How did Ellie's choice when facing the assassin influence the outcome of the story?

24. How does Dan's fate illustrate the theme that jealousy, greed and betrayal lead to tragedy.?

Acknowledgments

Many thanks to everyone who read early drafts of *Body Merchants* and provided honest feedback, particularly my sister, Lee Newberg, for her enthusiasm and support; Eileen Herman, longtime friend and seasoned novel reader; my son, Eric, who questioned things I never would have thought of; Elaine Hutt and fellow writer Ted Hutt, who read with critical eyes and cheered me on. Thanks also to Lisa Krinsky, M.D., whose medical expertise was invaluable, and to author Dr. Brenda Dressler, whose excitement after reading a final draft was uplifting.

Without my cheerleading team—my sons, Eric and Glenn, and my husband, Ray—who supported me in countless ways along this creative journey, this book would not have been written. I'm especially fortunate that they have extraordinary writing, editing and art skills.

Special thanks to my son, Glenn, who was instrumental in helping me develop this novel from an original screenplay that we co-authored in 2013. His vision and editorial expertise made the transition from screenplay to novel possible.

www.ingramcontent.com/pod-product-compliance
Lightning Source LLC
Chambersburg PA
CBHW071656090426
42738CB00009B/1545